Also by the same author

Our Vinnie
My Uncle Charlie
My Mam Shirley
Blood Ties

JULIE SHAW

BAD BLOOD

YOU CAN'T ESCAPE YOUR FAMILY

Certain details in this story, including names, places and dates, have been changed to protect the family's privacy.

HarperElement
An imprint of HarperCollins*Publishers*
1 London Bridge Street
London SE1 9GF

www.harpercollins.co.uk

First published by HarperElement 2016

1 3 5 7 9 10 8 6 4 2

© Julie Shaw and Lynne Barrett-Lee 2016

Julie Shaw and Lynne Barrett-Lee assert the moral
right to be identified as the authors of this work

A catalogue record of this book is
available from the British Library

ISBN 978-0-00-814285-8

Printed and bound in Great Britain by
Clays Ltd, St Ives plc

MIX
Paper from
responsible sources
FSC www.fsc.org   **FSC‑ C007454**

FSC™ is a non-profit international organisation established to promote
the responsible management of the world's forests. Products carrying the
FSC label are independently certified to assure consumers that they come
from forests that are managed to meet the social, economic and
ecological needs of present and future generations,
and other controlled sources.

Find out more about HarperCollins and the environment at
www.harpercollins.co.uk/green

For my wonderful, and ever-expanding family. My parents, my kids Kylie and Scott, and my very patient and loving husband Ben. When I eventually leave this world, I hope that the one piece of advice that sticks with my children is this: Be the best that you can be. The best parent, the best husband or wife, and if you happen to be a toilet cleaner, be the best at that. Always wonder if you could use a bit more bleach or scrub a little harder, because that is what will bring you happiness.

Bailey Boo, Harvey Bear, Tylah Pie, Dylan, Delilah and Tucker, my beautiful grandchildren, you are my world!

Would you turn back time if you had the chance?
Would you run away or stay?
Like the smoker who thinks his time is up,
Then gets news of a clear X-ray.
His promises to God are forgotten then,
He dodged another bullet,
He continues to play Russian roulette,
Trigger finger poised to pull it.

Cross the line, step into the abyss,
Now there's no going back,
You've lost control, you've gone too far,
There's no defence, so attack.
You are no longer you, and you no longer care,
Join the ranks of the depraved.
One thing is sure from this moment on,
The pathway ahead is paved.

But would you change things if you could?
Can you see where it all went awry?
Would you not do that thing that set this course?
Would you really even try?
The past can't be changed, but the future can,
Starting right here, right now,
You don't have a lifetime to turn it around,
And no one can teach you how.

Chapter I

Bradford, July 1981

Christine squinted as her eyes met the bright July sunshine, and shuffled awkwardly down the front path to the car waiting in the road. Of all the cabbies in Bradford who could have picked them up, today of *all* days, it just had to be Imran. Imran who, in the absence of a female to leer at, would probably chat up a pot plant.

'Lovely day for it, innit, ladies?' he shouted conversationally, as Christine clambered awkwardly into the back. He had no choice. He was currently competing with a warbling Shakin' Stevens, because, as was usual, he had his car stereo turned up loud enough to wake the dead.

Not to mention the soon to be born, Christine thought wretchedly, as the next contraction began to build. It was like a giant elastic band, gripping vice-like around her middle, and the panic began engulfing her again. Why hadn't anyone *told* her how much it would hurt? Her own mum, for instance. The thought made her tearful. She'd never felt pain like this in her life. Ever.

'Lovely day for what?' her friend Josie snapped, as she climbed in beside her and slammed the door. 'And, Christ, Im, turn that frigging shit down, will you?'

Imran beamed at the pair of them through the rear-view mirror. 'Keep yer 'air on!' he said. 'I was only being friendly. Anyway,' he added, leaning forward to turn the volume down a fraction, 'where we off to today, girls? Somewhere nice?'

'St Luke's Hospital,' Josie snapped. 'And put your foot down as well. Seriously,' she added, as Christine began to wail. 'Or there'll be more than our Christine and bloody Shaky making a racket. Get a *move* on! She's already trying to push!'

It was only now, having twisted a hundred and eighty degrees in his seat, that Imran seemed to understand what was happening.

'You're about to have a *baby*?' he yelled, wide-eyed. 'A frigging *baby*?'

'No,' Josie deadpanned. 'She's about to have a wardrobe, you idiot. Now bloody *move* it!'

Christine sent up a silent prayer of thanks that Imran didn't seem to need telling again. He shoved the car into gear and they squealed away down the road towards the hospital, the strains of 'Green Door' filling the air in their wake.

It was only a three-minute drive from Christine's home to the hospital, but, in her terror, and with the lurching caused by Imran's panicked driving, every yard felt like twenty. That was the main problem, she decided through the fog of increasing agony. That it felt as if a wardrobe was exactly what she *was* having. How could a baby, so small and soft, feel so enormous and full of edges? More to the point, how was she ever going to get out of Imran's taxi and up to the maternity ward in one piece? She felt as if her whole body was trying to turn itself inside out; that if she moved so much as a muscle she'd rip in two.

But get out she must; they were now outside the maternity unit entrance and Josie, who'd leapt out and come round to open the other door for her, was tugging at her arm and trying to coax her out of the car.

'C'mon, mate,' she was saying. 'That one's dying down now a little, isn't it? Which is why we have to get you in, before the next one comes along.'

Not for the first time, Christine was grateful to have Josie here to help her. Calm, capable Josie, who'd not batted an eyelid when Christine's waters had broken and flooded the kitchen floor, because she'd done all this herself two years back, having her Paula. Who was nothing like her mother. Who was there for her. Who was her *friend*.

And Josie was right about the contraction, which was why it hadn't even been a question. The pain was dying off as quickly and as decisively as it had come. Gripping her belly, Christine shuffled her legs round and onto the pavement.

'You and all,' Josie said, sticking her head back into the car as Christine tried to climb out of it.

'Me?' spluttered Imran. 'What you on about, woman?'

'You,' Josie told him. 'Assuming you'll want paying. Come on, out. I need you to help me get her inside.'

Christine privately agreed. Josie was tiny. There was nothing of her. And though Christine had never dared to ask, she imagined that was why her friend's nickname had always been Titch. And there *she* was, like a whale, a great lumbering whale. And with the shakes now. She felt woozy and unsteady on her feet.

'Me?' Imran said again. Then he shook his head firmly. 'Sorry, love, but I can't be doing that. S'pose someone sees me? They'll probably think I'm the fucking father!'

'You wish,' Josie replied in disgust. 'Mate, she doesn't go near *your* type.'

'Mate,' Imran parroted. 'I don't go near *hers*. No offence, love,' he added, as he came round to the kerbside. He grinned and his fabled gold teeth both winked at her in the sunshine. 'Come on,' he coaxed. 'Let's be having you before the little bleeder plops out in the road.'

Christine cringed with shame and embarrassment as the two of them dragged her none too gently from the parking bay to the maternity-ward entrance, the words 'your type' going round and round her head. She loved Josie – couldn't manage without her, truth be told – but she wished she would shut up for once, because what she was saying to Imran was really too close to the bone.

Up until now, she had kept the paternity of her unborn child a secret. Told anyone who asked to mind their own business. But the time had come now. She'd be keeping her guilty secret no longer. In a couple of hours – probably less, given how her insides were feeling – everyone would know who the father of her baby was. Or they'd make an educated guess. And they'd be right.

The Maternity Department at St Luke's sat at the furthest end of the huge sprawl of hospital buildings, and seeing the familiar entrance calmed Christine a little. A place she'd never once so much as glimpsed before the nightmare had happened, it had become something of a sanctuary for her over the past few months – a safe place where no one ever questioned her or judged her. A place where they didn't care about the whos and whys and wherefores of her pregnancy – where they simply took care of her, were kind to her, were concerned about her well-being. Was she sleeping? Was the baby kicking? Was she taking her vitamins? Was she exercising enough? Was she eating the right foods?

It was a place she'd mostly visited alone, too, and that was fine by her. Though Josie had come with her on her first visit, when she was feeling so ashamed and scared, she'd since been happy to trot down to her antenatal appointments on her own – even had her mam offered to go, which, unsurprisingly, she hadn't. She had about as much interest in Christine's pregnancy as she had about Christine herself – which meant precious little, just like always. Christine hadn't minded. She didn't exactly want her mam involved. This was her kid, her future, and she vowed, over and over, that she was going to do things differently. Do it better. Do right by the child growing inside her. Be not at all like her own mam.

So she'd been happy to sit there with all the other expectant mothers – much preferred it, even. Here she was just one among many other waddling women, all chattering away, in the bright, busy waiting room; like a warm enveloping hug telling her everything would be okay. That girls just like her became mothers all the time. That it wouldn't be the end of the world.

But now it felt like it, and Christine was horrified to hear that Josie wasn't allowed to come in with her now. 'Sorry, lovey,' the nurse at the admission desk told them. 'Your friends will have to wait out here. We need to whisk you off for an examination. See how baby's doing, see how far you are along.'

Imran pulled a face, and let go of her as if jolted by a sudden electric shock. He was only lingering, Christine knew, because he was still waiting for his fare.

'Don't you worry, mate,' Josie reassured her, pulling a purse out from her handbag. 'You're in safe hands now, and I'll go and track your mam down, okay? Get her down here to look after you.' Though both of them knew there was a good chance, what with her mam currently being at the bingo, that she wouldn't get there in time even if she wanted to. Which, despite Josie's constant attempts to change things, Christine was pretty sure she wouldn't. Josie meant well, but she didn't get it – they just weren't like her and her mam.

So she tried to stay calm, knowing Josie was right. She was in safe hands, and now she was here, they'd take charge of things. Indeed, were already doing, because almost immediately Josie had left with Imran, a second nurse, after some consultation with a big whiteboard behind the first nurse, seemed to scoop her up almost – it felt as if she was being propelled along the corridor – and into an empty consulting room just off the waiting room, at the very point when the next contraction hit her.

The nurse helped her up onto the big trolley bed and, once again, being examined – as she had been, so many times, some on this very table – Christine was stunned by the intensity of the pain.

'No wonder you're pushing, love,' the nurse said, peeling latex gloves from her fingers. 'You're eight centimetres! This little one of yours is obviously anxious to be born!' Then she popped her head around the consulting-room door and yelled, 'Someone fetch me a wheelchair!', and within moments it seemed everyone was panicking.

This was it, Christine thought, as everyone hurried and fussed around her. All these months of wondering what labour would be like. She was frightened, but at the same time there was nothing she could do to stop it and all she could do was surrender herself to the inevitability. Only one thing was certain, or would be, she reckoned. That, good or bad, nothing in her life was ever going to be the same again.

The maternity wards were up on the second floor of the unit, and Christine was taken up in the wide hospital lift, which smelled of disinfectant and creaked as they rose. Only the week previously, a group of mums who had similar due dates had been shown around one of the wards, which, with its bright bays, patterned curtains and crisply made beds, had seemed a place in which nothing bad could happen. Though it had the same clinical smell everywhere else in the unit seemed to, it had a cheerfulness about it; a sense of homeliness, even. And there'd been a lull in labours – only one bed had been occupied, and the woman had been sleeping – and Christine had felt an unexpected surge of confidence. With the sun streaming in and the sense of calm and order, she could almost believe that whatever rows she had coming from her mam, it would, in the end, all be okay.

She was wheeled along the corridor, groaning now, almost growling – she couldn't seem to stop the embarrassing animal noise coming out of her – right past the wards to one of the delivery suites. Here there was no such sense of calm. There was no way of dressing it up. It was a room with one purpose – one all too evident from the huge cylinders of oxygen strapped to the far wall, evident from the scales and instruments, from the functional Perspex cot and, worst of all, from the leather foot straps that hung from the ceiling and swayed above the bed.

'Here we go, love. Let's get your things off,' the midwife commanded. Her name was Sister Rawson, and Christine was relieved to see her – even if a little earlier than expected. She'd last seen her only on Monday, and wasn't due to see her again till next week, because she was still a good ten days from her due date.

Sister Rawson was middle-aged and hefty. Her uniform strained across her huge bosom and she had chubby pink hands; hands that held Christine firmly as she helped her out of her hateful borrowed smock, and into a crackling hospital gown that did up with tapes down the back. 'Anyone coming? Baby's dad?' She held a monitor in her hand now. 'No, it'll be your mam coming, won't it?' she said as she began to strap the monitor around Christine's belly. 'She knows you're here, does she?' she asked conversationally.

Christine shook her head, gasping as a fresh wave of pain hit her. 'She's out. She doesn't even know I'm here yet. My friend is going to let her know.'

Though it really was doubtful whether Josie would be able to get word to her in time. She'd left only an hour back for bingo, leaving the girls to their own devices. Down the Mecca on Little Horton Lane with her cronies, same as always, all trying to win the big one; the jackpot that might change their lives.

They never did, of course. They spent as much on cheap lager as they did on the bingo, and on the slot machines that hardly ever paid out. And they'd stay there, through the afternoon and on into the evening, topping up on lager till they left to go down the pub. No, there was little hope of her mam coming to help her, even if she was struck by a sudden rush of love and maternal feeling.

Which was also doubtful, even *before* she saw the baby. Christine was under no illusions on that score, and never had been. She knew intuitively that whoever had turned out to be the father, her mother just wouldn't want to know. It was exasperating sometimes, how people didn't get it. How they kept saying, 'She doesn't mean it. She'll come round, just you wait and see.' How they imagined that when it came to it her mam would become somehow different – how she'd suddenly realise how much she'd be missing. How, when it came to it, she'd be so excited to be a granny.

Christine had long since given up trying to enlighten anyone about this. Not Josie's mam, June. Not Mr Weston, who she worked for in the café down on John Street. And though Josie knew better – one of the very few people that did – she still didn't quite get how bad it was, not really. She still hung on to the idea that there was this unbreakable maternal bond; just that it was very deeply buried. But there wasn't. There really wasn't. But no one wanted to hear that. So Christine didn't bother enlightening Josie further either. Her mam cared about two people, and that was pretty much it. Herself and her bastard of an on-off boyfriend, Rasta Mo.

At the moment, that was. That was all subject to change now. What hadn't changed so far was how her mam dealt with the pregnancy. First she'd been furious, then resigned, then just irritable and resentful. Especially in the last weeks, when Christine had had to give up her waitressing at the café. With the extra money no longer coming in, Christine's mum had all but washed her hands of her – at least (as she'd been fond of remarking, over and over) till she got off her fat backside and sorted out her dole. 'You made your own frigging bed and you're just going to have to lie on it, girl,' she'd told her. And she'd know all about that. Because she'd had to do exactly that herself. Not just when she had Christine, but also when she'd given birth to her older brother Nicky – neither of them knew who their dads were, and never would.

And it hadn't helped that Christine had stuck so resolutely to her guns. Because, like her mam before her, she hadn't told anyone who the father was, either. Hadn't and, in fact, couldn't, even though there wasn't a shred of doubt. Though, in the vain hope that things might not turn out as badly as she expected, she'd not rushed to contradict her mam when she'd reached her own conclusions; deciding that it was probably Paddy Sweeney's – the lad Christine had been seeing briefly before she'd left school. 'That bloody half-wit,' her mam had said. 'Trust you to pick that no-hoper. There'll be no hope of any support there – not from that bloody family.'

If only she knew, Christine thought. Because it was *so* much worse than that.

* * *

11

The monitor finally in place, and a second excruciating examination completed, Sister Rawson swept from the room, leaving Christine alone, with a bright-toned but ominous 'I'm just going to fetch the doctor!'

Then silence. Well, bar the beep of the monitor stand beside her, and the constant lub-dub, lub-dub from the microphone on her belly. Christine tried hard to focus on the baby's racing heartbeat. To lose herself in the strange, urgent sound the machine made; such an odd sound, she'd thought, when she'd first been able to hear it. Almost as if it was coming from under water. Which, of course, it sort of was. But it was hard to concentrate – soon impossible. Would the agony never stop? There seemed no break now from the pain; it was as if her body was no longer hers. It had become uncontrollable, unpredictable, an unstoppable alien force.

This was it, she knew. There was nothing going to stop her baby coming. And as the urge to expel it became ever more urgent, Christine realised quite how hard she had tried not to believe it. That the day would really come. And now it had. And now they'd know.

'I can't push any more!' Christine sobbed as someone mopped her clammy forehead. 'I *can't*!'

Time had passed. She had no idea how much time, but she had a definite sense of having lost some. A vague memory of an injection, of a mask placed on her face, of sucking up gas, and the unrelenting, dreadful, searing pain.

It felt different now, somehow; more a terrible burning – like she was about to be split in two. As if whatever was inside her was now fighting to get outside of her – hacking at her insides with a knife.

She felt sick, and cast about her, terrified she'd throw up all over herself. A bowl appeared, as if from nowhere, but, though she retched several times, nothing came.

There was still no sign of her mam, either, which, though entirely expected, made her tearful all over again. And she really, really, *really* didn't want to break down and cry, because she didn't want to be treated like a kid. If she wasn't being already, which turned her tears to anger. That people made assumptions about young girls like her.

Did this midwife? She looked between her knees, at the indistinct navy blue bulk of Sister Rawson, who was standing at the end of the table, bending forward, her bosom huge.

'Course you can push, girl!' Sister Rawson answered. Her tone was different now – sharp and snappy. 'You and a million other girls before you, my love. Natural as breathing, is giving birth … what a woman's body was made for. Now, come on, love. I need you to *push*!'

There were others in the room, too. A man in white. The doctor? And another nurse, a younger one, bearing a small trolley. The plastic mask replaced the kidney bowl. 'Come on, love, suck on this,' a gentle voice said. 'Suck on this, then a *big old* push. Listen to Sister, okay. Listen to Sister.'

'That's the way, love.' Sister Rawson's voice again. 'Hold it tightly. Deep and slow now.' She kept glancing at the monitor, across which a jagged line travelled left to right. 'That's the way,' she said. Something glinted in her hand. What?

Panicked now, Christine strained to see but couldn't. She well remembered what Josie had said about what might happen if she didn't push hard enough; if she couldn't get the baby out by herself. That was what had happened to Josie. She was too tiny. Much too tiny, so they'd used things called forceps. Enormous forceps, forced inside her, bigger than the baby's entire head …

'Christine! It's going to peak now! Christine, *look* at me! Baby's coming. Baby needs to come, *now*. Do you understand me, Christine? So this time you *have* to push. As hard and as long and as strong as you can. That's the way, lovey. Coming now. I can just see the head now.' Her voice grew hard then. 'But Christine, I mean it. You have to *try*. You have to give it everything you've got left, okay. Everything. You *have* to PUSH!'

It had been a pair of scissors, that was all. Not forceps, just scissors. Just to help. And they *had* helped, and she *had* pushed, and it had finally worked. The baby had been expelled from her so fast it was if it was entirely outside her control. Expelled and scooped up, and hung momentarily by its ankles, the face puckering, the mouth contorting, and then that single plaintive cry. And there it was – there *he* was. Her perfect child.

'It's a boy!' someone had said. 'You have a son! You clever girl, you!' And then the nurse by the scales had said 'bless her', though not *to* her. She'd said 'bless her' to the doctor, in tones not meant for Christine. 'She's only just seventeen.' She'd sighed then. 'No more'n a child herself.'

They'd sounded relieved, though, which had helped. And here he was on her chest now, staring up at her from his swaddling of blue cellular blanket, her blessing; her little coffee-coloured son.

Sister Rawson was standing beside her, beaming, pulling off her plastic apron. 'A beautiful baby boy,' she said as she balled it in her big pink hands and deposited it in the bin. 'Well done, lovey. Seriously. You were a brave girl. Well done.'

She reached across then, her expression strange, and swept a strand of Christine's wet hair from her eyes. It was an action so gentle that it made Christine want to cry. The sort of tears you couldn't help, because someone was being nice to you. And for a moment, she almost let herself give in to them. 'And your mum'll be here soon, I'm sure,' Sister Rawson said softly. 'Not too long now, eh? And, aww, he's beautiful, isn't he? Just look at him. A little stunner, he'll be. Look at those lovely, lovely eyes.'

Christine looked – it was all she could do *not* to, ever since she'd been handed him. And tried to find something in the baby's eyes that reminded her of his father. But no.

There was nothing. He was perfect. And he was hers. And she knew in that instant that she would always, always love him. That her bond to him, unlike her mam's, would be unbreakable.

Yes, his existence was about to cause hell for her, she knew that. So she was scared. She could imagine her mum's face, and she was scared.

But in that moment she didn't care. He was hers and she was his. No one else could matter more. She felt blessed.

Chapter 2

Josie held the phone receiver away from her ear. And then brought it quickly back again, mindful of a nurse hurrying past her. Lizzie Parker was known for many things, and one of the chief among them was the way she could scream and yell when she lost her rag. 'Calm down, Lizzie,' she hissed. 'I'm only the pissing messenger! And anyway, all I've told you is that he's black. That doesn't automatically mean it's Mo's.'

Lizzie laughed down the line, the bitterness in her voice evident. 'Course it's fucking Mo's kid. Who else's would it be? I fucking knew there was something going on. I *knew* it. And don't pretend you didn't. She's a fucking little slut, she is. Just you wait till I get my fucking hands on her.'

In the end, a while earlier, it had been Josie who'd seen the baby first. Knowing Lizzie wouldn't be at home when she and Imran had left the hospital she'd had him drive down to the Mecca and made him wait outside, planning to let Lizzie know that Christine had been admitted and, if she wanted, that she could use the cab to hurry back there. But she'd missed her. She'd already gone to the pub.

Josie could have gone looking for her at that point – there were several pubs locally Lizzie and her cronies frequented – or she could have gone home and tried again later. But knowing how far gone Christine had been, and that Paula was safe round her own mam's, she paid Imran and this time walked back to St Luke's. No, they wouldn't let her in till the baby was safely born, but it felt all wrong that there was no one there for her, and once it had been she'd be grateful for a friendly familiar face.

And Josie was glad she'd come back, because the baby was born just as she'd been finishing up her WRVS sandwich and, as all was apparently well, she'd been allowed in almost right away. And right away, the suspicions she'd had for a while had been confirmed.

'So it *is* his, then?' she'd asked. Though she hadn't really needed to. Christine's drawn, anxious expression had said it all, really – said in an instant what she'd been unable to say for the whole sodding pregnancy. But which Josie had worked out all by herself.

But had Lizzie? It hardly bore thinking about.

Christine sniffed, a single tear running down one pale cheek as Josie peered into the little plastic cot beside the bed. 'Isn't he beautiful?' Her voice wobbled. 'Oh, Josie. What the fuck am I going to *do*?'

Josie found herself overcome with a terrible rush of fury. The bastard. The sodding bastard. She had to work hard to keep her voice light because it was all too close to home for her. 'He is, mate. He's gorgeous. No thanks to his *twat* of a father. Doing the mother and then the daughter? That's pretty low. Chris, what happened? You have to tell me. Come on, truth. Did that bastard rape you?'

This suggestion only produced a fresh bout of tears. 'Oh, Josie ...' Christine started.

'He bloody did, didn't he?' Josie fumed. 'Fuck, Chris, why didn't you *tell* someone?'

But Christine was shaking her head. 'It wasn't ...' she began again. 'Josie, I ... Josie, I *let* him. I can't lie. I ...'

'You *what?*' Josie could almost sense her pulse throbbing in her temples. She sat on the edge of the bed and tried to calm herself. It was always like this. 'How exactly did you *let* him, Chris? Was this a thing that was already going on with you? Please don't tell me you –'

'No! Josie, *God*, no. He'd never been like that with me before. Which was why it was all such a shock. He was just like there, and Mam was out, and we had some wine – he'd brought some wine with him – and ...'

'And one thing led to another? Christ, mate. What were you *thinking?!*'

'I was drunk, Josie.'

'I'll bet you were. I'll bet he saw to that bit for you.'

'And it was like I was kind of there but not there ... and ...' She trailed off, remembering, and put her hands to her face.

'Great. So he slipped you a pill as well, did he? Christine – *Jesus*.' She sighed heavily. 'That utter, utter bastard. He did you good and proper, didn't he? What were you *thinking?'* she said again, because that was what she kept coming back to. 'No, scrub that. You weren't thinking, were you? Incapable of thinking, more like. The bastard.'

Christine pulled a paper towel from the dispenser by the bed. 'I don't know how I could have been so bloody idiotic, Josie, I really don't. So bloody *soft* …'

Josie blinked at her friend. 'Not soft on *him*? You being serious?'

Christine shook her head immediately. 'I told you. I don't know *what* I was thinking,' she said, but there was something in her tone that told Josie otherwise. That whatever nonsense he'd spun her to get her into the sack was still swilling around in her head even now. A whole nine months, and a whole baby, later.

'Chris, truth now. It was just that one time? You've not been –'

'God, no!' Christine's response was too immediate to be anything other than truthful. 'Christ, no! He's not been near me since and I wouldn't let him, either!'

But Josie still wasn't sure she had the full unvarnished truth. Not where Christine's feelings were concerned, anyway.

'So does he know? Has he sussed it? Christ, that was *so* bloody unlucky.'

'Tell me about it!' Christine said. 'I nearly died of shock when I realised.'

'And you've always known it must be his, have you? All along, I mean. For certain?'

'Course,' Christine said. 'There's not been anyone else.'

'So *does* he know?'

'Course he does. I told him straight away. I didn't know what to do, so –'

'So he told you what to do, did he?'

'Pretty much. He told me to get rid of it and when I said I wouldn't, he told me – well, he basically told me to sod off. That I could do what I liked and that he'd deny everything even if I didn't get rid of it. He didn't seem to care about what mam would think …'

'And that surprises you, does it?'

'No, but … I just thought … I didn't know what …'

Her eyes were brimming again. A vale of tears, Josie mused, looking at the sleeping newborn in the cot beside the bed. How could something so beautiful come out of such shit? She put one arm around her friend and reached for another paper towel with another. 'Here,' she said. 'Come on, mate. Blow on that. That's the way.' She nodded towards the cot. 'So you never wavered? You know. In keeping him.'

Christine shook her head. 'Not once, Josie. Never. I know what you're probably thinking. That I'm an idiot.'

'Some would say that, yes.'

'But I just couldn't. Not in a million years. It would be like getting rid of a part of *me*. And –'

Josie kissed the top of her head. 'You don't have to explain, mate. I know. Something of your own. Something to love. Someone to love *you*. I understand.' Then she smiled ruefully. 'Christ, I sound like a bloody soap opera!'

Christine balled the paper towel. 'My *life* is a bloody soap opera!' she said, with feeling. 'But at least now I can get out of it. Get away from that shit hole. Get away from *her* and make a life of my own. But, look, Josie, you've got to tell her for me. Tell her before she comes here. Give her a chance to –'

'To what? Build up a proper head of steam before she gets here?'

Christine shook her head. 'Just to get used to the idea before she arrives. Not that he's Mo's kid. Just that he's a half-caste. Just to get her used to that idea first.'

'Love, you're not thinking straight. You think she won't work it out? *Really?*'

'She's no reason to if I deny it. And that's what I plan on doing.'

'And you'll say it's whose, exactly? Like who exactly might be in the frame, here? Like you really think if you tell her it's some anonymous bloody Indian bloke she's going to *believe* that? Like, say, Imran? I think you're clutching at straws, love, I really do.'

Christine looked across at the cot. Reached a hand out to touch her baby. 'She's going to kill me, isn't she? She's going to hate him for ever. Even if I …' She started sobbing again. 'She's going to *kill* me.'

Josie sighed as she reached for her handbag. 'I'll try her again now, okay?' she said, squeezing her friend's arm, then passing yet another paper towel to her. What a mess. What a complete fuck-up. 'I'll see what I can do, okay? See if I can at least get it down to life without parole.'

Josie put the payphone to her ear again, reflecting on the irony that she'd initially thought it a bonus that Lizzie had picked up. She'd not expected her to – thought she'd probably stay out for half the evening, so she'd tried the house phone again more in hope than expectation. But she was now seeing the error of her ways. It would have been so much better just to leave it. Leave it all till tomorrow. Tell Lizzie Christine was staying at hers for the night. She'd have believed that, because she often stayed over.

Josie could see that now, of course, and mentally kicked herself for not thinking it through. Because Lizzie was currently two things – furious and drunk. A bloody nightmare of a combination.

'I will, you know,' she was saying now. 'I'll fucking kill her. Everything I've done for that little bitch and how does she repay me? By sleeping with my fucking boyfriend!'

Josie considered pointing out that Lizzie wasn't quite right on that score. However much she might bury her head in the sand about it – and she clearly had – it was common knowledge that Rasta Mo had a number of girlfriends scattered around the estate. Not to mention kids – and quite a few of them, if talk was to be believed. And besides, to mention that would be to confirm that it *was*

Mo's. Which, despite her knowing it was pointless, Christine had made her promise she wouldn't.

And it was pointless, because another thing everyone knew about Mo was his penchant for a bit of young flesh. And Lizzie knew that too, however much she might try to kid herself otherwise. One day, as far as Mo went, she'd be deemed over the hill.

Josie pondered how to play it – whether she should state the bleeding obvious; that her beloved boyfriend might have somewhat forced his hand there. That Lizzie knew what he was like, how he'd have groomed Christine in preparation. Then raped her, to Josie's mind, for all Christine denied it. She wasn't yet convinced he hadn't told her to say that. Commanded her to say that. Or else.

But there seemed little point. Not right now. Because Lizzie was half-cut. Best just deal in facts, not recriminations. 'What's done is done, Lizzie,' she said firmly. 'So you're just going to have to make the best of it. Oh, Liz, I tell you, he's *so* gorgeous. Just wait till you see him. I know it's … complicated, but can't you just –'

'Make the fucking best of it? What are you on about?'

Okay then. Time to fight fire with fire, Josie thought. 'Lizzie, will you just get over yourself?! We're talking about your fucking grandson!'

'My *grandson*? My grandson! I tell you what. Give that slut a message, will you? That that sprog she's popped out is no grandson of mine! Actually no. Don't do that, Jose. I'll fucking tell her myself!'

The receiver went down with a clatter.

It was around a ten-minute walk from Lizzie's house on Quaker Lane to St Luke's, and Josie's immediate thought was to hurry back there and attempt to head her off. But no sooner had she got halfway down Little Horton Lane (having opted not to waste time going back to the ward and explain to Christine) than she saw a car flash by, hooting – a car that she recognised. It was Gerald Delaney's, a young lad off the estate, and she could see Lizzie glaring at her from behind the windscreen. She silently fumed. How much unluckier could you get?

She turned around and began jogging back where she'd come from, watching the car swing into the hospital grounds and disappear out of sight. Where it would soon disgorge Lizzie, a spitting ball of bile and fury.

Breathing hard, she reached the entrance, the car having long gone now, wondering quite what she was heading back into. It had been a vain hope – a mistake – trying to play the 'happy grandparent' card, clearly. This was a woman without a maternal bone in her body. Which wasn't all her fault. Josie had sufficient empathy to understand that. Josie might have had a tough childhood, what with what had happened to her and everything, but at least she had a mam and dad who'd loved her, in their way. And her brother Vinnie. Always Vinnie. All things Lizzie had never had – she'd been not so much brought up as dragged up, when they could be bothered, by a pair of neglectful, preoccupied drunks. It was a miracle they hadn't lost her to a foster family years back – she remembered her own mam saying that. Or, if you looked at it another way, a shame.

Either way, Lizzie Parker was on the warpath, and she needed to catch her.

Chapter 3

It didn't take long. Though Lizzie had obviously had sufficient presence of mind to present a calm, motherly exterior
at the reception, Josie was still outside the post-natal ward
when she first picked up more familiar tones. What was the
stupid woman thinking of? Turning up there, hanging out
all her dirty washing in public? No, she might not give a
flying fuck about who heard the torrent of abuse she
intended for Christine, but did she not have sufficient
pride to worry about how it would make her look? Like a
pissed-up old fishwife with a mouth like a sewer – and it
was odds on there'd be someone in earshot who'd know *of*
her, even if they didn't know her personally.

But it was clearly too late to try and lead her away and
talk some sense into her. As Josie approached the double
doors, she was already behind a small gathering of nurses,
who were hurrying to the scene in a blur of blue.

She spotted Lizzie right away. It wasn't difficult, as she
was dressed to be noticed, in spray-on drainpipes and a
clingy long-sleeved vest top. And Josie could tell from her
stance that she was as drunk as she'd sounded on the phone
– slightly wide-footed, as if recently dismounted from a

horse. The same stance she remembered from her own childhood, when her mam had returned from a lunchtime session down the pub. She'd stand in front of the mantel-piece, randomly prodding her hair, and trying to focus suffi-ciently to apply her signature blood-red lipstick. Like a kid holding a crayon and trying to colour inside the lines. One of the reasons Josie never adorned her own mouth.

Christine was still in bed. She'd given birth less than two hours ago, for fuck's sake! And to the side, standing protectively in front of both mother and baby (and looking like she'd happily deal with any nonsense) stood a nurse – senior by the looks of it, probably the ward sister – with her hands held out in front of her, at chest height. She put Josie in mind of a football referee trying to stop an angry forward starting on a defender.

She hurried up. Touched Lizzie's arm, which was imme-diately shaken off. 'Lizzie, it's *me*,' she hissed. 'Will you please calm the fu—' she quickly swallowed the expletive – 'down!'

Lizzie glanced at her, but only briefly. She was already engaged in conversation with the nurse, clearly. 'Of course I'm going to fucking leave!' she was saying. 'Does it look like I want to stay here? I've seen everything I need to see, thank you very much. And, yes,' she added, in response to some pointed nodding and gesticulating by the nurse to one of the others, 'feel free to call whoever the fuck you like, love. I am *outta* here,' she finished dramatically. Josie rolled her eyes. Had she heard that expression off the telly?

'And as for you, you little bitch –' she stabbed a burgundy-tipped finger in Christine's direction – 'don't even *think* about coming back home.'

Christine, whey-faced and visibly shaking, said nothing in response to this.

The nurse did. 'Mrs Parker!' she exploded. 'That's *enough!*'

Josie became aware now of the occupants of the two other beds in the bay. Both young-looking. Both wide-eyed. One with a hand to her mouth. There was the sound of a baby crying. Christine's baby, she realised. She saw her friend glance at the cot. Watched Lizzie's eyes swivel too, towards the source of the noise. Josie touched her arm again. Grabbed onto it more firmly this time. Was she bloody going or wasn't she? The nurse was moving towards her, perhaps to take hold of her other arm.

The nurse didn't, though. She just strode up and was right in Lizzie's face. 'Out.' She didn't raise her voice now. She didn't need to. A noise from behind alerted Josie to the reason why – the arrival of more support. She let Lizzie go and glanced backwards, relieved. She wouldn't put it past Lizzie to engage in a spot of brawling, but perhaps not with the three burly young porters who were now approaching.

Lizzie wasn't done yet, however. Stepping round the nurse, presumably keen to add a pithy parting shot, she headed straight for her daughter. But then turned her head away again and, as if on impulse, cleared her throat.

Oh, no …

Josie realised what she was about to do, and reached out in vain to stop it happening. Too late. As Christine's expression changed from fear to disgust, Lizzie filled her mouth, noisily, and then spat into the cot. 'That *thing*? My *grandson*?' she said. 'Not fucking likely.'

She even laughed – a weird, almost Disney-esque moment, Josie thought – as, like the bad fairy godmother, she was quickly escorted out, and everyone was suddenly talking all at once.

Thankfully, Lizzie's phlegm missed the baby's face by inches. A new blanket was fetched. Both cot and baby were changed. And after an intense round of chatter – the sister and Josie comforting Christine, the junior nurses reassuring the other mothers – within no more than fifteen minutes the ward was once again quiet and orderly, the echoes of the whirlwind that had so recently invaded it reduced to memories (and gossip, for when new visitors came) of the unpleasant scene that had been witnessed.

Christine was shaken, but surprisingly sanguine on the surface, but then, she'd just given birth and was shattered, no doubt. Josie suspected it would only properly hit her later. There was also the small matter of expectation and familiarity. Lizzie had always been fiery. Had always had a temper. She wore her heart on her sleeve, said what she thought, and Josie couldn't recall a time when she'd cared the slightest jot who happened to hear her.

But this was rich, even for her – this thing had clearly sent her reeling. Which made Josie anxious; could she really be *that* blind about Mo? As for Christine herself, perhaps now, for all the excruciating embarrassment, she was relieved it was done now, finally over, this secret that she'd been carrying. A weight that, emotionally, must have felt almost as big as the baby's. Which, positive though it was, still frustrated Josie greatly – why on *earth* hadn't she confided in her?

Still, that was done now, and Josie knew she could only follow Christine's lead. Perhaps she'd always known, after all, how her mum was going to react. Perhaps things were panning out entirely as she'd expected.

Well, from Christine's point of view, perhaps, but certainly not the nurse's. Who was indeed the ward sister. And a ward sister who now had a problem.

And once tea had been bought – the hospital trolley having rattled up in timely fashion – it was one she was keen to address. And in doing so (and this was unusual, so a testament to the difficulty of the situation) she was only too happy to include Josie. The problem was simple and quick to establish; that, from the sound of it, Christine – and her baby – had nowhere to go.

'Which leaves us with a problem, my love,' she told Christine gently. 'Because I can't discharge you till I know you have an address to be discharged *to*. And, with the best will in the world – and I obviously don't know the circumstances in the way you both do – I can't see your mother coming round. And that's assuming we were entirely comfortable with you taking the baby there anyway. Which, given what we've just witnessed' – she grimaced – 'I'm not *entirely* sure we are.'

Christine shook her head. 'No, that's fine. I don't want anything to do with her ever again. For as long as she lives,' she added, for good measure.

So now what? Josie was conscious of time marching on. What had begun as a dash to drop her friend off in hospital had now become something very different. It was already gone four and she knew her mam would be wondering where she'd got to. It was Friday in her house just as much as in Lizzie's, and she'd be wanting to get ready for her night out. It didn't happen often but, as Josie thought about the mess Christine was in, she found herself really appreciating her mother.

Not to mention understanding the background to the extreme way Lizzie had reacted, even as she'd been completely appalled. Lizzie was clearly reeling. She'd been that blind about Mo – was still that blind, clearly. She'd obviously had not the tiniest inkling what Mo had been up to, so he'd obviously covered his tracks well. He was a master – had effectively washed his hands of Christine, and carried on, business as usual, with her mother. And as for Christine – Josie sighed; it was all such a needless mess, this – she'd simply buried her head in the sand.

But Christine was still a *child*. That was the crux of it. An innocent. Something Josie hadn't been in a long time. And a victim, every bit as much as if Mo *had* raped her, rather than just seduced her. Something Josie still wasn't ruling out. The five years that separated them in age suddenly seemed like a gulf, with Josie, so much older and world-wearier and wiser – and Christine, for all that she too was now a mum, still on the other side. She'd been seduced by a fucking expert and was now about to pay the price. It was all a bit of a ball scratcher, as their Vinnie would say.

Christine started, shaken awake from a half-sleep. She opened her eyes to see one of the nurses trundling up the ward, on her way round with her box of tricks on wheels. Temperature. Blood pressure. Have you needed a pee yet?

She turned towards the cot, seeing but still not quite believing. Not even a full afternoon had passed since her baby had been born and here he was, already denied a grandmother and homeless. They both were. She tried to chase the thought away. What a life you've been born into, she thought wretchedly, as she looked at him. He was opening and closing his eyes, as if trying out being alive and not yet being sure about it. And why wouldn't he?

Christine glanced across at Josie, who was reading a magazine in the visitor's chair, and remembered her question about whether she'd not considered getting rid of it. Him. Not 'it'. Him. She shouldn't have said that, not now he'd been born. Christine knew Josie would brood on that now.

As if reading her thoughts, Josie glanced up and slapped the magazine pages back together. She glanced up at the clock, high on the wall. 'Good doze?' she asked Christine. 'Look, I need to be heading home soon, mate,' she added. 'Mam'll be doing her nut if I don't get my skates on. Question now, though, is what are we going to do with *you*? Because it certainly seems you've got your wish to get away from her, doesn't it? But to where? That's the thing. Where will you go?'

'I don't know,' Christine admitted. 'But if they need a new address to discharge me to, I was thinking I'll give them Nicky's. I was thinking I might ask him if I can move in with him – not permanently,' she added, watching Josie's expression become increasingly horrified, 'not for ever. Just for a bit. Just for the first couple of weeks, for when the community midwife does her visits.'

'Your *Nicky*?' Josie looked aghast at this development. 'Who I don't need to remind you lives with the world's druggiest druggy! Seriously, Chrissy, move in with him and Brian? Are you mad?' Her voice was growing shriller. 'Think about the midwife! What she'd see. What she'd *think*! She'd have the social on you before you've even changed a nappy, you div. You can't go there!'

Christine looked at her friend, feeling a mixture of anger and exasperation. It was all very well Josie stating the bleeding obvious – which she was; she was under no illusions where her brother was concerned. But didn't she *get* it? Where else could she and the baby go? She said so.

'So it *has* to be Nicky's,' she reminded her friend irritably. 'Because at least Nicky *cares*.' And she believed that. Whatever else was true, she had never stopped believing that. Even if she knew he'd be less than pleased to see them.

Josie sighed heavily. 'Oh, *Chris* ...' she began, in a tone that made it sound like Christine had suggested they relocate to one of the benches down by the market. 'Oh, Chris, you *can't* ...' She trailed off, running a hand along the baby's cot. 'Mate, look ... I tell you what ... *God*, I shouldn't even be suggesting this. My Eddie's a bloody saint, but he's still only human ... but –'

'No,' Christine said, shaking her head. 'We'll be fine. I told you, I'm going to ask Nicky if he'll have us. Which he *will*, so there's no need –'

'Yes there *is*,' Josie said, leaning forward towards the bed. 'It's not your Nicky – it's that druggy bloody mate of his. You really want your beautiful baby around *him*?'

Of course not, Christine thought, her eyes smarting with tears now. Of course she bloody didn't! But what choice did she have?

She tried to say so but the words caught in her throat, panic bubbling underneath them, like a welling tide.

'You're coming to us.' Josie put a hand up, even as she said it. 'Don't start. Not for *ever*. Just for a couple of weeks, till the midwife's finished with you.'

'Josie, no,' Christine said again, reaching for a tissue. 'What about your Eddie? Jose, he'll freak.'

'He'll do as he's bloody told. No. That's that. So no arguments. You tell the midwife that you're coming to live with us, okay? And while you're with us, we can go down the social and see about getting a flat for you. Because they've got to give you one. You are technically homeless now, after all.'

It was like the sun coming out when you were expecting rain all day. Almost too bright to bear. 'Oh, Josie, *really*?' she said.

'*Really*.' Josie leaned over and hugged Christine. 'I don't know why I even dithered about it. Some friend I'd bloody be if I couldn't put you up in your hour of need.'

'Only if you are *absolutely* sure,' Christine said, feeling the tears come again. 'Oh Josie, and I bet little Paula will love it – love *him*.'

Josie looked down at the baby. 'I wouldn't count on that,' she said, smiling. 'She's a toddler, don't forget. And used to getting all the attention, as well. Throw this one into the mix, and it could easily mean tears before bedtime. Speaking of which, now you know it's a boy, have you decided on a name?'

Christine had been reluctant to be drawn on the matter of names up to now. Oh, she'd thought about it plenty. Rolled names round her tongue like they were marbles. But to actually voice any preference … She had always been much too frightened to do that. Suppose something had gone wrong? On top of everything else – everything that was already wrong in her life, suppose in this – this one thing that was hers, her choice and responsibility ... No, she'd definitely not decided on a name.

But now she smiled at Josie. 'Joey,' she said, getting the syllables out at last. Liking the sound of the name, too, as she spoke it. She said it again. 'Joey.'

'That's perfect,' Josie said. 'He looks just like a Joey, too. And I'm glad you haven't come over all Bob Marley and given him a Jah name.'

Christine laughed, brushing the tears away, letting the happiness catch hold of her. She knew it would only be fleeting, so she grabbed at it hungrily. She was young, fit and strong. So was he. They'd be okay. 'No, it's definitely Joey,' she said, 'after this lad I fancied at school – Joey Brearton. He never knew I bleeding existed, but I always liked his name.'

Josie laughed out loud. 'You're priceless, you are!' she said. 'Naming your kid after a boy who never knew you existed. And what about his last name? I'm hazarding a guess that you won't be giving him Mo's?'

'Not a chance,' Christine said. 'He'll be a Parker, just like the rest of us.' She leaned across to stroke Joey's head. *Joey*. He *did* look like a Joey. 'Another kid in our family with just my mam's name to carry him. Poor little fucker. Another one without a dad.'

Josie managed a smile but didn't say anything to contradict her. She knew as well as Christine did that little Joey would be exactly that. Another kid who didn't know who his dad was, just like his mum and his uncle. 'But with a wonderful mam to take care of him,' she said, rising from the chair. 'And, speaking of mams, if I don't get back and fetch our Paula soon I'm going to have my ear chewed off, aren't I?'

Christine reached for Josie's arm. 'You sure, mate? You sure Eddie's going to be okay with me – *us* – staying?'

'Course he is,' Josie said. 'So let the nurse know, okay? I'll phone here in the morning to check you're still okay to be discharged, and if you are, I'll be back lunchtime to pick you up.'

'And you'll pick up my stuff and that from home?' Christine asked, realising there was still all that to sort yet. 'And all the bottles and nappies and stuff in my bedroom?'

Josie nodded, and promised she'd do exactly that. Though as Christine watched her leave, and returned the wave Josie turned and gave her as she disappeared, she wondered if any of it would actually *be* in her bedroom. Knowing her mam as she did she wouldn't have been remotely surprised if Josie told her tomorrow that it had all been dumped in the front garden. She sighed. Of the home that wasn't her home any more.

If it had ever really been in the first place.

Chapter 4

Josie looked out of the bedroom window and immediately felt guilty. It wasn't yet eight in the morning, and it was Saturday, too, but already Eddie was out the front, shirt sleeves up, spanner in hand, tinkering with his beloved Ford Escort. Well, not so beloved currently, as it was refusing to work, but she didn't doubt he'd eventually get it going again. If there was any justice, at any rate, given the amount of time he spent taking care of it.

She'd done wrong, landing Christine and the baby on them without asking him. Inviting trouble to their door, as he'd immediately pointed out. They both knew what Lizzie Parker could be like when she was roused.

But his concern was, as ever, more for Josie than for himself, and the fact that he'd taken it as well as he had made it worse. It wasn't just the business of getting involved in it, after all. It was also that it wasn't fair to expect him to put up with a newborn for the best part of a fortnight. He worked all hours, and Paula was a handful enough currently, being at that age when it was all 'me, me, me', day and night, and with the long days and short nights of summer thrown in, she was up before six every morning as well.

Paula was sitting on her parents' bed, flicking through a picture book and singing to herself. Josie glanced at her daughter now, and couldn't help but smile. She also wondered, as she often did, how she'd managed to be so incredibly blessed. There was her sister Lyndsey, off her head mostly, her brother Vinnie banged up in prison, and here *she* was, with her Eddie, her beautiful little daughter, and, since the spring, even their own lovely home. So much happiness, which she wasn't sure she'd any right to.

She hardly dare think about it. Dared not take any of it for granted, ever – if she did she had this horrible notion (which never seemed to go away and often visited her in nightmares) that something terrible would happen, and she'd lose it all again.

Right now, however, Josie's thoughts were on Christine, and she wondered what kind of night she might have had. Pretty sketchy, if her own first night with Paula was anything to go by. And with everything else – with her future so uncertain, she doubted the poor girl had slept a wink. 'Come on, missy,' she said to Paula, holding her arms out to pick her up. 'Let's go down and make your dad a cuppa, shall we? See if we can butter him up a bit.'

'Ah, bribery, now, is it?' Eddie remarked, as Josie went out to join him, mug of tea in one hand, Paula on her opposite hip. He threw the spanner he'd been wielding back into the rusty old biscuit tin that served as his tool box.

'Sort of,' Josie admitted. 'I do feel bad, love, I really do. I just couldn't think where else she could go.'

'Back to her fucking mother's, is where,' he said, accepting the tea. He'd been out there for some time now and had smudges of black on his nose and cheeks.

'Dirty Daddy!' Paula trilled. '*Dirty* Daddy!'

Josie set her down. Being early on a Saturday morning, the street was safe enough, being so quiet. And she was more interested in the mud in the front flowerbed than the road.

'Seriously, love, that's what *should* be happening, Mo's kid or otherwise. Can you imagine us treating our Paula like that? *Ever?* I'd fucking kill for her, I would.' He shook his head. 'How could anyone throw their own kid out?'

Josie loved Eddie for lots of reasons – had done since she'd first started seeing him. But never more than when he talked about their Paula. Even though, at the same time, she knew she'd lived a bit more than him, which meant she knew that, in real life, it wasn't always that simple. Thank God that, for him, it was.

'I know, love,' she said, 'but perhaps she'll come round.'

'That mad cow had better not come round here!' he said, and she could tell from his expression that he was purposely misinterpreting her meaning.

Josie smiled. 'She wouldn't dare.' And of that she *was* sure. For all that Lizzie could mouth off, Josie was still a McKellan. No, there was no danger of anything like that. 'Anyway,' she added, 'it's only for the ten days while the midwife is calling – and you'll be at work most of the time anyway, so you'll hardly see them.'

Eddie grunted, then put the tea down and picked up his spanner. 'Well, let's hope so,' he said, 'and I mean it, babe, really. I'm not having you running around like a mad thing looking after that bleeding kid of hers, all right?'

Josie tried not to grin. For all his big talk – which he liked to try out from time to time – Eddie was actually a teddy bear at heart. And a loyal one; another reason why she'd fallen for him so completely. He'd do anything for her and Paula, and he'd always fought her corner – never been afraid of her family (rare in itself). Even Vinnie. She felt safe with him, secure, and that was a feeling beyond value, her life before she'd met him having been no sort of life – her childhood destroyed by rape and, she'd thought, her future with it. But he'd saved her. Would poor Christine be as lucky?

She came around the side of the car and nipped his bum through his oily jeans. 'Thanks, babe,' she said. 'Now, how do you feel about a bacon sarnie? Only I've got to nip down to Lizzie's and pick up Christine's stuff for her, and –'

'And muggins here is expected to hold the baby? Bleeding typical!'

Josie turned and blew him a kiss as she scooped Paula up and headed back inside. 'Half an hour, I'll be, tops, babe,' she promised, deciding that this would probably not be the time to mention that she was going to have to shell out for another cab to fetch Christine back. No, that could wait and, who knew? He might yet fix the car. Miracles did sometimes happen.

Josie wasn't expecting any miracles on Quaker Lane, though. The sarnie made and eaten and the baby put down for her morning nap, she left Eddie to his tinkering and walked the short distance from their house to Lizzie's. It was a proximity that had, up till recently, been quite a plus.

Before all the business of Christine's pregnancy, Lizzie's home had been a friendly, familiar place, mostly because Josie couldn't remember a time when Lizzie and her mam hadn't been friends – that they'd make the trip there from Ringwood Road to catch up on all the gossip, or would have Lizzie, Nicky and Christine in their own kitchen. She'd been one of the constants in a difficult, traumatic childhood.

But this was trauma of a different kind. One that could drive a wedge between them. As she walked, she pondered the conversation she'd had with Lizzie yesterday, before she'd gone down to the hospital and made such an exhibition of herself. Was she regretting that now? She'd been adamant then that she was washing her hands of her daughter. Would she still be of the same mind this morning? Josie hoped not, but though she hung on to a vestige of optimism in her heart, her head said that Lizzie would have softened not a jot.

Reaching the house, and trotting down the cracked concrete path, she decided that, today, she'd not simply walk in. Instead, she bent down and lifted the flap on the letter box. There was a low whine, which she recognised as the hum of the vacuum cleaner. It being Saturday, Lizzie would be cleaning the house. She was no clean freak but she always did the housework on Saturday mornings, because Mo's 'weekly' visits – when they happened – always happened on a weekend.

And he invariably came bearing gifts. Drugs, often – usually just some weed or a bit of Lebanese black – a few cans of cider, and invariably ready cash. And to an extent that since becoming one of his 'regulars' five years back, Lizzie had even given up her job on the fruit and veg stall on John Street Market, fancying herself as some sort of pampered 'kept woman'. It was a point of contention, though Josie wouldn't ever dream of mentioning it. Just one of those things that made you realise the sort of woman you didn't ever want to be. Though Eddie brought the wage in while she looked after little Paula, that was a team effort, both of them doing their respective jobs; she would never in her life want to be 'kept' by any man. In fact, she couldn't wait to get back to work at the factory.

'Lizzie! It's me!' she yelled through the letterbox. 'Can I come in, mate?' But Lizzie clearly couldn't hear her, because the whine of the hoover carried on. She stood up again, tried the door. But it was locked, which surprised her. No one ever locked their doors on Canterbury. Was that how it was, then? That she was expecting her daughter – less than twenty-four hours after giving birth – to show up on the doorstep, babe in arms?

She was just bending down again when the sound of the cleaner stopped. 'It's me!' she called. 'Josie! Can you let us in, mate?'

She heard a noise on the stairs, then the door was flung open. Lizzie stood there, looking gaunt underneath her usual layer of slap; all in place, of course, despite her only doing the cleaning. Josie wondered if she'd ever feel that same sense of competitiveness with Paula as Lizzie had done since Christine hit her teens. No, she couldn't. Not at all. It was beyond her imagining.

But perhaps that was because she'd never seen herself as a looker. Far from it. She'd spent most of her childhood and teens doing everything she could to remove every trace of girlishness. First as a response to all the slap her own mam wore and after Melvin … She shuddered. After what he'd done to her … Well, it was almost a miracle, her and Eddie. She'd never forgotten that. He'd saved her. Made her whole again. She'd never forget that, either.

Maybe it was different for women like Lizzie. She'd been a looker, no doubt about it. Striking. Always a head turner. And when it seemed she'd given birth to an equally pretty daughter, Josie would have reckoned she'd be pleased. But it was never like that. The more Christine grew and blossomed, the harder Lizzie seemed to take it; dressing younger and younger, as if clinging desperately to a raft. She'd embraced punk like a drowning man might embrace a

lifebelt, and though she didn't know it, there were mutter-
ings from those who liked to mutter that, with Mo's thing
for young flesh well known around the estate, she was looking a bit raddled and desperate these days.

She certainly looked raddled now. 'Oh, so it's been
discharged then,' she said, turning around and stalking off
down the hallway. 'And you're putting her up, then, are
you?' she added. 'Like some kind of mug?' She turned
around in the kitchen doorway, her eyes boring into Josie's
reproachfully. 'I thought you were a fucking mate, Jose.'

'I *am*, Liz,' Josie said, shutting the front door and following her. The house smelt of furniture polish. Ordinary.
Clean. Funny how easy it was to create an atmosphere of
calm and normality. Just that whiff of polish and everything
was okay. Was on the surface, at least. There was still all
the crud swept under the carpet. 'And like I *tried* to tell you
yesterday,' she continued, 'there's no point going on one at
me. I'm just the bleeding piggy in the middle, me, as per
usual.'

Lizzie had picked up a packet of Regals from the kitchen
counter and now lit one, blowing the smoke across the
room towards Josie. 'Your choice,' she said coldly. 'What do
you want, then? All her worldly goods, I assume?'

Josie shook her head. '*No*. Look, Lizzie, she's only stopping at mine till the midwife's done her visits. She needed
a fixed abode, didn't she? You know that as well as I do.
And while she's with me, she'd going to put in for a council
flat –'

46

Lizzie sneered. 'Oh, she is, is she? Just like that, eh?'

Well, you should know, Josie thought, irritable at Lizzie's complete lack of insight. Wasn't the promise of getting a council place precisely why she'd decided not to abort Nicky? She'd said so often enough down the years, and Josie had understood – all her friends had. Having a baby – though unplanned – was her chance to create a better life. To get away from her horrible excuses for parents. Could she not see it was happening again? Was she *blind*?

'No, not just like that,' she replied, 'but she'll obviously get one, now she's got a nipper in tow.' Though what was going to happen between the midwife finishing and a place being found for her, Josie had no idea. She couldn't expect Eddie to keep her longer. Wouldn't. It wouldn't be fair. But maybe, just maybe, Lizzie *would* come round. She needed to hold the baby. Make that connection. That was key. That it registered that it was her own flesh and blood. That might just soften her up a bit. Right now, though, her expression said it all.

'Anyway, for the moment, I just need the stuff for little Joey. The bottles and nappies and that, plus a few bits and bobs for Chrissy. She'd got nothing but the clothes she had on when I took her in yesterday. And they're in a right state, as you can imagine, the poor thing.'

If Josie had hoped the mention of Christine struggling in labour might soften Lizzie's heart, she was mistaken. 'Oh, it's *Joey*, is it?' she said. 'Little *Joey*. *Diddums*.' The same implacable expression greeted this acid pronouncement as it had everything else.

But then, all of a sudden, Lizzie seemed to drop the attitude as swiftly as she might have a hot brick. She pulled out a stool from under the worktop and sat down on it heavily, her face beginning to contort as she did so.

She was crying. That was what was happening. She was sobbing. Josie hurried to put an arm around her. She felt bony. Brittle. 'Aww, mate,' Josie said, squeezing her friend's shoulder. 'I know this is all shit – I *do* – I really understand how you must feel about it, you know. But in time you'll work it out. I know you will. You have to. We're talking about your grandson here, Lizzie. It's –'

'Yes, my grandson by *my* fucking bloke, Jose! Don't forget that little detail! My daughter's bastard by my fucking *bloke*! You don't get it, do you? That's all I can think of – of her screwing my fucking fella! Where did they do it? When? I can hardly bear go in her bedroom without heaving. Were they screwing in there whenever I was out at fucking work?'

'Liz, it wasn't *like* that … He worked on her. Got her *drunk* …'

There it was. Out. If it could ever have stayed in. Lizzie angrily shook Josie's arm from her shoulder. 'How the fuck would you know? She give you blow by blow about it, did she? Fill you in on all the sordid details? The little bitch. I'm not interested in hearing any of her fucking excuses.

How could she *do* that to me? I never want to see her or that fucking kid again as long as I live.'

Josie felt the irritation well again. 'What about Mo?' she asked. 'Hmm? Where does he figure in this? What's his part in it, eh? I told you, it wasn't like that!'

'So *she* says.'

'Don't be so bloody naïve! That's the way you're determined to see it, is it? That he's just some poor helpless sod whose head was turned by your calculating, predatory daughter? I notice you're cleaning the house. Hoping to see him, are you, Lizzie?'

She had to stop herself saying more. From spelling out a few more home truths. Christ – like she even *had* to! He was the biggest bloody drug dealer around and the biggest womaniser to boot. How Lizzie could live in such breathtaking denial was beyond astonishing.

Josie sometimes wondered if life wouldn't be a whole lot less fraught with anxiety if she could be that blessedly naïve. Oh, yes, Lizzie had probably lived a bit – she was in her thirties, after all – but at the tender age of twenty-two, so had Josie. Too much, too soon. And as a consequence she knew exactly what some men were like. Not just the filthy nonce who'd raped her. But her own scumbag of a brother-in-law, Robbo, who'd tried to get himself between her legs too.

And who was she to say – in all seriousness – how that particular nasty memory could have turned out differently? Suppose he hadn't been a coke-head and a twat and a loser? Suppose he'd liked her, been kind to her, been a confidant and friend to her? How could she say, hand on heart, that she wouldn't have succumbed to his charms? And Mo *was* a charmer. Good looking, full of swagger, knew how to smooth-talk women. Whether Christine accepted the fact or otherwise, he *had* as good as raped her. Known exactly what he was about, confident of controlling her innocent teenage mind.

It had been playing on Josie's mind, that – that the reason Christine was adamant Mo hadn't forced himself on her was that she still harboured some sort of wildly naïve hope that, now the baby was born, he'd have a sudden change of heart, and sweep them both off on his white charger. God, she hoped not, but she wasn't ruling it out.

Lizzie sniffed and scowled at her, perhaps reading her mind. 'Fuck off, Josie,' she said, drying her eyes on her sleeve. 'Don't try to make out she's been Miss Fucking Innocent. And don't you worry – *he's* going to fucking get it an' all. You know as well as I do that men'll take it when it's offered on a plate, and that's *exactly* what that sneaky little get has obviously done.'

She stood again, coughed up some phlegm, and lit another cigarette. It had been revolting, what she'd done yesterday, and Josie wondered if she was regretting that today, too. But perhaps not. She was clearly still in too much of a state. She was looking at Josie through eyes which (it was now all so evident) had done a great deal more crying than she'd just witnessed. She had a moment of clarity. Lizzie really *was* that upset. Over fucking Rasta Mo, of all the people in sodding Bradford. A man who'd slept with half the women-of-a-certain-age-and-persuasion on the estate. And was still working his way through the rest. All of which Lizzie knew. All of which she had *always* known. It made no sense.

Or perhaps it was just jealousy of her daughter, pure and simple. And jealousy was a powerful emotion. 'I'm not interested in owt else you've got to say, Josie,' Lizzie told her. 'You've got ten minutes. I'm off next door for a cuppa with Barbara, so get what you need and take it. But tell her to keep well away from me, okay? And if I hear she's been looking for Mo, I'll fucking kill her.'

Josie opened her mouth – *really?* – but thought better of it and closed it. She watched Lizzie leave – slamming the front door behind her – then went upstairs to sort out what she needed to take. Despite what she'd said to Lizzie she decided to take as much as she could carry: all Christine's clothes and shoes, some of her toiletries, plus her precious collection of things for the baby, which she'd been saving up for and buying week on week. She might as well – she doubted there'd be a reconciliation any time soon.

And as she carried them down and then out and then along the road back to Exe Street, she tried her hardest to sympathise with Lizzie's point of view. It must have been hard; she'd had a shit childhood and a pretty shitty adulthood. And however small a part of Mo's harem she was, she was still *in* that harem. You could say – some did – that she was a constant in it, too. He might not cherish her (obviously didn't, since he was all too happy to fuck her daughter) but he saw her regularly, gave her stuff, gave her an *illusion* that she was cherished. And perhaps that illusion, in her shitty life, *was* the raft she clung on to. So, perhaps, she should judge her less harshly. After all, how would she feel if she found out Eddie had been cheating on her? Murderous, no doubt.

Still, in a couple of hours, hospital willing, she'd be bringing Christine and the baby home with her. For ten days, during which time a miracle needed organising. And maybe it would be. Which would be handy, since, last time she heard, miracles were a *lot* easier to whistle up than council flats.

Chapter 5

Christine winced as she passed baby Joey out to Josie, and then again as she climbed out of the taxi. It wasn't Imran's today, and she was glad. He'd take one look at her son and no doubt say something sarky, and she didn't trust herself not to burst into tears. So much crying. It was getting exhausting.

Or she'd thump him. Maybe that was more likely. Because in the last twenty-four hours she'd discovered something about herself. Something that she hadn't really reckoned on. A kind of fury, the like of which she'd never felt before, which rose up inside her, and took her unawares. An instinctive, protective fury that pitched her against anyone who seemed against Joey – and though she recognised that it might be what she'd heard called maternal instinct, the term seemed much too commonplace, the idea of it too benign, to have anything to do with the intensity of how she felt.

It had been the strangest, most draining twenty-four hours of her life. She'd barely eaten, barely slept, barely been able to shuffle to the loo, even – and that despite the night nurse's insistence that she wouldn't be allowed to leave till she'd 'passed water'; something she hadn't under-stood at first, like so much of the language and routines on the ward. She'd felt nagged at and violated and never left alone. Shall we see if we can get baby to latch on? Shall we check your down-belows? Baby sounds like he needs changing. Baby looks like he needs winding. Where's your mam, love? Expecting anyone? Shouldn't you be putting baby down?

And worst of all – that muttered 'oh', when the night nurse came on duty and peered into the little plastic cot while doing her rounds. She'd not said anything else to Christine after that. She hadn't needed to. Her expression, as she glanced from Joey and up to Christine and back again, had already amply made its point. And then Christine had seen her afterwards, up at the nurses' station at the far end of the ward, leaning over the desk and whispering to one of the other nurses. Then glancing back at her and whispering to the other nurse again. Christine hated her for that. *Hated* her. For Joey.

'You okay, love?' Josie was holding Joey like she knew exactly what she was doing. Holding him in the crook of one arm, jiggling him slightly so she didn't wake him, the Morrisons carrier bag with Christine's dirty clothes in dangling from the same elbow, and still proffering her other hand to help her friend out. 'Come on,' she said. 'Let me help you. Feeling sore?'

Christine took Josie's hand, thinking how the word 'sore' didn't *begin* to describe it. She'd remembered her mam mentioning it, a good while back, when she'd first confessed to being pregnant, and had ventured to ask what giving birth was like. 'Like having your fanny put through a fucking mincer' had been her immediate brusque reply.

It galled Christine, somehow, to realise she'd been right. To accept that in some things her mam did know better. The thought also saddened her. She'd ruminated on it miserably for half the frigging night. To think her mam had been through exactly what she had in order to give birth to her. And had now disowned her, apparently. She couldn't quite make sense of it. How it might have happened. How she felt about her baby – that she would kill for him, love him always – and how her mam now seemed to feel about her. How did you get from the one to the other?

She clambered out, with Josie's help, and grimaced as she did so. 'Jesus, Jose,' she said. 'I'm feeling *battered*. I thought once you'd done the birth bit that was it for the pain.'

Josie shook her head. 'You wish, mate. You've got stitches?' Christine nodded as she took her friend's free arm. 'That'll be it then. Then there's the after-pains, of course …' She'd already steered her in the direction of the house. They'd pulled up a couple of cars down as Eddie was outside tinkering with his Escort. 'And brace yourself, love,' Josie said. 'Because now the hard work begins. As in feeds round the clock and no sleep for the foreseeable future. Welcome to the wonderful world of motherhood!'

'Little ray of sunshine she is, isn't she?' Eddie had popped up from under his bonnet, his curly hair haloed by the sun. 'Full of sympathy and helpful little nuggets of advice, eh?'

Josie aimed a toe in his direction and Christine felt a stab of anxiety for Joey's safety. 'Piss off, Eddie,' Josie said, laughing. Then she took a step closer to him. 'Want a peek?' she asked, twisting so he could better see into the folds of blanket.

Eddie grinned. 'That's a whole bundle of trouble right there, that is. You all right, love?' he asked, turning to Christine, his expression sympathetic.

'S'pose,' she said, though she felt anything but.

Christine had always felt at home round at Josie's, where everything felt just that bit nicer. When her own house was full of tired, old-fashioned furniture, Josie and Eddie's place was almost like a show home. They didn't have much spare cash, she knew, but they had made the best of what they did have. There was a modern low-backed sofa, one of those huge paper lanterns hanging from the middle of the front room ceiling, a glass coffee table with chrome legs and a huge shaggy rug. They also had one of those enormous stone fireplaces along one wall, with a specially designed shelf for the telly.

Most of all, though, was that Josie's home was a place of warmth and calm, where no one ever shouted or got wasted. And watching her friend now, doing everything one-handed with the baby still tucked close beside her,

Christine knew immediately that she was going to dread having to leave.

But leave she must. She was a mam herself now, with a whole tiny life depending on her, and much as part of her wanted to collapse into a heap and sleep, another part was already struggling with the scenario before her – of both Joey *and* her being mothered by Josie. Of her friend taking charge, of having *already* taken Joey. And there it was again; this powerful urge to take him back again.

She didn't. The more rational part of her didn't feel equal to the task of doing anything but watch her friend gratefully, as she lay the baby on the couch and in seconds removed the woolly hat and knitted coat it had taken her so long to put on.

Joey stirred and kicked his tiny legs. 'There,' Josie cooed. 'That's better, isn't it, little man? Oh, our Paula's going to think she's died and gone to heaven,' she added, turning to Christine, who still felt incapable of doing anything but standing there, mutely. She felt dizzy now, foggy, as though her brain wasn't quite functioning.

Josie obviously noticed. 'Sit down,' she ordered. 'Go on, before you fall down.' She picked Joey up again and nodded towards the couch. 'I expect your blood pressure's through the floor. You must be dropping on your feet. You need a proper rest, Chris. You'll feel much better once you've had a decent kip. Tell you what, I'll leave Paula round my mam's for a bit longer. Look after your little man for you while you get your head down for a bit, okay?'

'Oh, Josie,' Christine started, 'I can't let you. I'm supposed to –'

'Nonsense. Now look,' she said, going round to the far end of the couch. 'Don't laugh, but I couldn't carry your Moses basket down on top of everything else. So I thought this would do for now … Least till I go back up to your mam's and fetch it …'

She'd hooked her heel round something and was dragging it across the carpet backwards. 'Had a bit of help from Paula – and a gift – of her second favourite teddy. Just on loan, mind.' She grinned. And what she'd pulled out was a drawer. 'It's from the chest up in the spare room,' she explained. 'And trust me, this is luxury. My nan used to put my dad to bed in a drawer.' She laughed then. 'Only difference being that it was still *in* the chest of drawers, and if he played up, she'd shut it – with him still in it!'

She stopped laughing then, and came across, sitting down beside Christine, who had started sobbing so hard that her shoulders were shaking. It had come out of nowhere. It was seeing the cot. The wooden drawer. The whole emotional whump of it. That she was a mum, with a baby, and had nowhere to go.

But for her friend, anyway … Life suddenly felt so precarious. 'It's all right, love,' Josie soothed. 'You're just tired, overwhelmed. Come on, let's get this little fella tucked up – and don't worry. He's quite safe. Come on, to bed with you. *Now.*'

* * *

Joey's cry cut through the fog like a knife. So distant, yet so powerful, as if designed specifically to seek her out. Which she supposed it was, and the fierce protectiveness washed over her immediately, but now it was accompanied by a feeling of something like claustrophobia, as the thoughts that had assailed her before she'd drifted off to sleep all returned with a vengeance. She was on her own. She had a child to support. Her life was changed beyond recognition. No more could she ever do what she liked when she liked. Her life would instead be governed by the cries and the needs of her tiny infant, who needed things she didn't yet really know how to give. She was clumsy. Inept. Fearful of breaking him or dropping him. Had nothing to offer him except her love. Which counted for nowt, really. Not in the real world. And the glances of the nurse and midwives were beginning to hit home. Because, even if sympathetic, which she conceded they mostly were, the taint of disapproval, of regret, was still so obvious behind the smiles. She'd been a stupid girl. Irresponsible. And not at all up to the job she'd been given as a result. A job that would last for longer than she'd been alive.

She had no idea how much time had passed, only that it was still daylight and that she was sweaty. She'd not got into the bed – she'd had no energy to undress – but had pulled the candlewick bedspread over her, more for comfort than heat. She thrust it off, and ground the heels of her hands into her stinging eyes.

She felt a gentle hand on her elbow, and started. She'd not heard Josie come in. She rolled over to see Josie standing there, holding a mug of something. Christine could still hear Joey mewling downstairs. 'Feeling better now?' Josie asked.

'Much,' Christine lied. 'What time is it?'

'Just after five. And that little one of yours needs a feed. I'd make up a bottle, but, you know ...' She let the statement lie there. And Christine *did* know. That was her job. To make up a bottle and feed her one-day-old baby. Just thinking about it made her breasts stab with pain. The midwife – not at all happy that Christine said she'd bottle feed – had promised her it would stop in a few days, but in the meantime it was as if they had a life of their own.

It had all seemed so straightforward, deciding to bottle feed. There never seemed any question but that it was the sensible thing to do. It was what her mam had done, and what everyone else seemed to do too. And if she'd needed convincing – which she hadn't – her next-door neighbour would certainly have put the lid on it; whipping her saggy tits out here, there and everywhere, not seeming to give a stuff who clocked them. Could she imagine doing that, *ever*? No, she couldn't.

But perhaps she'd been wrong. Her boobs were actually leaking now, under her bra. Doing what they were supposed to, she realised. Why hadn't that ever occurred to her? But now she was at Josie's there was nowhere properly private to do it anyway, and she certainly wasn't getting her tits out in front of Eddie. She swung her legs over the side of the bed, stretched and stood up. 'No, no,' she said. 'I'll do it.'

'Good,' Josie said, already turning to go downstairs again. Christine followed. 'All important for the bonding.' Another word she'd kept hearing. As if she wasn't 'bonded' to Joey more that she'd ever felt possible to be connected to anyone, ever.

She followed Josie down the stairs and into the front room. Joey's wail cut through the air like a speaker cranked up to high. How could something so little make so much noise?

Paula's eyes lit up when she saw Christine and she rushed towards her, arms spread. 'Kissty!' she sang, seemingly oblivious, over the racket. 'Kissty! You got a baby!! Baby Doey!' Her excitement made Christine want to cry all over again.

Josie had already set out everything Christine needed to make the feed up. The steriliser sat on the draining board, bottles and teats bobbing inside it, the tin of formula on the worktop beside it. Joey himself, still in his drawer, was now up on the little table, eyes screwed up, lower lip quivering as he screamed his fury, fists clenched, cheeks scarlet. Christine felt a jolt of fear at the idea of picking him up.

Josie must have seen her expression. 'Leave him be,' she said. 'Soon as he smells you, he'll only kick off even more, trust me. There you go. Know what to do?'

Christine nodded. 'They showed me.'

Paula was tugging at her top. 'I help! I help! Feed baby Doey!'

'He's a very hungry baby Doey, isn't he?' she said, scooping Paula up into her arms instead, and kissing her forehead. And then wincing as her little body squashed her still-stabbing boobs and her little feet drummed against her belly.

'I help you?' she asked again.

Josie calmly peeled her off. 'No you don't, missy,' she said. 'You've got to help me lay the table. Time for tea soon. Daddy's waiting. And he'll be kicking off himself if we don't get a move on,' she added.

And though she didn't mean anything by it, Christine felt it even so. That she was a nuisance, and Joey's crying was really getting on Josie's nerves.

She peeled the plastic lid off the can of formula, racked with guilt.

The community midwife was called Sister Davies and arrived on the doorstep at ten the following morning. It being a Sunday, there had obviously been no rush for anyone to get up, so Joey's dawn screaming session felt doubly bad. Anxious not to make things worse, having crept down for a bottle just as a watery sun was rising, Christine had stayed put in the spare room with him then for as long as possible, willing him to settle again, so he wouldn't disturb anyone. Then, once he was asleep again, had washed and dressed herself as quietly as she could.

But she could tell by Eddie's expression that all her creeping around hadn't helped. He was too nice to show it, but she knew even so. Having them stay was a nuisance he could do without. Having let the midwife in – he'd had little choice as he'd been on his way back out the front to work on his car – he immediately made himself scarce.

Josie seemed keen to leave Christine alone with the midwife too. 'That's my husband,' she explained briskly, her offer of coffee having been declined. 'We're putting Chrissy and Joey up for a few days, just till she gets herself something sorted out.'

The midwife clucked as she put her bag down. She looked fierce and disapproving, and, fearful of an interrogation, Christine wished Josie would stay. She had already been clear. She must keep her trap shut about her grandparents – and definitely about Nicky. She must make it clear to everyone who asked that she had nowhere to go. They'd not make her a priority otherwise. Christine didn't see how any of this would be anything to do with the midwife. How would she know anything about it? Why would she even care? Yes, she knew she had to do that when she called the council Monday morning, but was the midwife going to grill her about it too? She hoped not, but looking at the woman's doughy, unsmiling face, she was no longer sure.

As it turned out, it was obvious why Josie had taken Paula and left them to it – and also why she'd pulled the front-room curtains before she went. Because the first thing the midwife did after pronouncing Joey a 'handsome fella' was to ask her to take off her knickers and lie on the couch, in order that she could check that everything was 'as it should be'.

'And how are your breasts?' she wanted to know, apparently satisfied with things at the other end. 'Any heat coming off them? Any pain?'

Once again Christine was subjected to a quick but thorough pummelling, but though she said yes to both, neither admission seemed to cause the midwife any concern. 'Hot and cold flannels' was all she said. 'You're just going to have to grin and bear it, I'm afraid.'

Finally, Sister Davies turned her attention to Joey. Christine had been proud of her small success in managing to dress him relatively easily. Seeing the matter-of-fact way Josie handled him had begun to give her confidence. In fact, he seemed altogether less fretful when she held him firmly. But it didn't prepare her for the way Sister Davies handled him; undressing him unceremoniously, seemingly oblivious to how he shivered, weighing him in a little pouch thing and jotting a figure down in his notes, then inspecting him all over, at one point jiggling his legs alarmingly, before finally handing him back, naked, stunned and bawling, so Christine could re-dress him while she put away her things.

'Well,' she said at last. 'Baby seems to be okay. And how about you, young lady?' She eyed Christine quizzically. 'Are you eating well? Have you slept? Are *you* okay?'

Then she smiled – an expression that hadn't seemed to come naturally, but transformed her face – and Christine decided she wasn't quite as fierce as she looked.

'I think so ... I'm ... well, I don't know yet ...' she told her. 'It's all a bit ...'

'Overwhelming?' The midwife smiled again. 'Well, my love, why ever would it *not* be? Doesn't matter who you are. Black or white. Rich or poor. Young or old. Same for *all* of us. A woman's lot, is what it is. One day at a time,' she finished, standing up and patting Christine's shoulder. 'Take it one day at a time. That's the best way.'

It was only after she'd gone that Christine realised why she liked her. Black or white, she'd said. Just like that. Had just tripped right off her tongue. Sister Davies didn't hold it against her.

The same could not be said of the housing officer who was sitting on the same couch at Josie's house a scant six days later. It wasn't half an hour after Sister Davies had vacated it after her daily visit, and Christine wished she'd found some way to keep her there, to help her fight her corner.

The housing officer was a gaunt woman with a stern, unfriendly air, and a mouth that drooped down at the corners. The result, no doubt, of being employed in a job where you spent most of your life telling people 'no'. She was currently writing something in her folder with a Biro, having dispensed her latest nugget of unwelcome news: that because Christine and Joey *did* in fact have somewhere

Julie shaw

to go – i.e. her grandparents' – she couldn't possibly expect to be a priority.

Christine noticed that Josie's mouth was downcast as well. And once again, she felt stupid and guilty. She should have kept her trap shut about her grandparents when she'd made her application to be housed, just as Josie had warned her. Which she'd managed with Sister Davies, but had failed to once they were down at the scary housing office; out it had all come, before she'd been able to stop herself, and now she was paying the price.

Up till then, Christine had begun to feel the first stirrings of positivity, not least because the trip down there three days back – Christine's first proper outing anywhere with Joey – had turned out not to be the logistical nightmare she'd feared, but a welcome return to some kind of normality. Yes, she was shattered, and still sore, but she'd finally begun to gain in confidence; she'd managed to feed him and change him and dress him all by herself, and with hands that, increasingly, seemed to know what they were about.

And on the walk down there, pushing him in Paula's old pram, which Josie had lent her, she'd felt something new and strange – something she realised was not unlike pride. Though it didn't take long for it to vanish. She'd only been in the housing office once before in her life, when her mother had dragged her in there to complain about getting the garden fence fixed, and it was exactly as she remembered it. At the bottom of Leeds Road, near the dole office, it was a grim grey-brick building, set among others that

66

looked every bit as dingy and depressing, because the sun never shined in this corner of town. It was as if it had been chosen specially to discourage people to go there.

Happily, however, Josie knew the drill. They'd taken a ticket and waited to be called when their number came up, sitting down at the end of one of the long wooden benches, filled with other single mums, unsmiling families and the odd elderly drunk, coughing and spluttering all over everyone. Fearing the germs, Christine tried to squeeze herself up as small as she could so she didn't touch the dirty-looking old man at the side of her, who stank of beer and BO.

Thankfully, however, the wait wasn't too long. Within half an hour they were called by a kindly-looking girl, who smiled warmly as she showed them to her booth. And she *was* kind, unthreatening, listening to Christine's case without judgement, writing everything down on the lined pad in front of her, but all the while stealing glances across to where Joey was gazing wide-eyed at the strip light above their heads. 'Aww, love him,' she said. 'He's an angel, isn't he?'

Perhaps that was it – that she was *altogether too friendly*. That she looked like she understood. And that she cared. That, like Sister Davies, she didn't seem to hold it against Christine that she'd got herself in such a mess in the first place. In any event, when she asked Christine if she had any other relatives in the area, Christine just couldn't do it. She just couldn't tell a lie.

* * *

So Christine had told the truth. She was also fearful that they'd find out somehow anyway. And it was now going to cost her dearly. Just as Josie had predicted as they'd left the housing office and trudged home, now they knew Christine had family who could provide her and Joey with shelter, her need would be deemed not that urgent at all. Not compared with those who had no one.

And Josie had been right. Christine had known the minute she answered the door this morning. Miss whatever-her-name-was (she'd said it too fast for Christine to catch it) didn't look at Joey at all, let alone smile or call him an angel.

'She can't go *there*!' Josie said now, as the nameless housing officer continued writing. 'No offence, and that,' she said, glancing at Christine before continuing, 'but her grandparents are a pair of filthy drunks. It's no place for a baby, any more than her brother's flat is.'

'I appreciate your concern,' the lady answered. 'And I take on board your comments. And I'm not saying they won't get a place in due course. But there are certain protocols and I'm afraid Christine doesn't quite meet them. Not at present.' She put the cap on her pen. 'Not as things stand, at any rate.'

The way things stood, Christine thought miserably, as the damning notes were slid back into the woman's expanding briefcase, were that she was standing between a rock and a hard place. She could well imagine that social services thought she had somewhere to go because her nan and granddad lived in a big house on Canterbury front, and had a whole empty bedroom she could have. And wouldn't care if she *did* have it because most of the time they were off their heads on cider, or too busy arguing – usually both. They'd barely even register that she was there. Well, except when they were sober enough to have her running around after them as well and pinching her family allowance out of her purse.

And Josie was right. It was no place to be with a baby. It was way beyond unhygienic. It was a shithole of the first order – as her mum was fond of saying, 'so dirty that you've to wipe your feet on the mat on the way *out*!'

And her preferred option – to go to Nicky's – wasn't a lot better. Not least because, actually, it wasn't even Nicky's flat. It belonged to his druggy mate, Brian, as Josie kept reminding her. But in this – which, ironically, would probably help her case a little – she knew she really *did* have to keep her mouth shut, because Nicky, in reality, shouldn't even be there. Brian had only inherited the flat because his mam had had the foresight to add his name to the tenancy before taking the heroin overdose that had ended her life.

And how long before Brian went the same way? At just twenty-two he was already a well-known junkie – one who'd started off on weed when he was only seven or eight, and soon progressed onto the hard stuff like his mother. Christine wasn't stupid. She knew he was little more now than a needle-jabbing mess; already on the same ride his mother never got off.

But, for all that, he was a gentle soul – there was nothing difficult about him. And, crucially, at least Nicky was not on the hard stuff. All kinds of other things, yes, but not that. He'd never waivered on that point. And he was her brother. Her kin. Whatever else was true, she still knew in her heart that he'd take care of her.

And perhaps she didn't actually deserve any better, truth be known.

'So, how long d'you think, then?' Christine asked the housing officer politely. 'You know, just so I have some idea.'

In truth she was hoping that a miracle might still happen. That she'd say it would only be a couple more weeks and then Josie would decide that, since it wasn't going to be for long, that she might as well stay put with them. But it was a vain hope. 'Could be a month, could be six,' the woman told her flatly. 'Regrettably, I don't have a crystal ball.'

Christine caught Josie's disgusted expression out of the corner of her eye, but luckily she kept her thoughts – and expletives – to herself. One thing was clear – you didn't antagonise the people who held the power. And the keys.

The housing officer left soon after, walking with a brisk, stiff-necked gait, her tatty briefcase swinging beside her, as if she couldn't wait to be somewhere else. They watched her all the way to the corner. 'What a cow,' Josie said. 'What a miserable frigging *cow*.'

But though Christine agreed, her thoughts were closer to home. To the house round the corner and the mother who'd thrown her out. And closer still. Which provoked a kind of helpless, wretched fury.

After all, who could she really blame but herself?

Chapter 6

Hanging over the balcony on the sixth floor of Elizabeth Towers, Nicky Parker had only two thoughts on his mind. The first was that he'd be spending the foreseeable future sleeping on Brian's ratty futon. And the second – unbelievable, even a whole twenty-four hours later – was that, in theory (he'd have to see what Chrissy had to say about it), he was officially related to Rasta Mo.

'You're joking, right?' he'd said to Eddie down the Listers the previous evening. And, despite Eddie's stern looks (he'd already delivered The Lecture about shaping up while his little sis was staying) Nicky'd genuinely thought he was having a laugh. But he hadn't been. No, she hadn't actually admitted it, as such, not to him. But she certainly had to Josie, and why would she lie? And who the fuck else's would it have been, given that it was half-caste? And then Eddie had gone back to his droning, like he was Nicky's dad or something. No drugs round the baby. No weed. *Definitely* no heroin. And don't look so shocked. I'm not wet behind the ears, mate. Keep it clean. Don't fuck up. Don't fuck things up for your *sister*.

Nicky had had half a mind to tell Eddie he should bloody well keep the pair of them, if he was that worried about things at the flat. But, weirdly, given how mortified he'd been when Chrissy had asked if he could take them in, there was this strong, unlikely sense in him that it was his responsibility anyway. That with his fuck-up of a mother going ape – no surprises there, given Mo – it was his duty to step in and help out. So on one level he even resented Eddie thinking that he didn't have it in him to do so.

He took a drag on his joint and scanned the road below for signs of Chrissy and her baby's arrival. It was so hard to get the words 'her baby' around his tongue. Yes, it had happened, no doubt about it – it was coming to fucking *live* with him – but he couldn't quite square the thought of his little sister, who he still essentially saw as a kid, and the business of her having given birth to her *own* kid. And in doing so, making him an uncle.

Unbelievable. A fucking uncle! And – even more unbelievable – to Rasta Mo's son. Still, there was an upside, and it was the fact that it made his mam a granny. That was the most laughable part of it all. Her with her make-up, and her tart's clothes, and her pathetic denial – did she look in a mirror, ever, and actually *see* herself?

His mam a granny. She couldn't hide *that* under an inch of slap. And that was probably as much the reason she'd told Chrissy to fuck off out of it as anything else she'd come up with. Which made him smile too. She was like the *Telegraph* and fucking *Argus* when it came to gossip about anyone else. But her a *granny*. No, she wouldn't like hearing that one bandied about – not one little bit. She'd hate that as much as the other enormous bombshell. Nicky still couldn't quite believe it. That it was *Mo's*.

He recognised Eddie's Escort while it was still some way distant – one of the benefits of having such a lofty view of life – so there was time to take a last welcome drag before grinding the joint out under the heel of his boot, and for the tell-take smoke to blow away. That little ginger cow would do her nut if she copped him smoking. And then there'd be another tedious lecture.

He hoicked his jeans up and pushed open the flat door with his foot. 'They're here, Bri,' he yelled into the hallway as he entered. 'Fuck off into your bedroom for a bit, will you, mate? Not for long. Just till the Gestapo have gone.'

He heard a mumbled 'yeah'. Brian already knew the score. He shuffled about like a pensioner, and usually smelt like one too, and with his sallow skin and with him having a pair of pupils you could usually park a fucking bus in, Josie and Eddie would only have to take one look at him to set them off again. About fucking junkies and how they were a scourge on the world. Which was as ironic as it was boring, given that Josie was a McKellan. Her sister was one of the dealers he sometimes bought from. But perhaps – he had the wisdom to admit it – that was why. Lyndsey, a mum herself, was a fucking state.

Thinking of Brian and the impression he wasn't going to be allowed to get a chance to make, Nicky stopped by the wonky mirror that was hanging in the hall. Like his sister, he was only small in comparison to most of his mates, but, despite the inevitable ribbing he'd had in school, it had turned out to be to his advantage, and, as a consequence, had earned him a modicum of respect. If he was in need of money, which he often was, he could readily earn a few quid, as he had a reputation around Bradford (among the people who needed to know, anyway) for his unrivalled ability to squeeze through even the tiniest of windows. He was therefore much in demand to assist in local burglaries.

He also had the sort of features that caused grannies to declare that 'butter wouldn't melt', when he was a lad, and had subsequently stood him in good stead with younger females too, even if his last girlfriend, about whom he'd felt a growing affection, had dumped him for already being the person he knew he could all too easily become. He studied himself critically, trying to see himself as Josie might see him. A bit pasty. Unkempt. Sharp around the cheeks. Far too thin. All evidence of a life being very poorly lived lately. As were his T-shirt and jeans, which were now two sizes too big for him. One day, soon, he knew, he must make the break from Brian. Which he knew he could. But in his own time and on his own terms.

Which meant not today. Not next week. Not next month, now, in reality. Because right now he actually needed the stability of Brian's gaff. He had his sister and a baby coming to live with him, after all. Which could only highlight the fact that since escaping his shitty mother he at least had a roof over his head.

Christine huffed as she pushed her way into the flat. A new sound, a tired sound. She also looked like shit. 'Get the kettle on, Nick,' she ordered. She had the baby held in her arms. Well, he supposed it was in there. It was a shockingly tiny bundle, and nothing human was visible. 'And put the door on the latch will you?' she added, pushing past him. 'Josie and Eddie are fetching my stuff up.'

'Nice to see you too,' Nicky huffed back, but he couldn't help but smile. He'd not seen her since she'd been something like six or so months pregnant. And it was good to see her now. Face to face. Out the other side, so to speak. And she would look like shit, he decided. She'd just had a baby. His tiny little sis, giving birth to a *baby*. An image surfaced. Perhaps best not go there.

'Bloody hell, sis,' he added anyway. 'Giving orders already? You've only just set foot in the place!'

He leaned closer so he could see into the bundle of cellular blanket. It was *tiny*. He'd never seen such a newborn before. Well, not that he remembered. And yup. It was half black, as he'd already been told by Eddie. The baby opened his eyes, sleepily, and then with more focus. 'Now then, little Joe,' he said, 'how's it hanging? I'm your uncle.'

'Joe-*ee*,' Christine corrected. 'He's not Joe, he's Joey.' She took the baby across the sitting room and rearranged a couple of the cushions slung on the futon. Then, when she'd sorted them to her satisfaction, she lay the baby down.

'Cute,' Nicky observed, watching her. 'What d'you think? Anything like his father?'

Christine turned around. 'Nick, you know, I *really* don't want to talk about that.'

'I'll bet,' he said, then held up his hands in mock surrender. 'Oh, don't you worry. I'm saying fuck all, sis. Your business is your business. But –' he paused. Because it probably needed saying. 'I just don't want the fucking lunatic round here creating all the time.'

'What, Mo?' Christine answered.

'*God*, no! Don't be daft. Christ, does he even *know*? And I'm assuming if he doesn't you're not telling him.' Rumour had it, Nicky knew, that Mo had kids all round town. All denied, obviously. And no one challenging it, because no one challenged Mo. Him included. He shook his head. 'No, *mam*, of course, you ninny. What do you think?'

His sister pulled a disgusted face. 'Oh, don't worry about that. She's made it *well* clear she wants nothing to do with me or the baby and, trust me, that's just fine by me.'

The baby apparently dozing, Christine stalked off into the kitchen, where she rolled up her sleeves to fish a couple of mugs from the muddy washing-up water in the orange plastic bowl. Nicky grabbed the teapot and leaned past her to tip the old tea into the sink. She smelt sweetish, of baby, but not unpleasantly.

'Where shall Eddie put all this lot?' Josie asked, appearing in the kitchen doorway. She looked as officious as ever, and had a large cardboard box in her arms. 'And where's that fucking divvy Brian?'

Josie always had the usual McKellan swagger, and it irritated him. Her mam was a Hudson (and didn't he know it) and her brother Vinnie was a local hero. He'd been banged up – for a long time – for murdering a local nonce, who it was said had had a piece of Josie when she was little. Which probably accounted for the chippy way she tended to address *all* men – Eddie excluded – and though Nicky kind of understood that, it still riled.

He stuck his head out of the kitchen doorway and pointed out his bedroom to Eddie, who was close behind with another box and a couple of bin bags.

'I'll come and help you,' Chrissy said, drying her hands on a tea towel as she followed him down the hallway.

'He's in his room, Jose,' Nicky said, as Josie took over with the mugs. 'And you don't need to worry. Everything's sorted. Like I told your Eddie, I've told him none of the hard stuff while Chrissy's staying, and whatever else he does, he does it in his room.'

'Like you can tell him what to do in his own flat?' Josie said, swilling the mugs out under the tap. She wasn't being sarcastic, he realised, just stating a possible truth. But still it irritated him that, on the one hand, she could say that, and on the other, that being *exactly* what she was pretty much ordering him to do. Like he was being auditioned for the role of his sister's fucking landlord!

'Course I can't, Jose,' he shot back. 'Like you say, it's his flat. But I think he's being a diamond about it, as it happens. He could have just as easily told me to fuck right off, couldn't he? And, by the sound of it, it's not like there are a whole lot of other options.'

'No, but if he –'

'Oh, shut *up*, Josie,' Eddie said, returning to catch the end of their conversation. 'He's only in the next bloody *room*. He's been right as rain letting them stay, so I think we should keep out of it.' He glanced meaningfully at Nicky, even so, as he said this. Then added, albeit lightly, 'at least for now'.

Nicky knew a warning when he saw one, and would normally have bridled, but he had a lot of time, not to mention a lot of respect, for Josie's Eddie, and he genuinely wanted to help his sister out. Even so, he couldn't wait to get rid of the pair of them, because the truth was he was already craving something stronger than the hurried joint he'd just had, even if he'd have to sneak around to have it.

By the time half an hour had gone by, and they were still all camped in the sitting room, Nicky was having a rethink. Not about the tab he was looking forward to, but his whole morning's strategy; emptying all the ashtrays, sweeping the carpet with the useless battered carpet sweeper (he'd have been quicker picking the dirt off bit by bit) and the wipe round with the lemon Ajax he'd found under the sink, which gave the sitting room the impression that it was properly clean. To the nose, if not to any eagle eyes like Josie's.

Because with them all so apparently comfortable in the unusually clean and tidy flat, they were lingering much longer than he'd reckoned on. Sipping their teas, chit-chatting about weird baby nonsense, meaning it was getting increasingly likely that Brian would release himself from his self-inflicted purdah. And he did.

He appeared in the doorway, scratching his ribs, seeming insubstantial and unbalanced. Like a wraith or a ghoul from a bad trip or a dream. 'All right?' he said, to no one in particular. 'Is there a brew going?' He nodded towards Josie's mug. 'I could murder a cup of tea.' He staggered out of sight then, leaving an after-image of inky stubble and fright-wig hair, only pausing to tip his head back round the door and, for reasons Nicky couldn't fathom, saying, 'Oi, Chris, are you breast-feeding that sprog? I bloody hope not. Can't have those fried eggs of yours spilling out all round the place!' He then laughed at his own joke and ambled off to the kitchen – simultaneously coughing his guts up – leaving Christine scowling and Josie shaking her head. 'Give me strength,' she said. 'Jesus fucking Christ. Give me *strength.*'

'Sorry, Jose,' Nicky said, feeling the need to say something. 'He's normally sparko at this time. We must have woken him up.'

Josie stood up. 'Oh that's Bri in "awake" mode, is it?' She looked at Christine and something passed between them.

Nicky knew what, too. A look that said sorry. Sorry we can't take you straight back to where you came from. And for a moment, Nicky wished she would change her mind and do it. That solid dependable Eddie would do the kind thing and let her stay with them after all. How long could it be before she got a council place, for fuck's sake? Because the look said it all. This place – *his* place. Brian's druggy shithole really *wasn't* the right place for a baby.

But that wasn't going to be happening. So his dump it would have to be.

Josie was hugging Christine now. 'Now, are you sure there's nowt else you need me to get for you? Just say if there is and I'll get it and bring it up.'

She was obviously headed to his mam's, probably because her own mam was round there with their Paula. They were thick as thieves. 'Long as you don't bring the old witch round here too,' he said, collecting the mugs up.

'No danger of that,' Josie said. 'Though, actually, now you mention it …' But then neglected to finish the rest of what she'd been thinking. That she could stage some sort of reconciliation? Make his mother take Chrissy back? Who knew? All he knew was that it wasn't happening. His little sister, who his mam *didn't* love, had shagged Mo, who she did love. It was all wrong. But at the same time, those were the facts.

So no question. He knew his mam. There'd be no going back.

Chapter 7

Christine opened her eyes and tried to focus. Somewhere in the back of her mind she could hear the baby crying, and she knew she should get out of bed and see to him. She closed her eyes again for a moment but soon opened them again. It was all too easy to get sucked back into blissful unconsciousness; more and more now, since she'd been living with Nicky and Brian and the bright morning bustle of Josie's busy home was no longer there to pull her along.

Instead, she was constantly pulled under. Neither Nicky nor Brian lived anything like normal lives; their comings and goings seeming to have no relationship whatever to the time of night or day. They would sleep in till late – often late into the afternoon – and often went out in the small hours of the morning. Other times they'd be up with mates till gone six in the morning, filling the flat with dope fumes, popping pills or snorting coke, sometimes cackling uncontrollably, and, though at other times they were quieter, there seemed hardly a night where at some points she'd not be woken up – with a start – by music blaring loudly out of nowhere. Though both lads were unfailingly nice to her, and always cooed over Joey, it was like they were living inside a madhouse.

A shithole of a madhouse as well. Christine had no more love of housework than any other sane person. And it was all she could do to take care of Joey currently. But the filth and the mess and the stink made her yearn for home; a yearning that shocked her to the core.

Most of all, though, she yearned for the life she had lost. For her little bedroom, for the reassuring routines of her life. For her job down the market – a greater shock, to discover that – and for the sleep she had once taken so much for granted. For the freedoms she had never once considered to be freedoms – to sleep, yes, but also the simplest of freedoms. To get up and shower, put some clothes on, sling her bag over her shoulder, leave one place and walk or run – hop, skip or jump, even – to another, without having to consider anything – any*one* – but herself.

Joey was building up a head of steam now, and, her situation being what it was, she knew she must silence him, and quickly. For all that Nicky and Brian could bring in a brass band and have it play all night and all day outside her door, she felt the weight of her indebtedness to them constantly. She must at all times try to minimise Joey's presence in their lives. Much as they would chuck him under the chin – and in Brian's case, with his disgusting fingers, to Christine's great anxiety – she was always alert to the expressions of irritation that she would catch cross their faces when they thought she wasn't looking. She was a nuisance, an inconvenience, an imposition and a pain, and she knew full well that they were counting the days till she got a flat sorted as much as she was.

She plucked Joey from the pram that was also doubling up for a cot. Josie had a proper cot at home, all ready for her to borrow, but he was too small for it yet and, all being well, she'd be in her own place before it came to putting it up. He kicked his little legs out as she pulled him to her face, nuzzling into her cheek, rooting, going pink in his annoyance. He really was little more than a machine, she decided. One that lived just for two things – milk and sleep.

He felt hot, soft and squidgy, and smelled uniquely of baby – a scent she only now understood. 'Ooh, that gorgeous baby smell!' Josie said that often. 'I could breathe it all day. They ought to bottle it.' And she'd been right. They really should.

Joey's other end, predictably, smelled rather less lovely. She knew just from the weight of him that his nappy was drenched, even though he was in one of the two-sizes-too-big ones that were all she'd been able to get from the Co-op. She lay him down on the bed, undid the poppers on his babygro and removed it, recoiling as the ammonia hit her nostrils. 'You're going to have to wait, little man,' she whispered, as he started up yelling again. 'Hush now. I've got to go and warm your bottle!'

In that, at least, she did have a modicum of order, having learned the hard way that if she didn't make his night and

morning bottles up, life became all that much more unbear-
able for both of them. As it was she'd still have to wait for
the kettle.

She stepped out into the hallway and immediately felt
her foot hit something solid. 'For fuck's sake!' she mouthed,
as a can of Special Brew started spewing its contents all
over the ratty carpet. She leaned down to pick it up – she
no longer wondered why she'd find such a thing in such a
place – and, looking across to the lounge, saw Nicky sparko
on the futon, and, judging by the fetid smell, he'd not been
asleep that long.

She lifted the kettle, found it full enough, and switched
it on, surveying the kitchen with her usual distaste. There
was washing-up piled everywhere, in tipsy, random towers
– pretty much the only thing that stood apart, in the corner
of the windowsill where'd she'd cleared a space for it, was
her big yellow transparent steriliser, in which bottles and
dummies bobbed and which, on a bright day, when the sun
hit just so, painted golden puddles on the lino.

She took the jug from on top of it and went to the fridge
for the bottle, wrinkling her nose almost as much as she did
when changing Joey's nappies. It was like one of those
things Mrs Goodson, her PE teacher, had once identified
when surveying the furthest reaches of the school changing
rooms – a whole ecosystem, right there.

Waiting for the kettle to boil, she ventured into the
lounge, not to wake her brother – God help her if she did
– but to do as she always did at this time of day, make a stab

at restoring some sort of order. The room was completely trashed – and even more so than was usual, as a result of the windfall she'd been responsible for when she'd finally got her social money the previous day. She'd hung on to what she could – there was stuff to buy – not least nappies and formula – but, as she'd pretty much sponged off Nick and Brian for the best part of three weeks now, she felt it only right that she give them most of what she had left.

Which had gone quite a way – all the evidence was in front of her. The coffee table was scattered with Rizla cigarette papers, overflowing ashtrays, and the dust from the cocaine powder and rocks they'd had the night before. Take-away containers vied with crisp packets and chocolate wrappers and shards of smashed poppadoms, and the makeshift pipe Nick and Brian used for burning their crack cocaine was overturned on the floor.

Yes, twenty quid had gone a long way. A ridiculously long way. There had even been enough left for cider and lager which, as Brian had pointed out, giving her one of his explosive back-slaps, was 'a bit of a bonus – the icing on the paaaaarty cake!'

The smell in here was as bad as the one in her bedroom and though she didn't dare open the curtains on her slumbering brother she could at least reach behind them to let in some air. If not, she decided she would have to seriously consider feeding Joey out on the frigging landing.

She did it soundlessly, but he heard it even so. 'Oh I do wish you'd fuck off, Snow fucking White,' he groaned amiably. 'Damaged at fucking birth, that's what you were, you know that?'

Christine couldn't help but smile. For all that he drove her mad, and lived like a pig in the proverbial, Nicky didn't have a bad bone in his body. 'Yeah, by being born into a family that had *you* in it,' she countered. 'Don't worry. I'm not hanging about. I have this thing. I need to *breathe*.'

She ducked the answering cushion, and headed back into the kitchen with some empty glasses. Today, she thought, as she half-filled the jug and set the bottle in it, today I shall tackle this mountain of washing-up. Do something useful. Set an example to my waster of a brother – who seemed to be calling her now.

'Chris!' His voice was low but the urgency in it was unmistakable. She popped her head back round the living room door to find him up on his feet. He stabbed a finger in the general direction of the window. 'There's someone outside!' he hissed. 'Some fucker snooping around on the landing!'

Christine spread her palms. 'Maybe the postman? Or the milkman?' As if. No such luxury. But she couldn't see or hear anything.

Nicky ran his hands over his face. She could hear the stubble rasping on his chin. He listened for a bit longer, then his shoulders dropped a little. 'Maybe not, then. But it was like someone was hovering outside. But you're right. Maybe not. Make some tea, yeah?'

Christine went and refilled the kettle and popped teabags in two cleanish mugs. Then wrung out the cloth she used to wipe Joey's bottom. Nick and Brian were always twitched on that score – people turning up uninvited – which made her worry about the sort of characters they hung out with. But it was obviously nothing, so she told him the kettle was on, then picked up the jug and went to sort out the baby.

He was still squawking, and continued to complain while she cleaned him, but was soon soothed when she picked him up and popped the bottle in his mouth, though with the stench, she decided she'd feed him in the lounge. With Nicky up – even if he went back to sleep shortly after – she'd at least have a modicum of fresh air.

She'd just settled on the futon – Nicky was now in the kitchen, doing the tea – when she heard the knock on the door.

So he'd been right. 'See?' he mouthed at her, clearing a space on the coffee table for the mugs. 'Told you, didn't I? Someone's snooping around.'

'Hardly snooping,' Christine whispered. 'They've knocked on the door, haven't they?'

'Fuck's sake!' Nicky whispered back. 'And it's not even half nine!'

He went across to the window that looked out onto the landing, and carefully moved the curtain a couple of inches to one side. A stripe of white sunlight divided the carpet into two, dust motes dancing around above it. 'Trust me, *no one* comes at this time,' he said, peeping out through the narrow slit. 'Shit!' he hissed then. 'Are you expecting someone, sis? It's a woman with a fucking briefcase!'

Galvanised, now, Christine glanced anxiously around the living room. '*Shit!*' she whispered. 'Nicky, clear some of this crap away! Oh, *God*. Typical. I bet it's someone from the housing.'

'The *housing?*' Nicky gawped at her.

'Yes, the housing!' she snapped at him. 'They said they might visit before I got an offer off them, didn't they? I *told* you. So they could check on –'

'Check on what?'

'Check on *me*, you numbskull! Check where I'm living!'

'Brilliant,' Nicky said, going immediately into action, grabbing up all the evidence of his and Brian's drug taking the previous evening and kicking curry containers under the coffee table. Christine could only watch him, because Joey was still sucking hungrily on his bottle and if she moved now he'd probably freak. Not that he needed her help. It was a long-practised manoeuvre and he was like a whirling dervish. And fair enough that he was doing it, anyway, Christine thought. What a bloody state they'd made of the place. Thank God the woman hadn't come half an hour earlier.

The knock came again, more sharply this time, while Nicky was still in the kitchen, stashing everything out of sight. So she obviously knew they were in there. Probably heard them talking earlier. And it could be worse, Christine thought. Brian could be spark out on the floor, as he often was. Thank God for that at least. Chances were that he'd be comatose in his room for hours yet. 'So I *do* let her in, right?' Nicky said, popping his head around the door again.

'Of *course* let her in,' Christine said, gesturing with her free hand. For all that the woman had come at the worst moment possible, this might finally be her chance to get away.

She trawled her hand through her knotted hair and wished she could do something about her face. Not to mention her clothes, or, rather, lack of. She was wearing nothing but an oversized T-shirt – one of Nicky's, which had an old stain down the front. Great. She adjusted Joey slightly, to better hide it, while Nicky stomped off to the front door.

She heard the door open, and the sound of an unfamiliar female voice, and though she couldn't make out anything from the sounds of their conversation, it only took one look on her brother's face when he returned to know she wasn't from the housing department after all.

Christine would have known anyway, just as soon as she saw her. There was just something about her expression, and the way she looked generally – slightly down at heel, slightly hurriedly put together. She had one of those trendy puff-sleeved shirts on, but the neck tie was wonky, and with her hair, which was big and mad and full of chunky blonde highlights, she didn't look properly 'office-y' – much less officious enough. She was young, too. Christine reckoned not yet into her thirties. But sharp. Her gaze, even hidden behind a pair of pink glasses, was cool and assessing – and roving all over the place.

'Carol Sloper,' the woman said, holding her right hand out for Christine to shake, and then withdrawing it as she realised Christine's was otherwise engaged with Joey's bottle. 'No, no, stay as you are,' she said, cracking a smile finally. 'Sorry to call so early. I'm from social services.'

Christine's mouth twitched politely but her heart sank to her boots. She knew the woman's smile meant sod all. Social services, in her world, was a dirty, scary name. They were the enemy of every good parent – June McKellan was always saying that. They were the ones who silently watched until you slipped up on something and then swooped in and took away your children. She glanced at her brother, who was ploughing a hand through his own dishevelled hair.

'Oh,' she said, not having any other response ready. The woman's gaze seemed to bore into her. 'Social services? Um, why, exactly?'

'She said it's nowt to be worried about,' Nicky offered. He still looked anxious.

'Quite,' the woman said. 'No, it isn't. You're Christine, right?'

Christine nodded. 'Yes, but –'

'Good,' she said firmly. As if Christine had just answered a question in a test. 'I needed to come and see you, love,' she went on. 'Check you were still living here. Only you've not been to clinic and your midwife was worried. Asked me to pop in and check you're okay, that's all.'

Christine relaxed a little. Though Joey was now wriggling on her lap. She realised she'd let the bottle tip and he was now sucking on air. She lifted it again. 'Course I am,' she said. 'Where else would I be? I'm still waiting to hear from the housing about a flat, aren't I?' She let it hang.

'I know, love,' the woman said. How, exactly? How'd she know that? 'And all being well,' she added, making another visual circuit of the shabby lounge, 'they'll find you something soon. But in the meantime we need to know you're coping okay with little Joey here, don't we?'

Christine didn't like that 'we', nor the fact that the social worker then plonked herself down beside her on the futon, moving the greasy pillow on which Nicky's head had only recently lain. Just shifted it and sat down. Just like that.

'So how *are* you doing?' she asked pointedly, but not unkindly, her eyes now on Joey, who, having drained the bottle, was entering that floppy stage – all drowsy and replete – which usually signalled an hour or so's peace.

'I'm managing,' Christine said, wishing it was true. Up close, she could smell the woman's perfume, which she recognised but couldn't bring to mind.

'Well, he certainly looks a bonny lad,' the social worker said, smiling. 'Certainly seems to have an appetite, anyway. But, you know, Christine, you need to bring him down to the clinic. I think you agreed with Sister Davies that, well, given the challenges of your situation, that you'd take Joey down to be weighed every week, didn't you? Yet you haven't been.' She smiled again. 'Have you? Which is why I'm here. Because Sister Davies was worried about you. How you're getting on. Whether something's stopping you from attending.' She paused. Glanced back at Nicky. 'Christine, we have a duty.' She stressed the word 'duty'. 'To check on Joey's progress. Check his weight. Check his height. Check he's *well*. And it's been three weeks now. You do know when the baby clinic runs, don't you?' Christine nodded. 'You don't need an appointment. You can come down any time at all. And perhaps should. Get you out. Get you both some fresh air and exercise.' Again, the sweep round the room, like she was a sniffer dog, looking for evidence. 'And if you attend every week, it will give *you* peace of mind. And you'll meet other mums. Share your stories. Swap tips and so on. You'd be *amazed* how much of a support it is to be with other new mothers … Christine, tell me,' she added, her tone subtly different now. 'Tell me, *is* there a reason you're not going?'

There was a part of Christine that wanted to tell the woman the exact truth. That she'd overslept and missed the first clinic and then, *having* missed the first one, she'd been determined to make the second one – and she really, really had – and for all the reasons the woman was telling her. Pretty much all of which she already knew.

But the truth was that, when it had come to it, she'd hit another obstacle. It had been raining – tipping it down

– and she didn't have a rain cover for the pram. Which left her with a problem she couldn't seem to solve.

Her brother and Brian had been off their heads after a party the night before, which had gone on almost till the dawn, and she hadn't dared risking nipping round to any of the neighbours to try and borrow one, because how could she? How could she leave her tiny baby by himself? But, it being so wet, the thought of getting him dressed up and carrying him around the flats in her arms had seemed even more preposterous and herculean a task – all those stairs, in the wet, carrying him, and him getting drenched anyway … it had all felt far too much of a nightmare.

And then, somehow, it hadn't seemed to matter quite so much after that. Joey was fine, and he was growing, and there seemed nothing whatever wrong with him. And the thought of the telling off she might get for missing the first two appointments was sufficient an additional stress to put her off.

But she found she couldn't tell the truth. Not to this organised-looking woman. Couldn't imagine her understanding just how big a thing it was, having a baby glued to your side day and night. Couldn't imagine her understanding how big a task it was just to get out of the flat. How big a *production*. No, she really didn't think she *could* understand.

There was also the fact that Nicky was still standing there, silhouetted in the window. He'd flung open the curtains now – why, oh why? It's just made everything look so much *worse* – and was just standing there, like he was a guard dog, arms folded across his chest. But it wasn't just that, either. This was a *social worker*. They'd sent a social worker to check on her. And wasn't that *exactly* the sort of admission – that it was all just so *hard* – that would see Joey on a list? Even spirited away?

'I was going to,' she said instead, trying to think how to put it. Having a baby, she decided, was like going back to school. Your life wasn't your own again. It was back to following rules. 'But it was raining, and … well, I haven't got a proper pram for him, have I? I mean, I'm getting one. Soon as I've got enough money together. But at the moment …' She sensed Nicky's eyes homing in on her. 'Till my money comes through …' She tailed off and shrugged.

'I see,' the woman said. 'Christine, you know there's help available, don't you? If you're suffering hardship –' Again the eyes, which lingered again on Nicky. 'Then we can get help for you.'

'She doesn't need any help,' Nicky said. The social worker turned and looked at him. 'She's fine. She'll be down at the clinic next week, right? It's sorted. The baby's fine. So –' His expression said 'sling your hook'.

'Indeed it seems,' said the social worker. And there was something in the way she said it – to Christine directly, locking eyes with her – that said that, for all her niceness, the likes of Nicky didn't faze her one bit. 'So,' she said.

'Now. You have your own room here, do you? You and Joey,' she added, moving her back ever so slightly, but enough to effectively block Nicky out.

'Course,' Christine told her.

'In which case, can I see it?'

'Um … why?' Christine asked her, and immediately regretted it. It just made her sound like she had something to hide. Which she did, in a way, given there was a frigging Silver Cross in there. Old yes, and rusty, but still a proper pram. Why the hell *hadn't* she told her the truth? Why had she said pram and not rain cover?

'No, it's fine,' she said quickly, lifting Joey against her shoulder and standing up. 'It's this way. I was going to put him back down now in any case.' Then, ignoring Nicky's eye-roll behind the social worker's back, led the way into her brother's former bedroom.

Once inside, the strength of the ammonia smell hit her anew. As did the sight of the sodden nappy on the bed. 'I'd just changed him,' she felt compelled to say. 'And he was hungry, so I made his bottle up. You know how it is …' *Did* she, though? Did she look like she'd had a baby? Christine couldn't tell. How could anyone tell? She went across to the pram and lay Joey down in it, aware of the woman standing close beside her in the cramped space.

'So you *do* have a pram then,' she said.

Christine turned around. 'Not exactly. I mean, yes, it's a pram, but it's ancient. It doesn't run right. The brake's faulty. Like I said, I'm going to –'

The social worker stopped her with a hand on her arm. 'Christine,' she said, 'there is help out there for you. Money. Support. Support which could *help* you. Support that could help you become more *independent*. D'you understand what I'm saying? You don't have to struggle. That's the very last thing we want. We want Joey to thrive every bit as much as you do. But you have to *let* us help you, by attending the baby clinic. Being honest with us about how you're managing. Straight with us. D'you understand?'

Christine was horrified to realise her eyes were filling up. That she could all too easily burst into tears, right there, right then. She turned away, busying herself with straightening Joey's already straightened blanket. Then the hand was on her arm again. And another now, held out. 'Here,' said the social worker, who'd clearly rummaged in her case. 'This is my number. Christine, call me, okay? Call me if you need anything. Call me even if you *don't* need anything.' She smiled as Christine took the proffered piece of paper. 'If you just need to talk, okay? *Call* me.'

Christine straightened up. She was suddenly becoming aware of the sound of movement – ominous movement – from the other side of the bedroom wall. Brian stirring? This early? That would just be the *worst* luck. 'I'll get down there. I promise,' she said. 'I was going to go anyway ...'

But the social worker was closing up her battered briefcase anyway. Was leaving. Thank *God*. She just hoped it would be in time.

'And that's a promise?' the social worker said, preceding Christine out of the bedroom. Christine glanced into the lounge. Nicky was no longer in there.

'A promise,' she agreed.

'Because they're looking forward to seeing you. And like I say,' the woman said again, 'if you need anything, *call* me. That's what I'm here for, Christine.' She paused again. 'You understand me? We're not the bogeymen some would probably have you believe.'

She unlatched the door herself. How many flats like this did she go in and out of, Christine wondered. Plenty, she decided. God, she so wanted to be gone from here. It was like a weight on her, for all its lofty views and grass expanses. A weight, pressing her down to a place she didn't want to go.

'I know,' she said. 'And, um, thank you.'

The woman smiled again. 'There is no need to thank me. Just heed me, okay, Christine? For you *and* for Joey. Take care, love.' And then she was gone.

Christine looked down at the note. At the number. At the woman's tidy writing. 'Carol', it said above it, with a big emphatic underline.

'Well, that's fucking great, I don't think,' Nicky said, the second the front door was shut again. 'Fucking social sniffing round. That's *all* we need, that is. The fucking SS on our case. No offence, sis, but I bloody hope they hurry up and find you a place. If Brian hears about this, he's going to kick off about it royally. He'll go apeshit if he thinks we're

Bad Blood

going to have the authorities sniffing round. Sod the bloody baby clinic, you need to get yourself back down to the housing office. Sheesh, they never change, do they? Won't leave anyone alone. And how's it their business anyway? The baby's fine, and it's not like we're hurting anyone, is it?'

Christine sighed. 'I know,' she said, 'and I'll sort it, Nick, I promise. And I'm really grateful ...' She stopped, feeling the tears welling again.

He opened his arms then and pulled her in for a hug, taking care, as he did so, with the joint he'd already lit.

Then he laughed. 'They can fuck off, the lot of them, can't they? Tell you what,' he said. 'Fancy a toot on this, sis?'

Chapter 8

Christine banged the pram down the last flight of stairs, a familiar frustration welling up in her. It was all very well that Carol woman telling her she needed to attend the baby clinic – quite another for her to understand just how *hard* it all was. And would continue to be till the still-awaited miracle happened and she had somewhere of her own to go and live. Somewhere on the flat. Not stuck half-way up a tower block in Brian's wretched flat. But another week had gone by and she'd still not heard a word.

She backed herself and the pram out of the glass doors to the car parks (another thing she was getting good at doing now, she mused), at first frowning because bumping down the four flights had woken Joey up, but then smiling – she couldn't help it – at the sight of his happy little face. Which soon couldn't help sour her mood again. He deserved better, even if she didn't. Though it wasn't as if she wanted handouts or anything. Just a place to live, for which she would pay rent, out of her own hard-earned money, just as soon as she could find a way to look after him *and* go to work. Just a chance, that was all, to do her best for him.

She tried not to think about her mam, though it was hard. Josie was so lucky; she had her mam to help her out with little Paula. Almost *every* girl had a mam, or a gran they could depend on. And what did she have? No one. Well, apart from Nicky, obviously. But though he cooed over Joey when the mood took him, which was often enough, admittedly, there was no way in the world she'd expect – or want – to leave Joey with him.

But she didn't want to *be* like her mam. Her mam, who saw work as a take it or leave it option – who'd not worked since she'd fancied herself as Rasta Mo's 'kept woman'. And that was true of Nicky too, much as she loved him. He too seemed to live by their mam's familiar credo – do as little as possible, get away with as much as possible and, if he went the way of Brian, which it looked like he might, live in a drug-induced stupor every frigging day you could.

Which was fine for them, and she *was* grateful for the roof over her head, even if not quite so enamoured of the four floors of flats underneath them. She just wished she could give Joey something more.

Out in the car park, in the open, she felt better. The sky was full of scudding clouds, and the trees were turning red and golden, shedding leaves to be scooped up by the light autumn breeze that was fresh and sharp-smelling in her nostrils. She had a sudden image, and held on to it, of a time in the future when she and Joey could tramp through all those fallen leaves together. 'Look at you,' she cooed, as he waved his little arms at her. 'All right for some, eh?

Snug as a bug in a rug, you are, aren't you?' Which was something of a miracle, she decided, as she turned onto Little Horton Lane, given the jolting of those four flights of steps.

He responded by sucking on his dummy all the harder, his lips widening into a chuckle as she made faces at him, clearly oblivious of the struggles that had become the large part of her daily life. For all that she loved him, who knew being a mother could be so stressful? Just leaving the house was a major operation, and, increasingly, one that felt like a battle. Just organising feeds, finding clean clothes, packing just-in-case spare clothes, remembering nappies, and extra nappies, and all the wipes and paraphernalia, including a spare dummy, just in case Joey spat it out and she didn't notice.

Add to that the layers of clothing, despite it still being mild; the hat, coat and gloves, the blankets and rattles, the all-important rain cover Josie had finally tracked down, and Christine had gratefully cadged. Sometimes, it just felt so easy – *too* easy – to stay holed up in the flat, in her trackies and jumper, and let the world crack on without them.

The walk, however, energised her, and as she approached the doctor's surgery and clinic, it was with a strong sense that getting out and doing things with Joey was the *right* way. And as she did her usual turnaround and backed through the clinic doors, it was in a more positive frame of mind than she'd felt in days.

* * *

In contrast, the walk had had the opposite effect on Joey, who was now in a deep, untroubled sleep. He would create merry hell, Christine knew, once he was woken. And woken he would be, because Christine had asked Josie what would happen, and, as a consequence, suspected the baby clinic would be his least favourite thing. He'd be stripped off and weighed, measured, pushed around and prodded, and, if Josie was right, given he was coming on three months now, he'd be getting an injection as well.

And a scant ten minutes later her gloomy predictions came true.

She'd not known who to expect – the midwives did the clinic on rotation, apparently – but on first seeing Sister Rawson her spirits lifted again. She'd not forgotten the midwife's tenderness towards her after Joey had been born.

But Sister Rawson's expression made it abundantly clear that Christine was in for a ticking off. And that was what she got. 'I'm not very impressed with you, young lady,' she said, as Christine shuffled in with a now disgruntled Joey in her arms.

It made Christine's hackles rise, that 'young lady'. It reminded her too much of her mother. Sister Rawson indicated that she should take a seat and shook her head.

'I explained to the social worker,' Christine said, sitting down on the indicated chair, feeling defensive. 'I haven't been able to make it down because of the weather – not having a rain cover, or a decent pram, and that.'

'So I hear,' Sister Rawson said, looking not in the least impressed.

'But we're here now,' Christine continued, 'and, as you can see, Joey is doing fine.'

Sister Rawson held her hands out – the same pink podgy hands that had brought Joey into the world. She handed him over, thinking what a thing it must be to be a midwife – to be the first human touch for so many newborn babies. Did Joey have a bond with her too, because of that?

Apparently not. Sister Rawson took him across to a flat plastic cot – well, more like a cross between a cot and a baby bath – where she stripped him of his clothes and, despite his furious bucking and crying, proceeded to assault him just as Josie had described, yanking his limbs around, putting an obviously cold stethoscope to his naked chest, weighing him and generally making him furious.

Christine felt a powerful urge to wrestle her off but remained in her chair. *It's completely natural, that,* Josie had assured her, when she'd confessed to such feelings. *Just the normal maternal instinct coming out.*

It felt anything but natural, but Sister Rawson's manner seemed to change then. 'Oh, for goodness sake, there's no need for all that noise,' she chided Joey. She chucked his little cheeks, and glanced back at Christine, her smile warm now. 'The sooner you stop fussing, young man, the sooner you'll be back with your mummy!'

Your mummy. Christine still marvelled at being called that by other people.

'Here you go, love,' she then said. 'D'you want to pop his nappy and vest on while I write up my notes? Leave the babygro.'

Christine went over to the cot and began dressing Joey, while Sister Rawson returned to her desk. 'Well, be it by accident or design, Christine, he seems to be doing fine. He's a good weight and he's got a good pair of lungs on him. Which I imagine he'll soon be exercising. Bring him over when you're done, love, so I can give him his jab.'

Despite knowing to expect this bit, Christine was no better prepared, and as the needle went into Joey's arm, and as predicted he screamed blue murder, she felt her own eyes flood with tears.

'It's just the shock,' Sister Rawson said. 'He'll have forgotten it in an instant.'

Christine wasn't so sure. He looked up at her as if he couldn't quite believe his own mummy would have allowed that to happen. She hurried to dress him again, turning her back so Sister Rawson wouldn't see her snivelling.

But perhaps she didn't need to. 'So,' she said, her notes completed and the needle disposed of. 'Everything else. How are you coping generally? Any problems you need some help with?'

Christine shook her head. 'Everything's fine,' she said.

Sister Rawson's gaze bore into her. 'Really, Christine? Everything?'

'So far,' she said.

'And what about your living arrangements? Any progress with the housing?'

'Not yet,' Christine said, realising she probably knew everything. That the social worker would have come back and described it all in detail. The ratty flat. The dirt and squalor. Her own state of dishevelment. But maybe that had been a good thing. Perhaps they might have put a word in.

'And how about your mother?'

'My mother?'

'Have you managed to patch things up with her?'

Her voice was gentle, concerned, and Christine sighed inwardly. So she knew all about that too. But then, why wouldn't she? The way her mother had kicked off, it would have been the talk of the ward. 'Have you seen anything of her?' Sister Rawson said when she didn't immediately answer. 'You know, Christine, she might be regretting things. But she might feel she can't make an approach to you.'

'I don't think so,' Christine said, feeling a rush of irritation. Sister Rawson obviously didn't know the half of it. But she seemed keen to keep on, even so.

'You know, my love, whatever water has flowed under the bridge you're not in the best kind of circumstances right now, are you?' She paused, as if keen to press that point home. 'Now, I don't know all the circumstances,' she went on, 'but a lot of things that are said in haste are repented at leisure, and while I'd never suggest you put you or Joey in harm's way, I'd definitely counsel trying to patch things up if it's feasible. It's not good to be where you are – either practically *or* emotionally. Bad blood and all that … You so *vulnerable*.'

Christine didn't know what to say to that. Her instinct was to tell Sister Rawson she was living in fairyland. But that tone she was adopting – there was something about it. What was she hinting? Vulnerable to what?'

'She hates me,' she heard herself say. 'She's disowned me.' She dropped her eyes to Joey. 'And I can't blame her, can I? I just need the housing to –'

'I know, my love,' Sister Rawson interrupted, nodding. 'And under the circumstances I understand that. Of *course* I do. I'm just suggesting that it's probably not the whole picture, that's all. That you shouldn't discount the option of trying to mend things. That's all I'm saying. For *Joey's* sake,' she added, offering a finger, which he took in his tiny fist. 'For *his* sake, my love. That's all I'm saying.'

The sun was shining out of a clear blue sky by the time Christine came out of the clinic, Joey once again settling to sleep and armed with the date of Joey's next appointment, which was written in pencil on a small card. This was for his booster, but Sister Rawson had made a point of reminding her that 'doing right by' Joey involved her coming down *every* week to have him weighed and measured. That she should 'be extremely mindful of her situation'.

Christine ran through everything Sister Rawson had said to her – that included – and felt anxiety stirring inside her. Her choice of words, her expression, her keeping on calling her 'my love'; all of it conspired to make Christine scared rather than reassured. She was being watched, she felt sure of it. That was it. She was on some sort of list. It was tantamount to them telling her she'd better be careful, because they were onto her. Sister Rawson had probably only stopped short of actually saying so because she didn't want to frighten her.

But she was frightened even so. She headed back up Little Horton Lane, glancing up at the Brigella Mills clock as she passed, which was still working, despite the factory itself having been closed down for years. It told her it was still only half past eleven – not even half the day gone – and the thought of returning to the flat on such a bright, hopeful day felt all wrong. She thought she might walk round to Josie's; tell her the things Sister Rawson had said to her. It had been almost a week since she'd seen her, after all. And would doubtless have done so, had she not turned into Louis Avenue and seen June, Josie's mam, walking towards her.

June McKellan was a larger than life figure on the estate. She bore the maiden name of Hudson, so it went without saying. And, in Vinnie, she was also mum to one of the most notorious local heroes; currently incarcerated at Her Majesty's pleasure, he was still as well known, and well loved, as he'd ever been. June herself was as hard as a whole box of nails and for all that she'd thump anyone who said or did a thing against her Josie, they'd not had the easiest of mother–daughter relationships down the years either. She was also thick as thieves with Christine's mam.

Christine could, therefore, think of happier encounters she might had had, and felt her stride growing shorter, almost as if by itself, as she pushed the pram up the pavement towards her.

June waved and smiled as she saw her, however. 'Hello, love,' she said, as she got within a few feet. 'You on your way to our Josie's? If so, you're out of luck. She's just left for the community centre. Took our Paula down to that new play group thing they've opened.'

June peered into the pram and Christine could smell her distinctive Charlie perfume. It was as much a part of her as her bleached hair and deep crimson lipstick. Where her own mam had always embraced all the latest fashion fads – often appallingly, to Christine's mind – June, like her sister Annie, who also lived on Canterbury Estate, still modelled herself on Marilyn Monroe.

'Ooh, he's a stunning little bleeder, he really is,' she pronounced. 'Funny how half-castes are always so good looking, isn't it?'

Christine cringed. But June had no side to her. It was a genuine observation. And she was right. His caramel skin did make him stand out. Make him handsome. Especially among the pasty-faced type you usually saw in Bradford – the legacy of everyone being holed up in factories all day, and there being fuck all, most of the year, in the way of sun.

June now turned her gaze to Christine herself. 'And how about you, love? How you doing?'

Christine shrugged. 'I'm okay.'

'You look it too,' June observed, casting her gaze over her. Christine had made an effort for the clinic and, with Sister Rawson's scrutiny, she'd been doubly glad she had. Washing her hair, despite there being no hot water. Putting some make-up on her face. Even finding the prehistoric iron under the sink in Brian's kitchen, and ironing her one decent blouse, on a towel draped over the coffee table.

She was glad of it now, too. That she looked like she was coping. She couldn't shrug off this idea that everyone was waiting for her to prove them right and fail.

'How's my mam?' she asked June, the thought prompting the question.

June, to her surprise, shook her head. 'Not good,' she said. 'I don't mind telling you. Not good,' she said again. She glanced back into the pram. 'Look at him,' she said, continuing to stare down at Joey. 'Her only grandson. You'd think, wouldn't you … that …'

'Not good *how*?' Christine asked her. 'In what way?'

'She's just not herself.' Now June looked back up at Christine. Even in the heels that were as much her trademark as the hair and lippy, June was a good two or three inches shorter than her. She sighed. 'You don't really need me to tell you, love, do you? She's not taken it well, this.'

Christine didn't have an answer for that because she didn't need telling. Instead, she shook her head. 'Not a lot

I can do about that now, is there? Not sure there's much I *want* to do about it either, the way she's treated me,' she said. She lifted her chin. And she thought she meant it. But there was still this ache she couldn't shake ... She was a mere couple of streets away but *so* far from home. The closer she was to it, the worse the feeling seemed to be.

And Sister Rawson's words still lingered. It wasn't just about her, was it? Wasn't just about her *or* her mam. It was about Joey.

'What about Mo?' she asked June.

'Mo? Oh, she's given him his marching orders.'

'*Really?*' Christine was shocked to hear this, and not at all sure she believed it. But June seemed very sure.

'What do *you* think?' she added. 'He's a lying, cheating bastard and thank God she's finally come to her bleeding senses. Oh, make no mistake, love. He's history.'

Christine tried to digest this. Which was not to say her mam didn't still blame her, utterly, but, given what she had said to her at the hospital, this news was the very last she'd expected to hear. She'd had this whole picture sorted – of her mam and Mo, carrying on as they always had, both discarding her as easily as if she'd never existed. Was that not, in fact, the case? Could Sister Rawson have been right? That her mam *did* want to patch things up? Get to know Joey?

June stopped short, as Christine knew she would, of telling her to go and see her mam. June wasn't daft. She knew her friend well enough, and also long enough, to know what kind of row Christine might still expect. Lizzie Parker was not a mam in the sense that most mams were – even by June's less that earth-motherly standards. But as she said goodbye, Christine resolved that she'd walk round there anyway. She had nothing to lose, after all – her mam's ranting couldn't hurt her. But if it was true – that she *had*, unbelievably, sent Mo packing – then perhaps she'd come to realise that he *did* bear responsibility. And that she did want a relationship with her grandson after all.

Christine reassured herself again. Going round there couldn't *hurt* her, even if her mam kicked off royally. Sticks and stones, that was all. And given that there was no sign of a council flat in the offing, she should perhaps heed Sister Rawson's well-meant but thinly veiled threats.

She should try again with her mam. For Joey's sake.

Chapter 9

Though it felt strange to be knocking on her own front door, Christine did just that, before stepping back self-consciously and waiting, jiggling the pram handle absentmindedly.

The front looked as it always did – ignored. Dismissed. Written off. Wholly short of a bloke's attention. No neatly tended garden, or car out front, like at Josie and Eddie's. They always talked about a 'woman's touch', but there was a man's touch as well. Which they'd never really had, especially since Nick had left.

She stiffened as she heard the catch moving, braced for the probable explosion, but when her mam appeared from behind it, all she did was stare. First at Christine, then at the pram, and then back to her daughter.

'Christ, tell me this is a fucking dream,' she said eventually.

Christine was shocked by the look of her. It had been weeks since she'd seen her mam, and she could understand what June meant now, because the first thought that came to mind was that her mother looked like shit. She had no make-up on for one thing, though she was dressed as if to go somewhere, and beneath the baby-blue fluffy jumper – a jumper? In this weather? – and a pair of drainpipe jeans, she looked insubstantial and gaunt.

She looked so un-mam-like that any normal, sharp response seemed unthinkable. 'I just saw Auntie June, Mam,' she said.

'Oh, you did, did you?' her mother drawled at her. She opened the door a little wider and stood there glowering, with a hand on each hip. Christine wondered if she was drinking herself into oblivion every night.

'Yes, I did, and she told me you're done with Mo now. Look, Mam … Look at Joey. Just come out and say hello to him at least. He's got grandad's hair. It's so *thick* …'

She knew she'd started to gabble. Couldn't seem to stop herself in the face of her mam's withering glare. And something else. She was finding herself increasingly transfixed. To beyond her mam, now the breeze had pushed the door further open. To the hall, in which a sun shaft arrowed down onto the carpet. To the brightness beyond, where the kitchen was. The back door to the little garden. The ache intensified. It was that simple; she wanted – *needed* – to be home.

'It's thick because he's half bleeding West Indian, you stupid dolt,' Lizzie barked. 'And look at him? Look at him? Be reminded of that fucking low life? You've got more chance of plaiting fog, you silly mare!'

She almost snarled then, seeming to make a point of looking anywhere but at the pram. 'Just piss off, Christine, will you. Go running off to him, why don't you? I'm done with him. You're welcome to each other.' She took a step back, lifted her arm behind her and gripped the door catch. 'And we're done as well, you and I. You got that? So why don't you piss off back to that brother of yours and his dozy mate.'

Despite the sting of her mother's words, Christine stood her ground. She couldn't not. 'Mam, you've got to stop this! I don't care sod all about Mo – you *know* that! I'm done with him too! I was always done with him. It was ...' she exhaled. This was pointless. Her mam's hand was still on the doorknob. She seemed to be needing the door for support. She really did look like shit.

'Mam, you okay?' she asked.

'No, I'm fucking *not* okay,' came the swift response. 'Would *you* be in my shoes? I'm fucking *not* okay! Now piss off. I'm sick of looking at you.'

It was the tears, mostly, that made Christine step forward. Her mother's tears. She was actually struggling not to burst into tears. She, who shouted, but never cried – not in front of Christine.

But she had to snatch her outstretched hand away before she caught it in the slamming door. A breath of scented air followed the bang. It smelled of home.

'Bollocks to her!' Christine said to herself as marched back up Quaker Lane. 'You hear that, baby? We're on our own now and that's just fine by me.' And it was, she decided, sending the longing back where it belonged and slamming a determined lid on it. If her mother wanted to cut off her nose to spite her face then it was up to her.

Joey gurgled his delight at her stream of animated chatter, kicking out his legs and pumping his arms up and down. 'Exactly. Bollocks to her!' she said again, just because she could.

She headed straight back to the flat. Despite the sunshine the day had lost all its light and hope. It was all very well going to baby groups and parks and all that, but when your insides were churned up it was pointless. No, better be back with Nicky – who at least she knew loved her, and who wouldn't mind listening. And that was all she really wanted. To be listened to. For someone to care. And it was now approaching one, so he should be up and about.

He was. Was sitting on the futon he'd only recently slept in, greasy jeans covering legs that were splayed across the floor. He had a fat spliff in his hand and he grinned as he saw her, replacing the smile with a frown as he saw the look on her face.

'Hey,' he said, 'what's up, sis? Hang on …' he added, pulling himself up. He then placed the spliff in the ashtray, nudging the collection of butts up to make room for it. Then he reached behind the futon and pulled out something huge and soft-looking and grey.

'This help?' he said, thrusting the oversized soft toy at her. It was Eeyore, the sad donkey out of *Winnie-the-Pooh*.

'Where'd you get *that?*' Christine wanted to know, her distress diverted momentarily. It was made of plush and at least three times the size of Joey.

'Down the market,' Nicky answered. 'And before you pull a face, no, I *didn't* nick it. Couldn't say no to it, could I? Little Joey's going to love it, don't you reckon? Well, when he's big enough, of course. Might be a bit of a while yet.'

Christine couldn't speak. She had a rock in her throat. Nicky put the toy down. 'Hey, come on, sis, get a grip will you? Come on.' He gently took her hands from the pram handle and steered the sleeping Joey into the bedroom. 'Go on,' he said, gesturing towards the futon. 'Take the weight off those feet.'

Christine flopped down, sniffing and snivelling, and picked up the enormous toy. So like Nicky. Not a bean, yet he'd spent a packet on this most probably. And even if he hadn't – and she wasn't going to press him on that point – it was the thought. And what it meant. Just how much it meant. It meant she and Joey weren't just a nuisance. An inconvenience to be borne.

Nicky flopped down beside her moments later. 'Go on, then, spill, sis,' he said, propping the toy up against the wall.

So she started telling him – about what Sister Rawson had said, about seeing June, about their mam, all the while accepting drags on the spliff, gratefully, as she spoke. She still didn't like all the drugs they took, but the dope didn't count. It really didn't. They were even trying to legalise it, and with good reason. It didn't make anyone shout and scream and punch. It didn't do that thing you saw all the time down the Listers on a weekend. It didn't make lads brawl in the street.

Quite the opposite, she'd come to realise. Dope was gentle, and kind. It helped to soothe troubled thoughts. Helped you calm down and relax. Helped put your troubles in perspective.

'Fuck that silly cow,' Nicky said, raising his free arm and putting it around her shoulder. 'You got me and Brian, sis,' he said, planting a kiss on the top of her head. 'You're fine here. We'll sort you out. See you right. You're fine *here*.'

'I know,' she said. 'I know, Nick. It's just –'

Nicky pulled back. 'Do you?' he asked, holding her gaze. 'Do you *really*, Chris? I'm not sure you do. But let me tell you, I'll *always* do right by you, you know that? You and Joey. You're the only family I've got and I'll take care of you, okay?'

Christine took another drag, then sank back gratefully into the cushions, feeling the weight and solidity of her brother's encircling arm, and finally starting to feel a little less broken.

Chapter 10

Brian stumbled into the living room, barefoot and stinking of booze, but looking unusually animated.

'Fuck me, I nearly forgot,' he said, laughing. 'It's only me fucking birthday, Chris, innit!'

Barely two weeks had passed since Christine had been to see her mother. And though she'd dutifully attended baby clinic, and met up with Josie to pour her heart out, nothing had changed. No word from the housing, and nothing either from or about her mother.

She'd thought more than once she might phone the social-worker woman, Carol Sloper. But the idea had somehow not translated to action. When it had come to it, she hadn't quite found the wherewithal to actually go to the phone box and make the call.

Brian was hopping from foot to foot, looking around, as if for something. 'Where's your Nicky?' he asked. 'We'll have to have a party or summat, won't we?'

Christine studied him, taking in the state of him. Even with her sense of smell being so accustomed to the general rankness now, he stank. 'He's nipped out to cash his giro,' she answered. Then had a thought. 'And, if that's the case, maybe you'll be thinking of having a bath?'

Brian really did stink. Especially his breath, which she could smell from across the room. Not to mention his clothes, which he usually slept in, only changing them under duress. She'd learned he could usually be persuaded to, if she offered to do a wash for him, but, other than that, it was as if he either didn't notice or didn't care.

'Cheeky git,' he said, laughing again as he stretched and scratched luxuriously, before stepping out on to the balcony that served the fourth floor.

She watched him hoick up his jeans and bend dangerously far over the railing. 'C'mon, Rodders!' he hollered down. 'It's only me bleedin' birthday!' He then leaned back into the front room, grinning from ear to ear. 'Your Nick,' he explained, for what must have been the umpteenth time. 'Rodders. D'you get it, Chrissy? Like off that *Fools and Horses* thingy. Del Boy and Rodders. I'm Del Boy and your Nick is that plonker – that Rodney. Suits him, don't you think?' He mimed what Christine assumed was some ducking and diving. 'Suits him down to the ground, that does. That plonker.'

Christine carried on picking up the stray rubbish that habitually littered the living room. Where did it all *come* from? It was as if it bred in the night. 'Yeah, yeah,' she said. 'And this is Peckham, and this is Nelson Mandela House. Yeah, you've told me, Brian. Several times. I *get* that.'

Brian went back out onto the balcony and eventually returned with Nicky, who was carrying a paper bag from which a delicious smell was coming. 'Bacon sarnies all round,' he announced, holding the bag up and smiling. 'Get the kettle on, Chrissy. And see if you can find the brown sauce.'

They all trooped into the kitchen and while Christine popped the kettle on, the sauce located, Nicky started doling out his booty. The sink was, as usual, overflowing with filthy dishes – which always struck Christine as odd, since Nicky and Brian mostly ate out of take-away containers. She ran the hot tap, somewhat optimistically, while Nicky plopped sauce onto the butties, and once it was lukewarm, squeezed the last dregs of washing-up liquid onto the stacks of crockery. Joey'd not long gone down, so, not waiting for the kettle, she followed them both back into the lounge.

'So what's the plan then?' she asked. 'How shall we celebrate? Go out? Maybe I could ask Sonia to sit Joey.'

Sonia, who lived on the landing above them, was always on hand to babysit, it seemed. A half-caste fifteen-year-old – which made Christine warm to her – she'd long since dumped school for the more profitable business of looking after other people's kids. And it *was* profitable. She had no shortage of work. Chances were she might already be booked up.

Brian, predictably, was already halfway into his sandwich. He ate pretty erratically, which was why he was so scrawny, but when he did, he consumed food like it was the last he would ever see.

'Nah, mate,' he said, wiping ineffectually at the butter dripping down his stubble-coated chin. 'I thought I'd get a few of the lads round for a bit of a knees-up. It's cheaper than the pub, and besides, we'll be getting some gear, won't we? And some Charlie, if we're lucky. Can't do that in the pub, can we?'

Nick snorted. 'And who exactly do you think is gonna bring gear round here, mate? You still owe half the fucking estate for what you had last week.'

Brian winked at his friend. 'It's your best mate's birthday, innit? And you got your giro this morning. You work it out.'

'No way is all this going on smack, mate,' Nicky said, patting his back pocket. 'Be happy you got a sarnie for your birthday, cos that's *all* your getting.'

Brian wasn't to be deflected though. If there was money around, he was having some. It was his flat. As Christine was never allowed to forget when she got her family allowance either. 'Listen, I swear, Nick,' he said. 'I've got something coming up on Saturday. I'll be able to drop you a few quid at the weekend, promise. Tell you what – in fact I'll *double* what you spend.'

Christine had heard conversations like this on an almost daily basis since moving in, and she knew how it would go. Nick would say no. Brian would continue to plead, then Nick would cave in. But then he'd tell Brian he wasn't going to pay any rent until he got paid back. This time was no different. Nor would it ever be, she reckoned. Much as she loved her brother, what she wouldn't give to get out. And what the fuck was she supposed to do with Joey while all this was happening? Yes, she could keep him in the bedroom, and hope he'd sleep through most of it, but the flat would be crawling with the sort of idiots who saw a closed bedroom door as an opportunity (for either a quickie or a kip) and on the evidence of what she'd seen so far – even though in other flats, not this one – the whole thing could go on for bloody hours.

'Fuck the rent, Nicky,' Brian said amiably. 'I'm telling you, I won't need it this month. Rasta Mo is fetching me some right gear round on Saturday. I'll get rid of it the same day – no problem – then I'll be sorted. Tickety boo, like. It'll clear my debt with him as well. Happy all round.'

Mo. Christine's stomach flipped. Mo? Coming *here*? She looked anxiously at her brother, who had already looked in her direction. 'Is he for *real*?' she asked Nicky. She felt scared suddenly. Even as she knew she was being ridiculous. Scared and at the same time not a little defiant – even expectant. Let him come. Let him see what he'd produced. What they'd created. As much as anything she wanted to see his reaction when he did, even though Josie had told her over and over that he produced kids all over. That he couldn't, wouldn't give a shit.

'You can't have him round here!' Nicky said, pointing at Christine. 'Aren't you forgetting something?'

Brian's expression told Christine that he had. Then he shook his head. 'Don't worry, he won't come *in*, or anything. He told me not to tell anyone, didn't he? Not even you, Nicky. He'll wait down in the car park. It'll be one of his Joeys who comes up with the gear.'

Christine glanced towards her bedroom door, distracted and cross. Her poor boy. Having him for a sodding father. Then she turned to Brian, having processed what he'd said. 'Joeys?' she said.

Brian was busy scratching his crotch now. 'Eh?'

Nicky shook his head. 'Boys, sis. One of his boys is what he meant.'

Christine shrugged. 'Well, it doesn't matter anyway,' she said. 'Fuck Mo. He's a waste of space. So. Who's for tea?'

She wiped her hands on one of Joey's muslins, and gathered up a couple of stray mugs, suddenly feeling up for it. Feeling bullish. Feeling like she too had a right to a life. 'Let's plan this party then, shall we?' she said brightly. 'It's about time I let my hair down.'

Though initially looking shocked at Christine's sudden change of mind, Nicky and Brian soon got up to speed, deciding on whom they would or wouldn't bestow an invite, and discussing how they'd come by sufficient quantities of drugs and alcohol. In reality, their list of 'friends' mostly comprised fellow junkies from the flats, but perhaps that was the definition of 'friend' for the likes of Brian and, increasingly, Christine mused, for her brother.

Bad Blood

She decided to leave them to it, her brief moment of enthusiasm quickly beginning to seep from her, revealing itself for the impostor it really was. She slipped into the bedroom quietly, anxious not to wake Joey, and wondered, as she so often did, how she was going to fill another day.

She thought about going out, deciding that perhaps she'd nip to the post office to get a card for Brian, then immediately dismissed the idea as being pointless. Brian would much rather have a joint than a card. Fact. Indeed, he'd likely as not use it, assuming it was sufficiently thick card, to tear into strips to make filters.

She lay back on the bed, laced her fingers behind her head and stared up at the ceiling. It was covered in damp patches; great swathes of dirty grey, liberally spotted by spreading black mould spores. It had spread even since she'd been there and could only get worse – both from the condensation (it was too cold to air the room properly) and from the imminent approach of winter.

She had to get out. She *had* to. For Joey's health, as much as anything. They both seemed to be permanently snotty and snivelling. Which couldn't be good for him. And above all things, she wanted things to be good for him. She just felt powerless to make anything right.

She also felt anxious about seeing Mo. No, that was wrong, she decided. Her anxiety was more about him seeing *her*. Anxious about feeling scrutinised by him. About his gaze running over her – up and down, as was his way – and then deeming her unworthy of a second glance.

Her position angered her. Her assigned role of being one of his pathetic cast-offs – too stupid even to have got rid of his baby, and now saddled with a kid he had no use for. She hoped he did stay in his car – his look-at-me-I'm-so-hard BMW. She wondered if he even realised that round their way they called BMWs Black Men's Wheels, because every black wannabe gangster aspired to drive one. Probably, she conceded. And he probably didn't care. He was so full of himself he probably thought it was appropriate.

No, she hated the idea of seeing him, because she knew she'd find it hard to play the role *she'd* been assigned. That she'd want to slap him, put him down, give him a piece of her mind – like absolutely no one, as far as she could tell, ever dared to do. But at least she had the knowledge that her mam had sent him packing. No one sent Mo packing, but her mam had had the strength to.

She had another thought then. Why was Mo supplying Brian with gear to sell anyway? Mo hated Brian. Everyone knew that. He called him 'blow job' – a name he had earned very famously when he'd gone down on another dealer to pay for a spliff. Mo thought Brian was a joke, just like all the other dealers did. So why Brian? Why now? It made little sense. Except … A new thought slipped into Christine's mind and stayed there. Was there another reason for Mo's sudden interest in the flat?

She continued to study the ceiling while she played with possibilities, chief among them – and despite herself, she couldn't help but consider it – being that Mo, having been dumped by his ever-faithful doormat, Lizzie, had decided he might as well seek Christine out again. She might have a baby but she was still very young. And everyone knew, her included (she had the evidence in the pram beside her) that Mo had a liking for young flesh.

She shuddered inwardly, as the murky memories of their coupling revisited her. She'd loved Mo back then. Like a caring kindly uncle. Found him captivating, since she was eleven and he'd arrived with a toy for her. A Barbie doll equivalent that he'd chosen especially for her. 'Look at that!' her mam had raved. 'Aren't you the luckiest girl *ever*?' And he'd smiled his smooth smile, ran a hand over her head, and she'd drunk in his presence and the smell of his aftershave, and thought fleetingly how nice it would be – how *amazing* it would be – if Rasta Mo came to live with them and became her daddy.

When Christine emerged from her bedroom with Joey, to make up his bottle, Brian was alone in the living room. 'Change of plan,' he said. 'Your Nicky's been knocking on doors, and we've decided it'd be a better plan to leave the party till Saturday, so's people have got their money. Plus there's another benefit –' He talked like a teacher, presenting a lesson plan to a class. 'I'll have the gear, then, off Mo, and I'll be able to cut a bit of it, which means you, me and Nicky won't have to pay for any of it.'

Christine wondered at the mindset that seemed to see life as a series of obstacles in which success was measured in terms of what you got away with. She needed her bene-fits – needed them badly – but there wasn't a day when she cashed her giro without a sense of guilt and frustration. She wanted to work. To have her job back. To feel she mattered.

But this was good news. Far better to have it at the weekend, when there was much less chance of people kicking off about the noise.

Though Brian winked at her. 'Doesn't stop us having a little blast on our own tonight though, does it? Your Nicky said he'll bring us a couple of rocks back in a bit, if you're up for it.'

Christine was about to shake her head, but something stopped her. Now her head was sorted, she felt a lot braver. So instead she shrugged. 'Yeah, perhaps,' she said, shifting Joey to her other hip. 'Perhaps.'

Brian came over and lifted a hand to chuck Joey under the chin, and it was an effort of will not to flinch under the twin assault of filthy hand and fetid breath. 'Oh, go on,' he said. 'You know you want to.'

Chapter II

For all that the possibility of Mo turning up had been on her mind, Christine hadn't actually expected to see him. It wasn't even noon yet, for pity's sake – pretty much the middle of the night for the likes of Mo. He slept late and worked late and partied till sun up. Christine knew this because she'd observed his comings and goings for many years. So when she'd popped out with Joey, after a full morning's tidying and scrubbing, the last thing she expected to see when she turned the final corner to home was the sight of his BMW parked up in the flat car park.

Much less the sight of Mo himself. Yet here he was, large as life, leaning against the car, legs crossed at the ankle, one hand holding the cigarette he was lifting to his lips, the other slipped inside the pocket of his jeans.

He didn't even pause when he saw her. Not even for half a second. The cigarette continued its journey to his opening lips as smoothly as if propelled there by a motor. He took a deep drag, released it, then blew a steady stream of smoke out, while he flicked the ash off the tip onto the concrete.

Christine stopped in her tracks, her mind whirring and racing at the sight of him. Seeing his black jacket – leather, but styled like a suit jacket. The bright T-shirt beneath. The trademark Bob Marley dreadlocks, which were still such an arresting sight. Still one of the many things about him that had the power to unsettle her. How could such a bastard still exert such a power?

She looked down at Joey, who was stirring now the pram was suddenly stationary, and wondered for the umpteenth time whether the sight of him would change anything for Mo. Not with her – she was done with him. She was unshakeable on that point. But as a fatherless child she had a strong sense of outrage that while he cruised around in his fancy drugmobile, dispensing favours to those who pleased him, his son – his flesh and blood – had no such advantages. No, he was forced to live in a shithole, with his penniless mother. It was all wrong. All *wrong*. It was criminal, in fact. There should surely be a law, shouldn't there? If there was any kind of justice. To *make* shits like him support their offspring.

Her anger made her stronger. She started walking once again. He must see Joey. Must be made to meet his warm, innocent gaze. Try to hold it, if he was man enough. At least for long enough to understand that he had a fucking *responsibility*.

Joey's eyes were closing again, so she shook his rattle as she walked. Another gift from Nicky, the thought of which made her bullish; thank God that Joey had a half-decent uncle, at least. 'That's it, baby,' she cooed at him, determinedly not looking over at Mo now. And was rewarded with both the eyes and a beatific smile. 'That's the way,' she said, smiling back at him. 'Let's show him, shall we? Let's show him just how beautiful you are.'

More so than she was, she thought miserably, despite knowing she shouldn't even care now. But she did. Whatever else she wanted it was for Mo to realise what he'd lost. But here she was, looking shit, the sour tang of Ajax probably still clinging to her. In grubby jeans and Nicky's elderly bomber jacket. Which probably stank as well, she thought wretchedly – she wouldn't know, would she? Because her senses were so dulled now. It also drowned her, hanging off her shoulders like her dull, uncut hair.

Smoothing her fringe back, she crossed the small stretch of road that still separated them and wondered quite what she might usefully say to him, given that 'fuck you' was probably best saved for another day.

She regrouped as she approached him, finding strength in the fact that, close up, he did look a little ruffled. Nothing like scared, or even anxious – just ever so slightly off balance. She could tell from the way he quickly scanned the area around and above them, including the balconies, and she knew in that instant that it was because above all things, Mo had to have the upper hand whenever in public. He aspired to it anyway, but on the street it was essential. And she suspected, most of all, that he was expecting a row off her. Which is why she decided not to give him one.

'What you doing round here?' she asked, feigning surprise. 'Not your usual neck of the woods.'

He took another drag from his cigarette while he studied her. Then threw it to the ground and screwed the heel of his boot into it. At no point did he so much as glance at the pram. Then the familiar slow drawl. 'The fuck's it gotta do with you?' he asked her amiably.

Christine felt the adrenalin flooding through her and gripped the pram handle tighter. He'd been almost like a father to her, for such a long time, and then a seducer. A groomer. Shape-shifting seamlessly from one to the other, she realised. 'Why are you being suck a dick?' she asked, the words seeming to come from her mouth unbidden. 'And why don't you look at your son?'

That's what really struck her. That she'd known Mo for *years* – he'd been a constant at home right through from her early adolescence. She knew his mannerisms. Knew his style, and how he got what he wanted. So she really didn't expect what happened next. Quick as lightning, he shot out his arm and grabbed her by the throat, then squeezed steadily, his face expressionless, almost until her eyes bulged.

'You silly little fucking slag,' he hissed, his face looming so close that she could smell him. The same smell. The same aftershave. It took her back, even as he gripped her, to the night he'd come on to her. And on to her, and on to her, telling her she was beautiful and that he ached for her. Had ached for and ached for and couldn't stand it any more. That same night she caved in and gave in to him, high as much on his adoration as the alcohol he'd plied her with so steadily. As dizzy with lust as she had been from the wine. That night when a part of her knew, even as he feverishly tugged her clothes off, that it would destroy everything. That she should fight him.

That night when she hadn't.

He shoved her against his car, loosening his grip only once it was clear how hard she was struggling to breathe, her hands pinging off the pram handle automatically, for fear of toppling it.

'My *son*? If I hear you say *anything* like that again, I'll kill you,' he said slowly. 'You got that?' He let her go then. Put the back of his hand against his mouth and cleared his throat politely. 'Now fuck off, and take your little bastard with you.'

Christine glanced up to the balcony automatically. Was anyone witnessing this? Nicky, maybe? But no. As she should have realised. He'd already checked that no one was around. She grabbed the pram handle again, glad Joey had been unable to see it either. Though the thought re-fuelled her anger, just imagining how things could so easily pan out. She'd heard more than enough stories about men who knocked their women around. She didn't want that for Joey. She *wasn't* having that for Joey. She was as well rid of Mo as was her mam. She turned the pram. 'Fuck you, you black bastard,' she said through gritted teeth.

She heard him laugh. 'Black never stopped you before,' he said. '… By all accounts.' She carried on walking as he continued to taunt her. 'What's next? Bit of rough? Toothless dope heads? You know – what with you shacked up with old blow job himself. Classy. You mucky, fucking tart.'

Christine didn't turn the pram around and back through the entrance doors as she normally would. Just used it to force the doors open. Her eyes pricked with tears and her whole body shook now. What a bastard. What a wanker. What an evil fucking shit. Now she did back up, in readiness for bumping the pram back up the stairs. He was exactly where she'd first spotted him, lounging against his flashy car, another fag already on the go. She paused to wipe her nose against the sleeve of Nicky's jacket. Now she *could* smell it. It smelt of rancid chip fat and smoke. Of sweat and utter hopelessness and poverty.

'Whoah! Slow down a bit, will you, sis? Hold your horses!'

It was dark. Proper dark, which had happened without her noticing, any more than she'd noticed the comings and goings that had punctuated the bright afternoon. 'Gi's it here,' she commanded, keeping tight hold of the crack pipe, her mouth already watering at the popping sound that came from it, as once she had responded at the sound of the ice-cream van.

So *this* was what it was all about. This is what she'd been missing. Why had she never realised just how good it was? She felt euphoric. Loved the warm, rosy glow that now enveloped her. Loved the sense of peaceful contentment. She glanced around her. She was among friends. That was all that mattered, *ever*. The flat was filled with friends

– rich with friends, dripping with friendship. Friends who all cared about her. Friends who wanted nothing more than for her to be happy. Her and Joey. Who was content, too. Fast asleep in the bedroom. Sleeping the sleep of the contented while they partied on without him. And there was music – a little cheesy, but then that was Brian for you – and the booze and drugs were seemingly never-ending and she didn't know where one moment ended and another one began. All she knew was that she was safe, warm and loved.

Christine had never known anything about coke. She'd only ever known enough to know she didn't want to touch it – bar the odd spliff Nicky pressed on her, she really didn't *do* drugs. They were altogether too scary.

'But do *this*,' Nicky'd said, when she'd come up, snivelling and gulping, from the car park. 'Honest, sis, *do* this. It'll make you feel better. *Do* it. I promise. It'll help. It really will.'

It turned out that Nicky *had* seen everything, such as it was, and had been quick to reassure her it was nothing. 'Course he's not going to kill you!' he said, even smiling as he said it.

'I know *that*,' she'd sniffed back. 'Like he'd dare. Like he'd *ever*. I'm not an *idiot*, Nick! It's just … the bastard. The fucking *bastard*, Nick. I want to kill *him*!'

And despite him laughing at what she'd said – ho, ho, ho, wasn't it *funny*?! – she'd then started sobbing all over again.

But then, when she'd stopped, and she'd made up Joey's bottle, there seemed a definite satisfaction, even if the logic of it was shaky, in accepting Nick's offer of a try of some coke – some of the coke Mo himself had graciously supplied to them. 'Like, to get him back,' Nicky said. 'Because it's pure and we're going to cut it, and it's kind of like it's Mo who's paying for the party.'

Which it wasn't. Far from it. He'd be pocketing a decent profit. But the idea still appealed to her, in a 'stuff him' kind of way. And she'd taken it, snorting it first, using a rolled-up fiver to suck it up her nostrils from the coffee table, just as she'd seen Nick and Brian do, and bit by bit everything had gradually got better. And better still. Better than things had seemed in a long while. And within the hour it had become her new best friend.

Like pretty much everyone else, Christine was oblivious to the doorbell, the music drowning everything else out. Brian had bought himself a birthday present (as no one else had) of a record. Which he kept playing, over and over. Time had warped now. Christine wasn't sure if the song was on repeat or just going on and on and on. It was called 'Tainted Love' and it felt so appropriate. Dancing along to it felt almost like a rule.

There were fewer people now. She was dimly aware of a couple of people leaving, but there still seemed a lot of bodies strewn around. There were a couple comatose on the futon, and at least four or five laid out on the floor, limbs splayed as if slung there, like a row of carcasses in an abattoir. But half a dozen of them were still smoking and dancing and giggling, because it was a party, wasn't it? And she had to, had to, *had* to dance. And it didn't seem to matter – was hilariously funny even – that one or other of them would periodically lurch and knock something or other over. The coffee table had long since been toppled onto its back.

It was Brian, in the end, for whom the knocking filtered through. He was suddenly at the record player, having slid the volume slider down to zero, plunging the room and Christine's senses into silence.

He put a finger to his lips and Christine giggled. 'What's up, you divvy? Turn it back up!'

Brian's upper body swayed. 'Someone's banging at the door,' he slurred. She thought she could actually see his brain trying to focus. 'That's the coppers, that,' he said. 'I'd know that knock anywhere.'

Behind them, unknown to them, for fuck knew what reason, someone else had already gone and opened the door.

'Indeed it is, lad,' said the policeman who now stood before them. There were two more behind him. They looked dark and stern and huge. Christine found herself wanting to giggle again. She clamped her mouth shut.

'What the fuck's going on?' Nicky asked, looking pained. 'This is a private party. We're not doing owt wrong.'

Christine, gathering her thoughts, stole a glace to the coffee table, which was conveniently resting on a pile of detritus that included the pipe, the crack cocaine and what was left of the weed.

'There's been complaints,' one of the officers said, casting his eyes around the room. 'The music. Folk running in and out. You're causing a disturbance.'

Christine struggled to pull her mind to order. Someone had flicked the light switch – one of the coppers most probably – and in the sudden glare her thoughts immediately went to Joey. The place must stink of weed, she knew, and if Nicky got arsey they could get arsey too. Start looking around. Then they could all be in big trouble.

She stepped forward. 'We're sorry, officer,' she said, adding a bright, apologetic smile. It's his birthday,' she said, gesturing towards Brian. 'And it's all just gone on a bit longer than we thought. We're about done, though. No more music. We'll wrap it up.'

Christine had no idea how deformed and slurred her words might have sounded. But they'd come in the right order and apparently at the right time, because the officer to the left of the trio winked at her. She wasn't sure if he was being fatherly, or something else (she did have a skimpy top on), but either way she made the most of it and smiled shyly back. 'It's Brian's birthday party and it's gone on longer than we thought. We're about finished now, though, so, no more music, is that okay?'

'Right, well …' said the first officer, who was obviously in charge. 'So long as it's home time for everyone. And I *mean* it. No ramping it up again once we're gone, okay?

You're done.' He looked at Christine, presumably assuming she had the power to achieve this. 'We'll be parked downstairs for a bit, okay? And I expect everyone to leave quietly.' He then looked at Brian again. 'You're Brian Giles, aren't you?' he asked, as if it had only now occurred to him. 'And this is your flat.' It was a statement rather than a question.

Brian nodded. 'Yeah, it is, mate, and like she said, it's home time.'

'Right, Brian,' the copper said. 'I'll hold you to that. And you can count yourself lucky that we've got another call to make in here and are too busy to deal with the fact that it stinks like a bleeding cannabis factory.' His eyes narrowed. 'Or you'd be getting a warrant for your birthday, and all.'

The party guests left soon after, and, true to the copper's word, the police car sat four floors below them, for as long as it took to chivvy the last revellers out, half of whom were in such a deep, drug-enhanced sleep that it was like trying to wake the dead.

It was a good half hour before the three of them had the place to themselves again, and, fired up by their lucky escape from what Brian kept deadpanning was 'the long arm of the lawwwww', even did a little cursory clearing up.

Then they flaked out on the futon, all three of them. Christine felt a little nauseous now, a bit dizzy, and in dire need of a glass of water, but finding it impossible to complete the thought process that would see her actually go and get one, let the spinning in her head float her away.

'Fucking great party,' Brain said.

'Agreed, mate,' Nicky answered.

'A great night,' Christine added. 'Bloody *brilliant!*'

And though she was dimly aware of a sound that might be Joey grizzling in the bedroom, she couldn't complete the process that would actually see her get up and see to him. So she drifted off to oblivion, the smile still on her face.

Chapter 12

Apparently there was going to be a tornado. Or so they were saying on the telly, anyway – in fact, several of them were on the way, and Nicky glanced out of the flat window reflectively. The quarter light was open, despite the bitter cold. Though he couldn't remember who had opened it, much less when.

It was getting dark, and with the flat unlit, he was drawn back to the glowing screen – smiling to himself at the agitated-looking reporter, wondering idly what it might be like to have a tornado blow through Bradford. Would the flats stay up? Or might they be all blown away? Off to Oz. Now that *would* be pretty trippy.

He'd no energy to move, and had no idea where Brian was currently, but a snuffle from close beside him made him turn his head. Christine had been out for the count for ages – whether from drugs or lack of sleep he had no clear idea. He was only just coming round from the monster fix of heroin he'd taken – as far as he could recall – before dawn, and which had taken up most of the day.

A red triangle sign was flashing up. And the words 'Severe weather warning'. 'Set to hit almost anywhere in the UK,' the weather man was saying. 'Most likely strong and in clusters.'

He shook his sister awake, so he could share the compelling news with her. 'Hey, sis,' he said. 'Look. We're going to be hit by tornadoes. Look! I've never seen a tornado before. It'll be good.'

She mumbled something but seemed disinclined to move. Her lips were dry from sleeping so long with her mouth open.

Nicky ran his tongue around his own lips. He was pretty parched as well. He needed to stand up, go into the kitchen and get himself a glass of water – all of which still seemed too much effort. He managed it eventually, however, pausing only to ping the living-room light on, which produced a predictably angry whimper from Christine.

It was shit, this kind of come-down. Just about everything felt like too much effort. And seeing the state of the kitchen only made the impression worse. That was the thing, Nicky decided, as he fished around in the washing-up water for a glass to rinse out. It was the scale of it that caused the problem. The thing that stopped him from starting. If it was a manageable amount of mess he could deal with it – *would* deal with it – God knew, he felt guilty enough that Chrissy ran around him and Brian the way she did.

But there was just so *much* mess, and it occurred to him that she didn't do that quite so much now. That, actually, these days, she was often as pissed up and stoned as they were.

He spied Joey's bowl – or, rather, the bowl Christine habitually used for him. It was caked with something – perhaps Weetabix – and it crossed Nicky's mind that, with Christine completely out of it, it might have been a long time since he'd been fed.

Yet the baby was quiet. Not a peep – well, not as far as Nicky could hear, anyway. Which struck him as odd. Shouldn't he be screaming blue murder?

He drained the glass he'd filled, then refilled it and drank thirstily again, before shuffling off to Christine's bedroom (he no longer saw it as his) dizzy from the effort, and anxious about what he might find, and wondering if a snort of coke would help things along.

Probably, he thought. But he'd be good, he decided. He'd no business doing coke when he was looking after the baby. He'd no business letting Christine do coke around Joey, for that matter, and entering the bedroom – and being assaulted by a God-awful stench – he felt a rush of guilt that he'd allowed that to happen. That it was so infrequently that thoughts of this kind impressed themselves upon him. That he spent insufficient time properly looking after his little sister and taking some sort of fucking adult responsibility.

Joey was awake. Wide awake. And now he pulled himself upright, making the stench in the room even worse. He cried a lot these day, did Joey, so this was something unexpected, and it was only when Nicky got closer to the cot that he realised the reason the poor little blighter wasn't crying was because he'd obviously cried himself out.

Joey's plump little fingers gripped the top rail of the cot and he bounced up and down on the mattress. 'It's only me, mate,' Nicky told him. 'Your mam's having forty winks. Come on, let's get you sorted out, shall we?'

Nicky looked around to find something to hold Joey in, as he sure as hell wasn't picking him up with his bare hands. He'd wriggled his way out of his stinking nappy, which was laying flat on the floor beside the cot, and it looked like almost all of him was caked in his own shit – even the little vest he still had on and his hair.

Nicky diverted to fling open a window. The wind took it – perhaps there was a tornado already upon them – and a blast of freezing air bellowed in. Now Joey *did* complain, his mouth puckering then gaping as he took a breath in. And no wonder. He had almost nothing on.

'Don't you worry, mate,' Nicky told him, finding an old T-shirt to pick him up with. 'Nice hot bath, some clean clothes, you'll be right as rain, won't you?'

He didn't pick him up just yet, however, finding the presence of mind from somewhere to go back into the kitchen and fill the bowl for him first.

And maybe have a snort of coke, he decided, after all.

Pulling the pots and pans from the kitchen sink was as grim as he'd expected, as congealed food parted company with the plates it had been sticking to, and a whole new selection of disgusting stenches prickled his nostrils. But at least he had the pile more or less relocated to the crummy worktop and was able to swill out the sink and begin to refill it, added a few squirts of washing-up liquid for good measure.

'Come on then, kid,' he then said, going back into the bedroom. 'Let's be having you and get that shit off you, eh? And then a bottle. You'd like a bottle, wouldn't you? Bet you would, you poor bleeder. Then we'll wake your mam up and she can give it you, okay?'

Joey cheered up no end once he was sitting in the kitchen sink – gurgling happily as he played with a couple of old empty yoghurt pots, while Nicky – resisting the coke still – put the kettle on for tea. There was no formula, though. The can was sitting empty on the worktop. Nothing for it, then – he'd do what he'd seen Chrissy do the other day, and make him up a bottle of sweet tea. Though fuck knew what they'd give him for his dinner. The only baby food he could see was a half-eaten rusk. He picked it up – it was at least dry – and carefully placed it on the kitchen windowsill, priding himself on his presence of mind.

He heard a sigh, then, and turned around. It was his sister. 'Oh, gawd, Nick, I'm so sorry. Oh baby, look at the state of you!'

She hurried over to the sink where Joey splashed the water excitedly. She didn't make it. One minute she was grabbing the cooker handle to steady herself, apparently. The next she was clamping her hand over her mouth, and fleeing the room again, bumping into the door jamb as she went. Nicky could hear her throwing up shortly after.

He grinned at Joey, managing to find sufficient humour in the situation to say, 'State of *you*, mate? Talk about pots and kettles, eh?'

'God, I could *not* feel worse,' Christine announced minutes later, when she returned from the bathroom, clutching her head. By now, Nicky had cleaned the baby up and was drying him on his knee, while Joey sucked hungrily on the hunk of rusk.

'You couldn't *look* worse,' Nicky commented, truthfully.

'Thanks for that.'

'I did tell you.'

'Tell me what?'

'That you need to go easy on the crack. Sis, there's nothing of you.'

She ran her hands over her forehead and back across her scalp, revealing the taut blotchy whiteness of her skin. 'I need a top-up ...' she seemed distracted. 'Just to get me going again. I feel so fluey.'

'Sis, I'm not sure ...' Nicky began.

'Nick, for *fuck's* sake! Give me a top-up! You and Brian get most of my fucking baby money, don't you? And I've got to get to the shops,' she added. 'Pronto. Before they shut and we're all fucked for the day. He can't exist on tea and toast for ever, can he?'

Nicky sighed, but produced the goods anyway. Knelt down to fetch the plastic bag of powder he kept beneath a loose floorboard beneath one of the kitchen cupboards, and tipped a teaspoon full of it out onto the usual silver tray.

Joey pointed gleefully as Nicky fashioned the coke into a line for her to snort. 'You don't *never* wanna touch this,' he told the baby. 'Keep you poor, this stuff will, mate.'

But it was at least better than the crack they'd been using from the pipe and that she'd lately developed such a taste for.

'There you go,' Christine said, once she'd hoovered it all up. 'There you go, baby. Much better now, see?' She sniffed. '*Now* we can get to the shops. Get some fresh air and formula and food for you, yeah?'

Nicky handed Joey over so she could take him back to the stinking bedroom and get him dressed. 'There's tornadoes on the way apparently,' he called to her, suddenly feeling exhausted. 'Better wrap up.'

He heard a laugh. 'Yeah, right, Nick, of *course* there are,' she yelled back.

Chapter 13

Josie was livid. Not least because she should have seen it coming. It was only a matter of time, after all.

'Calm *down*!' Eddie was saying to her as she tugged off her pyjama bottoms. 'Being seen in a pub isn't a criminal offence!'

'Yes it *is*, actually,' Josie corrected him. 'Well, some sort of offence, anyway. She's seventeen, don't forget. Not eighteen yet. *Seventeen.* And who exactly was at home looking after Joey, do you think?'

'I could hazard a guess,' Eddie said, shifting Paula on his hip. 'But love, there is no need to go dragging off round there now, is there?'

Josie skewered her husband on the end of a sharp, assessing look. 'Love, if you hadn't wanted me to go dragging round there, then you shouldn't have told me, should you? Now, where are my jeans? Don't just stand there looking daft. Help me find them! I said I'm off round there and I am!'

'But it's got nothing to *do* with us, Jose,' Eddie tried, patiently, as he looked. 'I know you're narked, love, but if that silly mare wants to ruin her life, it's her business.'

148

Bad Blood

Josie glared at him. 'Not my *business?*' She yanked the bottom drawer on the bedroom chest so hard it almost toppled over. 'There's a baby not ten minutes away living in God knows what conditions. That same baby who spent the first fortnight of his life *here*. That same baby who you ask about every time you bump into one of those numpties down the pub. How can that baby not be our business?'

Eddie raised a hand, his usual signal that he knew when he was beaten. 'Okay, okay,' he said. 'I just think you should calm down, okay? I know you. I know what could happen here an' all, love. And I'm not having it, okay? Yes, I care about the little 'un. But I'm not having them living here again, okay? And not just for us,' he added, in response to Josie's scowl. 'And not only because we can't afford it. Because she comes back to us and she'll never get a council place, will she? Much less try to make things up with her bloody mother. That's all I'm saying, love, okay?'

Josie stepped into her jeans, leg by leg, then wriggled them up over her hips. Eddie was right. She knew that. He wasn't saying anything she didn't deep down agree with. Truth be known she had the same fears – if she took Christine home again, given the probable state of her, it would be doubly difficult to make her leave.

And she trusted what the numpties in the Listers had apparently told Eddie, however much she didn't want to. That Christine had been sucked down – as she'd been so bloody likely to – into the same crappy life of sloth and

149

booze as her brother. But not drugs. Please not drugs. Please let that not be true.

But that could so easily be true as well. Probably was. Because how long had it been now? A fortnight? Even longer? Over two weeks since she'd actually laid eyes on either Christine or the baby, despite having been round there four times. Twice there'd been no answer, even though she'd been sure she could hear voices, and twice more the door had been opened by that divvy, Brian, burbling on incoherently about how Christine was out with the baby and he didn't know when they'd be home.

Except she *had* been at home. Josie would have put money on it. So this – this latest news, of Christine boozing down the Listers – this was entirely, and depressingly, as expected. As was the consensus that Brian's flat was becoming party central. That he was earning off Mo and making plenty of money and that all kinds of shit were the norm now.

And it wasn't as if Eddie was the only bearer of bad news. Only the other day one of the lads from the other end of the estate had approached her, a well-meaning lad cruelly saddled with the name of Hilton Brown, who was well known both for drug taking and general not-giving-a-fuck – so to have *him* suggest she might want to involve social services, well, that really put the lid on it.

'I mean, I know I'm a twat myself, Titch,' he'd said to her, in his usual cheery fashion. 'But even *I* know that it's all fucked up over there. That baby deserves better than it's getting, no question. Honest to God, you should do something. Chrissie just doesn't seem to care any more.'

No, if the likes of Hilton Brown thought things were going too far, then they certainly must be. So today – not tonight, not tomorrow, not Monday, she was going round there to see for herself and nothing was going to stop her. She'd happily boot the door down if she had to. By fair means or foul, she was getting into that flat.

And if it proved to be true, then what? *Did* she inform the social? Not just yet, she decided. She'd simply threaten Christine with them. That and give her the bollocking of her life. And then maybe she'd stomp round her mother's for good measure. And give her a bloody bollocking too. Because Hilton was right. Poor Joey deserved better. Off his mam and his grandmother too.

Josie pulled a brush through her hair, then followed Eddie downstairs.

'I've had a thought,' he said. 'Why don't you take your mam with you? You know, safety in numbers and all.' She'd already dismissed his earlier idea – hence the heated exchange of views – that he should go round there with her, or she go not at all.

She shook her head. There was nothing in the flat that could frighten her. And besides, it was dry and crisp, albeit bitterly cold, and they'd already promised Paula a trip to Horton Park.

'I'll be fine,' she said, grabbing her big coat from the

151

under-stairs cupboard. 'Last thing their neighbours'll want is a mouthful of June bleeding McKellan – not on a Saturday afternoon. And besides, you know what my mum's like. She'd just make things worse. And if Christine's in a state, she'll probably give her a frigging battering, and I know from experience that'll do no good at all.'

Eddie nodded. 'You're probably right,' he conceded. 'But Jose, it's freezing out there and it looks slippy as well. How about I nip you round in the car and drop you? Come back for you in an hour or so?'

Josie was grateful for his offer. It did look freezing outside. And it made sense as well, seeing as little Paula was already dressed and ready. 'Go on then,' she grinned, her anger at Eddie forgotten. 'You've twisted my arm.'

She tugged playfully on the bobble on her daughter's woollen hat, smiling at her squeals of pretend protest. How could she? How could Christine neglect that little baby? For all that she knew they didn't live in frigging Disneyland, how could Chrissie – her friend – let that boy down so badly?

She planted a kiss on Paula's nose. 'You be a good girl for Daddy, won't you? And I tell you what, love,' she added, as Eddie fetched his car keys. 'You drop me round there, and if it's all not too bad at the flat, I'll walk down and meet you both at the park.'

'That's what you reckon, then, is it, love? That it'll be all not too bad?'

Josie smiled ruefully. 'I can live in hope, can't I?'

* * *

152

It was a hope that proved to be short lived. And dashed before they'd so much as driven into the Park Lane car park. Before the condensation had even cleared from the windscreen.

Eddie wiped it away with the flat of his hand, as if not quite believing what he was seeing – the same thing Josie was seeing from out of the passenger window, which even at first glance presaged something not very good at all. No, worse – presaged something very bad.

'What the fuck's going on, Jose?' he asked, leaning further and further forward, unable to park since there was nowhere he *could* park.

Three police cars, on the other hand, were parked. Well, not exactly parked, but more strewn randomly around the semi-circle parking area, two of them with doors gaping open. At least twenty residents were out, too, milling around, no doubt noseying – enjoying what was looking like an impressive spectacle at any time, but especially on a dull Saturday afternoon. Josie craned her neck, her eyes counting up to the fourth floor automatically, and noticing several more residents hanging over the balconies, and rewarded, if that was the word, which she doubted, with the sight of a substantial knot of people just where she'd hoped *not* to see one. Something too close for comfort was going down.

She was just about to say as much to Eddie, but then realised she didn't need to. 'Isn't that Brian?' he asked, pointing upwards to where a figure, clearly handcuffed, was being manhandled along the balcony towards the stairwell.

'Oh shit, love,' Eddie added. 'They've even got Nicky.' He nudged her and pointed across to one of the other cars, where Josie could now see him, sitting in the back seat, beside a police officer.

Eddie tutted. 'You know what, love. I think we should leave. Leave them to it, let the dust settle. Come back in a bit. You'll only be in the way now, after all.'

Josie saw that as her cue to beat a hasty exit. 'Not a chance,' she said, clambering out. 'I need to find out what's happening. To the *baby*. Go on, you go. Take our Paula to the park as planned. I'll follow on once I know what's happening with Joey.'

No one even really registered her, let alone tried to stop her – too busy, she guessed, making all those arrests. Even as she climbed the stairs she was passed by two further young men, both of which she vaguely recognised as mates of Brian's.

And it looked like the police had meant business as well, because when she entered the fourth-floor landing the first thing she saw was that the door to Brian's flat had been kicked in.

Oh well, she thought grimly, at least that saves me from doing it, feeling guilty even so as she stepped over the splintered wood, and felt glass and whatever else crunching underneath.

The dogged, pragmatic tone of her thinking soon changed, though, as she entered the living room and saw

Christine. Or rather, she decided, as she stared at her friend, a girl who bore a strong passing resemblance to Christine, but as if formed in waxwork, and of a much older relative.

Christine was slumped across the futon, dressed in a torn vest and trackies, a big stupid grin plastered onto her face. So it was true, Josie thought. It was all true, and worse. She was clearly off her head on something nasty.

Another of Brian's revolting druggy friends – the name Anthony surfaced from somewhere – was sprawled on the floor at her feet. And there was a third person she thought she recognised – the social worker, definitely. Carol Sloper, perhaps. The name again surfaced automatically. And who clearly didn't need the likes of Josie to put her in the picture, but whom – now she was slap bang in the middle of it – looked strangely lost, as if she didn't know quite what to do, other than stand there, her arms wrapped protectively across her briefcase.

There were also two hard-looking policewomen. And, thinking about it, Josie realised they were very much in charge. One was sitting next to Christine, obviously trying to get some sense out of her, and the other, who looked like she'd swallowed a wasp, who had evidently just returned from the bedroom.

'What's going on?' Josie asked. Her voice was shaking, she realised.

The woman with the briefcase turned and looked at her. It was definitely Carol Sloper. She'd seen her about on the estate, and also recognised Christine's description. 'And you are?' she asked Josie. 'Are you family?'

'All but,' she answered. 'I'm Josie Collins. Christine's friend. I think I know you, don't I? Are you Carol?'

The woman's expression softened. 'Ah yes,' she replied. Then, turning to the policewoman who was sitting down with Christine, she said, 'Josie here is the one who put Christine and the baby up when they first left hospital. She and her husband looked after them for a couple of weeks until they got sorted round here.'

The policewoman who had come from the bedroom snorted in disgust. '*Sorted*? Well, that's one way of putting it, I suppose.'

Josie couldn't help but bristle at her tone. 'I ask again,' she said levelly, 'can someone tell me what's going on?' She knelt down beside Christine. 'You all right, mate?' she said, lifting her chin. 'What's been happening?'

A male police officer entered the flat then and, without saying a word to anyone, he signalled to the policewoman who was sitting on the futon, and together they hoisted Anthony up off the floor, roughly shaking him to his senses as they did so. 'Come on, feller,' the copper said, his voice firm but not unfriendly, 'we've arranged a nice cement bed for you down the Bridewell.'

Bridewell was the name of the cells down in town. So that, presumably, was where Nick and Brian were headed too. He glanced at Carol Sloper then. 'I think that's us done, love,' he told her. 'Unless you need us for anything else?'

Carol Sloper shook her head. 'Thank you. I can take it from here, thank you,' she told him. Then she nodded towards Christine. 'Assuming there's definitely no plan to arrest her too?'

The male officer shook his head. 'I don't think so,' he told her. 'Can't say for absolute definite, but from what we've got from witnesses, I doubt it. It's a first for this one, and from what the neighbours are saying, a one-off. So we're happy to leave her in your capable hands – if we need her for something else, we know where she is.'

Brian's friend Anthony, growing restive in the hands of the two police officers, began trying to wriggle his way out of their grasp. 'Watch it, sonny,' the policeman said, his voice now markedly different, and it occurred to Josie, without a shred of accompanying compassion, that if he kicked off he'd get more than a clip round the ear on his way from the flat to the car park.

But her attention was now focused back on her friend. Who was now dribbling. Josie could hardly bring herself to look at her.

'*Now* can you tell me what's going on?' she asked Carol Sloper.

Carol seemed to be struggling with what she should and shouldn't tell her. Sighing as Christine groaned, her head lolling against the futon, she gestured that Josie get up. 'Come on,' she said. 'Follow me.'

Christine wasn't going anywhere, so Josie did as instructed, anxious now, seeing the look on the social worker's face and the fact that she'd yet to hear from Joey. Asleep, she told herself. He must just be asleep. Had anything bad happened, she'd have known it immediately. There'd have been no smiles from any policemen.

But it was her nose, rather than her ears, that would first be assaulted. By a stench as familiar and gross as it was intense; the smell of cannabis, ammonia and shit.

She put a hand up to her nose and mouth, as did Carol Sloper. Then saw Joey and immediately lowered it.

'Oh no,' she cried, rushing forward to pick him up and cuddle him – something she became all too aware she couldn't do. He was squatting in his disgusting cot, staring at her, completely silent, his face streaked with tear tracks, his body with faeces – and, unbelievably, it looked like he'd been eating it, too; it was smeared all around his mouth and his chubby fingers seemed caked in it.

She felt her own tears – tears of rage – threatening to spill. Yes, she'd seen it all before. Seen it more often than she'd cared to. Because babies born to druggies – her own crappy sister included – enjoyed a level of parental 'care' commensurate with most druggies' level of care for themselves in general. They were stoned, they were happy. They really didn't give a fuck. So, oh, yes – nothing new here. Nothing she hadn't seen before. She'd seen poverty as well – and how it compounded an already grim problem. Mothers whose only care was the care they took in selling their bodies to pay for gear – and, should the opportunity arise, when the kids were a bit older, selling their 'services' to get gear as well.

She cast miserably around for something she could pick Joey up in. This – this fucking *shit* – was something else. Christ, they were almost of an age. Had shared almost the same backgrounds. Yes her mam might be a head case, but that wasn't the whole of it, not by a long chalk. Whatever else was true, Christine had been given a half-decent start and had had plenty of promises of help from friends. She could have asked Josie, and several like her, for anything she needed. And she knew it. She *knew* it. There was *no* excuse for this. Heartbroken that she couldn't even pick Joey up in that state, she swung round to the social worker.

'Christ!' she said, exasperated, 'what the fuck's been going on here?' even though she doubted Carol Sloper could begin to answer. Then a thought hit her. 'Christ, you're not taking him into care, are you? Not today?'

She must either have been shouting, or it was simply a miserable coincidence that they heard an anguished wail from the other room. Carol Sloper turned and went back and, finding nothing with which she could usefully hold the baby, Josie followed. Perhaps there would be something in the living room. A stinking coat some druggy friend of Brian's had left behind, if she was lucky.

Christine, giddy and disorientated, was trying to stand. 'Not my Joey,' she wailed, tears streaming down her face. 'Please don't take him into care, please. Oh, *please*.'

Josie didn't trust herself to speak. Carol Sloper, on the other hand, seemed to find her composure.

'Calm down, lovey,' she said, 'nobody's doing that. Not today. We just need to find out what happened. You need to talk to me, Christine, and talk to me honestly. I'm not the bad guy, remember? I'm here to *help* you.'

'No you're not!' Christine shouted, suddenly animated. Though still not, it seemed, registering Josie's presence. 'No, you're not!' she said again, seeming suddenly more lucid. 'You just make everything *harder*. Just make everything so much harder! So I can mess up, and you can swoop in. And steal my baby!'

Christine's voice was becoming hysterical, and Josie had heard enough. 'Christine,' she barked, 'knock it off and bloody *listen*! The woman just *told* you – she isn't here to take Joey! But I swear to God, girl, you'd better think about what you say next. Because as God is my witness –' she stabbed a finger towards the bedroom – 'if any harm had come to that boy in there, I would have killed you myself.'

Christine looked at her, wide-eyed, as if trying to focus. As if only just realising that Josie was there. And having done so, she thrust her arms out, as if for a hug. 'Oh Josie, oh, *Josie* – oh, thank God you're here, mate. Is my Joey all right? Is he okay?'

Josie hugged her, then lowered her back down onto the futon. 'I swear down, Jose,' Christine said, meekly allowing herself to be manoeuvred, 'I don't even know what happened, honest I don't. They were all in here partying, and I was trying to get a bit of sleep. I had a headache. That was why. I had a headache, that was all. And all I remember was looking for some aspirin. And I took it and – I don't *know*. I don't know what *happened*! Next thing, I woke up and all hell was breaking loose. The police, the noise, everything. I couldn't even get off the couch to check on Joey – couldn't *move*. I swear, Jose. You have to believe me!'

Carol Sloper looked as sceptical as Josie felt. She also took a notebook and pen out of her briefcase. 'So, you're saying that someone else drugged you?' she asked. 'Is that it?'

Christine shook her head. 'No, I'm not saying that. I'm saying that what I *thought* was an aspirin clearly wasn't. But I didn't *know*. I swear down. I don't know what it was.'

'Or where it came from?' Carol Sloper was still busy writing.

Christine shook her head. Looked at Josie. Her skin was like parchment. The colour of washing-up water. She struggled to sit more upright, to see what Carol Sloper was writing. 'See,' she said, pointing at the notebook. 'And you can write this down, too. This is what happens when I don't get the help I was promised. If I'd have got my flat, like they promised me they'd get me, Joey and me wouldn't have to live here, would we? I could get childcare. Get my job back, get *sorted*!' Her voice cracked. Carol Sloper kept on writing.

Josie spied some sort of wrap, and picked it up. She had to hand it to Christine. Whatever the truth was, she was playing this perfectly. The way Christine was telling it, Josie wouldn't have been surprised if she came out of this with a new gaff *and* a Mother of the Year award.

'I'll go sort Joey,' she said, brandishing the tatty old shawl thing, all too aware that the person on whom all this centred was still in the bedroom, covered in shit.

'No, no, no,' Carol Sloper said. 'That's for Christine to do. Alone. Go on,' she said briskly. 'Time for you to walk the walk, love. Clean that baby up, dress him and feed him, the poor mite. That's assuming you've anything to feed him *with?*'

With Christine occupied and out of earshot (and on no account could Josie help her) she listened as the social worker explained what would happen next.

'Whatever Christine thinks, I have no intention of removing Joey from her. Though he's at risk and will obviously be recorded as such. To tell you the truth, I have grave concerns about Christine's ability as a mother, especially with the situation she is currently living in. But she deserves a second chance and I'm comfortable in giving her one. And a stern talking to, obviously, because she needs to recognise the seriousness of her predicament, not to mention the fact that there will *not* be a third.' She closed her notebook. 'And you can help. As her friend, you can help. She clearly looks up to you. Impress upon her that she's in a serious place now. Perhaps, if you can, give her a hand with things as well.'

'Oh course,' Josie told her. 'That goes without saying. I know Nick – her brother – wants to do his best by her, but this is the *last* place she should be. The last place *he* should be.' And in that instant her feelings become clear. If Christine was doing drugs, doing hard drugs, and often, Josie would be as decisive as it looked like Carol Sloper was going to be. She would have no qualms, she decided. She would support his removal. She couldn't, and *wouldn't*, sit by and do nothing. Make excuses for her friend when a baby was at risk. She left the flat feeling guilty, but strangely resolved, shaking out her coat to try and blow the taint away.

Chapter 14

Christine shivered as she cupped her hands under the icy water from the bathroom tap. She didn't think she'd ever felt so bone-cold. It wouldn't be much better in the living room at this time either, because the gas fire only heated up the area directly in front of it, though at least at this hour she and Joey would have it to themselves, Nicky having decamped to Brian's bedroom.

It had been a close call, what had happened, and it had scared her. Brian in prison – he'd got six months for possession and intent to distribute, as had his two druggy mates, Anthony and Phil. Thank God Nicky had got off so lightly; he could so easily have gone down too, but they'd thankfully dealt with him leniently. As it had been his first drugs offence, he'd got away with a community service order, which meant a weekly session with a probation officer – every Saturday for the next four months – which he was to spend cleaning the parks across Bradford.

But it was still a wake-up call – not least because, for the foreseeable future, anyway, it would be just the two of them responsible for all the bills. 'Lucky' was what Nicky'd called it, because he'd been bricking it, big time, but his solicitor had not only helped him evade a custodial sentence – because of Joey, he'd also persuaded the powers that be to let them be added to the tenancy of the flat.

Christine wished she could feel lucky, because it could have been so much worse, but now they were 'official' tenants, how did that leave her? She wasn't sure how all these people communicated with each other – only that they did. How else did Carol Sloper know all about their comings and goings? And she'd bet a pound to a penny she'd now be shunted down the housing list – if she was ever really on it in the first place. A tight knot of dread followed her everywhere now, and try as she might not to, she could only find one way to make it better. Pushing it away. Burying her head. Making it *go*.

She gazed into the cracked mirror above the porcelain sink and raised her fingers to the dark circles under her eyes. She knew she looked shit, and knew also that patting the bags that hung beneath them would not be banished – not even lessened – by dabbing at them with the freezing water. She did so anyway – she had to get herself washed and dressed, not to mention Joey – because Josie would be calling for her in less than half an hour, and if she wasn't ready and looking respectable she'd give her hell.

'You look like you've seen your arse this morning,' her brother greeted her as she walked back into the living room. He was squatting on the piece of carpet that served as a rug in front of the puttering fire. 'What's up with you?'

'Shut up, simple!' Christine snapped as she reached onto the coffee table for a Rizla paper, then thought better of it, chastising herself, then picked it up anyway. It was okay. It would calm her. It would smooth down the edges. Plenty of time yet for the smell to go away. 'Roll us a spliff, Nick,' she added, 'while I go sort Joey out. You know what Josie'll be like if I keep her waiting.'

Nicky took the paper and started to sprinkle some tobacco onto it. He looked and smelt like he'd slept in his clothes. 'I don't know why you have to go to the bleeding baby meeting anyway,' he muttered. 'What's the point? What's it for?'

'It's not a "baby meeting". It's a mother and toddler group,' Christine corrected. 'And I *have* to go. You know that. Just like you have to go and sweep the streets. I have no *choice*. That's the deal. Whether I like it or not. Or that Carol Sloper'll be on to me again.'

'How will she even know?' Nicky persisted. As if it made any bloody difference to him. He just didn't seem to get it – the potential shit she was in. She heard Joey calling and the knot moved and pulsed in her stomach. Just at the thought of the power Carol Sloper had over her. And Josie too. Nick didn't realise, but Christine was under no illusions. If she let Josie down, there was no two ways about it. She'd grass her up. She'd said she would. And Christine knew she meant it.

Nicky passed her the joint, such as it was, which was meagre. Then the lighter. She lit it and took a drag. 'I've got to go, Nick. You don't realise. I've got to do right by Joey.'

'Like you haven't up to now? He's all right, isn't he?' He really seemed to want to know. Just as, at the same time, he didn't seem to want to remember that party – that *fucking* party – and Joey being caked in his own shit. And how bad she felt. Didn't Nick feel bad about that? She felt wretched. But he *was* all right, wasn't he? Now he was. Nothing bad happened. And it wasn't happening again.

Christine blew a stream of smoke out, feeling stronger. 'He's fine, Nick. I just need to …'

'To what?'

'To … to get my head together. Get more organised. Get …'

Nicky turned to look at her. 'Get what?

In answer, she stabbed the spliff out. 'Fuck it, Nick. Get shot of *this*!'

Under his astonished gaze, Christine went into the kitchen and mashed some Weetabix into milk in the bowl she kept for Joey. Another of Josie's orders. That she kept his stuff clean and separate. Like she had any idea how hard that was, living here. Brian's shit still everywhere, and Nicky thinking washing-up was some sort of alien fucking activity.

She smashed the Weetabix to a pulp and took it into the bedroom, where Joey greeted her with the same beatific smile he always had. His hair was growing now – thick and long, though not as curly as his father's. She mused for a moment about how life might be different if Mo hadn't been Mo. How different it might be if he took some interest in his son. She smiled despite herself. He might even start making dreads for Joey, too.

But he didn't and he wouldn't. It was just them and Nicky. 'Hey, baby,' she said, as he held his hands out for the bowl, then plopped back down in his cot ready for her to feed him. '*Mum*-my,' she cooed at him. '*Mum*-my. M-m-m-*Mummy*.' One day soon, she knew – one day soon, he'd manage to say it. And perhaps one day she'd have enough saved to get him a high chair, too, so he could sit in it and properly feed himself. So much mess. Always mess. It was so hard to keep on top of.

'See? He's eating well, anyway.' It was Nicky's voice. Christine turned. He'd got up and followed her in.

'I forgot to say,' he said, leaning against the door jamb while he smoked his own spliff. 'I saw mum.'

Christine feigned indifference. 'Saw her where?'

'Down the Listers. She looked a right state. I mean, *really* shit. Lost a bunch of weight, too. June McKellan said she's ill.'

Christine digested this as she wiped Joey's chin. Registered the stab of something – what? Just the business of Nicky seeing her. Just that wrench that not once had she been round, or sent a message. Just that realisation that, actually, she didn't care. Didn't love them. 'Ill how?'

Nicky shrugged and took another drag. 'I didn't ask, did I?'

'Didn't ask June? Didn't she say?'

'I didn't speak to June, did I?'

'So how'd you know mum's ill then?'

'One of the lads said June told him.'

'And you didn't think to ask?'

'Why the fuck would I want to ask?' He smiled grimly. 'She might get me confused with someone who actually gives a shit, mightn't she? Besides, if she's that ill, what's she doing down the fucking Listers?'

'So did she see you? Try to talk to you?'

'Yeah, she ran over and bought me a pint, sis. Course she didn't speak to me.' He took another drag and shrugged. 'I just thought I'd tell you, is all. Didn't expect twenty questions.'

'You won't be getting them, either. Why should I care?'

Nicky shrugged again, and ambled off, while another sentence formed in Christine's brain. *Yeah, but you do. You fucking do. Just like I do. You DO.* Yet for some reason she couldn't seem to ever say it. Not out loud. It was like it wasn't allowed. For either of them. The big taboo.

Twenty minutes later, Josie was helping Christine bump the pram down the steps, their breath forming clouds in front of their faces.

Christine didn't want to – didn't really mean to – but out it came anyway. 'Nicky says Mam's ill. Is it true, Jose? Said he saw her in the Listers and she was looking really crap. Said your mam said.'

Josie let the front of the pram down and pushed the door open to let Christine through.

'Not that I've heard,' she said. 'But then I wouldn't know anyway. I've not seen much of Mam these past couple of weeks. But I know she's been round your mam's a bit, so maybe.'

There was nothing in her voice that seemed to suggest any different. But it was still there – a kind of niggle. No. It was guilt, that was what it was. She wished she could get her head together. Why the fuck should she feel guilty? If her mam was moping about, not looking after herself – well, that was up to her, wasn't it? It wasn't like she could put it all at Christine's door. *Fucking* Mo. Still, the feeling persisted. That she should see if she was okay. But *why?* Another part of her fumed. It wasn't like her mam gave a shit about how *she* was. How she was coping with Joey. If she was okay.

She tucked Joey's pram blanket tighter round him, to help keep the bitter cold out. And she'd been down the Listers, so, like Nick said, she couldn't be *that* ill. She should do like her mam did to her. Leave her to it.

'Maybe just got the flu,' she said to Josie.

'Maybe,' Josie agreed. 'Anyway, come on, earth mother. Let's get you down to this baby group, shall we? Notch up another brownie point or two.' She smiled at Christine. 'And, for God's sake, at least try to look like you're enjoying it this time, eh?'

As if there was anything to enjoy. That was the problem. There was no one there her age – obviously all had more sense. Just a clique – that was the word for it – of self-satisfied-looking mothers, all with fellas at home, probably, and nothing like the problems she had. And worse than that, they seemed determined to ignore her.

'*It's fucking 1981!*' she wanted to scream, every time she intercepted one of *those* looks. Like she'd brought a bloody alien along with her. And it didn't escape her notice either, how much Josie glared at everyone – on her behalf, probably. It wasn't like she had anything in common with the women there either. She never went. Never had done. Probably'd never felt the need to. With the size of Josie's family – there were, like, *dozens* of Hudsons – why would she ever bother herself hanging out with such a snobby crowd?

But what Carol Sloper said, Carol Sloper obviously got, and Josie was obviously dancing to her tune. 'It's for the baby,' she'd told her. 'And that's what they need to see from you. That you're thinking about that. Remembering to put Joey's needs above your own.'

Still, she conceded, once they'd plonked Joey down on the big blue play mat with the other babies, at least it was a change of scenery, and the hot chocolate was free. And biscuits too – one of the grandmothers usually brought a couple of packets in. And it wasn't like they were *all* quite so full of themselves. A couple had been friendly enough the last time. And it did occur to her that if she'd come on her own with Joey she might make more of an effort with them, and they with her.

Julie shaw

She was just about to say so, when Josie tugged at her sleeve. 'Oh, great,' she hissed. 'Look what the tide's brought in.'

Christine glanced towards the entrance, where a large lady was backing in a double buggy. And leading with a backside familiar to most. It was Sylvia Harris, who lived a few doors from home. A few doors down from her *mam's* house, she mentally corrected herself.

She'd come with two of her grandkids – a pair of over-excited toddlers – and once she'd freed them from their coats and left them to run amok among the various playthings, she wasted no time in coming over to look Joey over.

Christine stiffened at her approach, wondering what sort of greeting to expect. Sylvia and her mam had never seen eye to eye about anything. Even had the odd slanging match out on the street down the years. Would her enmity towards her mam turn out to be a good thing or a bad thing?

A bad thing. 'So that's him, is it?' she said, placing a hand on Christine's chair back while she looked across at Joey.

'That's my son, yes,' Christine answered, feeling the cold air coming off Sylvia.

'Black 'un, then,' she added. 'So it's true, then?'

'So *what's* true?' snapped Josie.

Christine wished she could have even a tenth of Josie's front. Where did she *get* it? Twenty-two, and she'd talk on a level with anyone. Talk down to them even. Even old bags like Sylvia Harris.

But Sylvia Harris wasn't to be deflected. 'That he's another bloody one,' she said, tutting as she nodded in Joey's direction.

'Er, *excuse* me?' Christine started. Josie placed a hand on her arm.

'Sylvia, what Christine's son is or isn't is really none of your business,' she pointed out.

'Oh, I think he is,' Sylvia responded. 'Try telling my sister that, why don't you? Help out, does he? Change the nappies? Lavish you with gifts?'

'*What?*' Christine said.

'Well, it's not like everyone doesn't know already, is it? What line did he spin you, love? Or are you as wet as your mother?'

'You know what?' Josie said, putting a hand up. 'Can we leave this, please, Sylvia? Whatever axe you or your sister have to grind with Lizzie, she's not here, right? So just leave it. Christine's brought Joey here for a bit of peace, not an interrogation.'

'Oh, *Joey*, is it?' she said. 'That figures. No doubt he'll end up being one as well.'

'Jesus!' Christine barked now. 'What are you *on* about, Sylvia?'

Again, she felt Josie's hand on her forearm. 'Do us a favour, Sylvia, will you?' she said again. 'Just leave us alone?'

Christine had a moment of sudden clarity – one of her mam and Sylvia's slanging matches having suddenly sprung into her mind. 'Has your sister got a kid with Mo, then? Is that it?'

Sylvia Harris scowled. 'Oh, *yeah*, like she'd be so fucking stupid, I don't think. She got it flushed, love. Same as you'd have done if you'd had any sense. More than enough black bastards in this world already.'

Christine didn't actively decide to slap her. It just seemed to happen. Though Josie's arm, ever hovering, meant it didn't quite connect.

'Whoah, Chris! Pack it in! She's not worth it. She really isn't. Now will you just piss *off*, Sylvia!' she snapped. 'Seriously, get out of my fucking face!'

Sylvia Harris took a step back, but seemed not in the least abashed. Not remotely concerned by the ripple of oohs and ahs from across the hall. 'Only too happy to,' she said quietly, but with the edges of a smirk appearing around her lips. Like Josie's mam's, her mouth was coloured a violent shade of red. Christine thought how very much she'd like to punch it.

They didn't stay long after that. Sylvia Harris, apparently not in the least concerned by what had happened, took up a position across the hall, with a couple of the other mothers, where she chatted away as if nothing had happened. Christine felt nauseous. Upset. Like Joey was some kind of pariah. Mo's kid. A black kid. A *joey*.

'Tell me,' she'd kept on at Josie. 'What's she mean by that – a "joey"?'

Josie had been reluctant to tell her, and for good reason. Because now she'd finally got it out of her, it made her even more upset. It was slang for a drug-runner, apparently. An errand boy – a bloody errand boy – for dealers just like Mo.

'Look, just forget about it!' Josie told her. 'It only means anything in their world, okay? And you're not *in* that world. *Joey's* not going to be in that world.'

Except she *was*. And she couldn't get beyond that. She really couldn't. She didn't want to be, but she was. And she didn't know how to escape from it. How to get Joey to a place where his name would mean nothing. Except what he called himself. 'And what's all that stuff about her sister?' she wanted to know. 'She was another one of his women too, was she?'

Josie opened her mouth to speak, but checked herself. '*What?*' Christine said.

'I was going to say "cast-offs", but under the circumstances it seemed a bit insensitive ...'

'I don't know why you're worrying. They *are* the bloody circumstances. They –'

She stopped then, catching the tail end of a gesture she recognised. Or at least thought she recognised. Enough, at least, to convince her she needed to finish what she'd started, because the gesture was happening while Sylvia Harris held a monkey glove puppet in her hand. Christine leapt to her feet, pushed her chair back, and rounded the play mats, then marched straight up to a now startled Sylvia Harris.

'You fucking racist *cow*,' she said. 'What the fuck has my little boy ever done to you?' And this time, very gratifyingly, the slap connected.

'Well that's fucked that up,' Josie said as they marched briskly back towards the flats. 'That must be a first, mustn't it? Being ordered out of a fucking toddler group!'

She burst out laughing then, and, despite the dregs of anger still eddying around inside her, Christine soon found herself laughing too.

Because it had been funny. Especially when the slap dislodged Sylvia Harris's false teeth and, rather than slide them back, she'd popped them out and handed them to her friend.

'I don't think I've *ever* seen anything quite so hilarious,' Josie said. 'Oh my God, I cannot *wait* to tell them all in the Bull. I couldn't believe it!'

They stopped at the corner of St Luke's, where they would part ways, and, looking ahead towards the flats, her laughter disappeared again almost as soon as it had started. Carol Sloper. It was her 'suggestion' that Josie take her to the group in the first place. 'Oh, shit, Jose,' she said. 'D'you think I'm going to get reported?'

'To Carol Sloper?' Josie said, obviously reading her mind. She shook her head firmly. But also, to Christine's mind, a little too quickly. 'No,' she said. 'Why would they even know who she is? It was me she suggested it to, wasn't it?'

'Ordered,' Christine corrected.

'Okay, ordered. But that's between her and us, isn't it? Nothing to do with the women that run that place. Besides,' she added, leaning into the pram to give Joey a farewell kiss. 'Even if they did, by some chance, speak to her, or it got to her some other way, I'd be right there defending you, okay? There's laws against being racist – making racist gestures and that – aren't there? So she hasn't got a leg to stand on. And all you did was slap her. The rest was just bloody fuss. She could play for the first bloody division at football, that one.'

'You think so? You think I'm all right?'

'I *know* so,' Josie reassured her. 'But you'll see. It won't even come to that. No. forget it. We'll go back next week and it'll all be forgotten. They all know the old trout only got what she deserved.'

Christine tried to keep telling herself that as she bumped the pram back up to the flat. But she cursed herself for rising to it. How was that going to help Joey? It wasn't as if the likes of Sylvia Harris would stop being racist because of it. Of hating her poor innocent Joey just because of him being brown. Because of him being Mo's.

Whatever she deserved, Joey deserved so much better.

Chapter 15

Nicky tried to focus on the TV screen. He wondered where he was. There was a man. A grinning man. Some sort of commotion in the background. Shapes and colours. Lots of laughter. Altogether too much *brightness*. A sudden wave of nausea made saliva flood his mouth.

He looked away, and then back. It was Noel fucking Edmunds. Which – he groped for comprehension – meant it must now be Saturday. How'd he get from Friday lunchtime to Saturday so quickly? Or, on the other hand, he decided, how'd he get there so *slowly*? The mushrooms. Just the thought made his gorge rise again. He needed to be sick and, like, *now*.

He staggered up from the futon and grabbed the door jamb to steady himself. He'd never really got to know Smiffy, the girl from the fifth floor. An ex of Brian's – who naturally didn't have a good word to say about her – she'd always been completely off his radar. But with Brian out of the picture, and Chrissy seeming to like her, she'd started coming round the flat quite a lot.

And it was yesterday – yes, the details were beginning to come back to him – that she'd brought round the bag of magic mushrooms. Which she'd cooked, and they'd eaten from a spoon, washed down with vodka. And very soon … yes, the mushrooms were now coming back to him. Though more importantly, right now, coming *up*.

He retched till he was emptied out and covered in beads of sweat. And would cheerfully have stayed there, on his knees on the bathmat, but for the incessant banging on the door. 'Nicky, is that you in there?' It was Christine. Who else did she think it would be? 'Hurry up, mate!' she whined. 'I need a piss!'

'Give me a minute,' Nicky shouted back. 'I'm throwing me fucking guts up. You and your friend's magic frigging mushrooms!'

He heard her laughing outside the door, sounding completely A-OK, and wondered why the fuck she wasn't feeling as rough as he was. And she clearly wasn't, because once he'd wiped his face and washed his mouth out under the cold tap he trudged into the kitchen, every move sending daggers through his head, to find her busy at the stove, making porridge for the baby, like she was Mrs fucking Beeton or something.

He went straight to the mess on the tiny patch of worktop, and rummaged in search of aspirin. 'I don't know how you're so chipper,' he said. 'My head's fucking splitting!'

'Because it's *Sat*-ur-day,' Christine said, as if explaining to a baby. 'And me, you and our Joey are off Christmas shopping, aren't we? You know, I was thinking. It's the first time in my life I've actually done that. You know, as in have a proper amount of money to go out on a proper shopping spree.' She beamed at him. 'I feel all grown-up, all of a sudden!'

'Yeah, proper grown-up. Getting in hock with the club cheque woman. Welcome to the world, eh?'

'Oh, but it's *Christmas*. We've got to make it special for Joey, haven't we?'

Despite the axes in his head, Nicky couldn't help but smile at her, even if the idea of traipsing round town was just about the last thing he felt up to doing. This was a gift, after all, this first probation-fucking-officer-clear-the-shit-up-free Saturday. The first in weeks when he'd not had to get up in the dark to go and do his 'bounden civic duty'. A proper stroke of luck, the guy being ill. Hence the mushrooms. The business of not having to give a fuck. Of going off fuck knew where – Christine had turned into a duck at some point, hadn't she? – and experiencing something unlike anything before it; a something, he was now beginning to realise, that, for all that it had been pretty damned amazing, still seemed to hover round the edges of his consciousness, in a distinctly unsettling way.

Didn't they say that? That mushrooms could cause terrible paranoia? He finally found a blister pack of Aspro, and ate two straight from the packet. His main paranoia was that he must be getting past it. How come his sister was bouncing round like Tigger?

'Because I went easy,' she told him, when he asked her again.

'Not *that* easy,' he snorted. 'You were fucking mental for a bit, you were.'

'Not *that* mental,' she corrected him. And then the penny dropped.

'You've done some coke this morning, haven't you?' he said.

'Just a bit,' she said, grinning. 'And mind the nappy bucket. I had to pee in it. Now go and get yourself dressed while I sort Joey out. Half an hour, right?' She made a little shooing motion with her free hand. 'And I'm timing you from *now*!'

Feeling guilty was a new thing, and Nicky wasn't sure he liked it. Feeling guilty about his little sister even more so. It wasn't quite how he'd planned it, Chrissie hoovering up coke the way she seemed to. No, it wasn't like she was going to the dogs or anything – far as he could tell, she was perfectly functional. There was just this constant niggle in his mind that it wasn't quite panning out. He was supposed to have been putting her and the baby up for a couple of weeks, that was all. Doing his bit – and he had no axe to grind about that, the poor cow. But that was all he'd expected. To help her out when she needed it. To step in when their useless bitch of a so-called mother kicked her out.

Yet here they were, months down the line, and the pair of them even had their names on the bloody tenancy! Which he knew wasn't Chrissie's fault. He knew how much she wanted her own place. Or *had* wanted. And that was the real crux of the matter. She didn't seem to bang on about that any more. She'd adjusted to the life he and Brian liked living. Which was no way good, and he felt the guilt about that crowding out any justification he could come up with.

He kept down the bile that was threatening to come up while he threw some clothes on, taking care to drag a brush through his rat-tails – he really needed to see about getting his hair cut – and finding the least bogging of his shirts to throw on. No, it would be good to get out; might help soften the downer Chrissie was soon going to be suffering; give her a bit of boost that didn't involve shoving chemicals into her body. Which, fuck knew, she deserved, after everything.

She was already out on the landing when he was done, blowing raspberries at a chuckling Joey. Her own hair hung down in front of her, lank, he saw, and stringy. And she looked painfully thin, wasted – even to his habituated eye. But for all that, little Joey was okay. She'd not done half bad, he decided. Had a lot to be proud of. Drugs or no, she was a far better mother than their own had been, for starters. He felt a pang of sadness. Because she actually *loved* her kid.

He shook his head to clear it – try and clear the strange tendrils of impending doom away. 'Hey, you know what, sis?' he said.

'Oooh, you look quite respectable!' she said, turning.

'Your hair,' he said, shutting the flat door. 'Why don't we treat you to a hairdo?'

She grinned at him. 'Ooh – a *hairdo*!' she parroted.

'Well, whatever you call it. A cut and blow job.'

Now she laughed. 'Nick, you're priceless, you pissing doylum!'

'Well, whatever you call it.'

She shook her head. 'I don't think we can spend the vouchers on hairdressers. It has to be toys and stuff. Baby clothes. And I think stuff from British Home Stores, if I remember rightly, so's we can get some Christmas decorations. And a Christmas pudding. That would be nice, eh? It's fine. I don't need a "hairdo" anyway.'

'But you're getting one. My treat,' he said, decided. He had a few quid put away for the rent, so he'd use some of that. He could easily put it back when he got his next giro, which would be double bubble, on account of the Christmas break.

Course, they'd struggle come January. But January felt a whole world away.

It was heaving in town, even more than he'd expected. Like the whole of Bradford had chosen this particular Saturday to do every single bit of Christmas shopping. But they managed – in truth, he was pulled along not only bodily, but by the infectious nature of Chrissie's unbridled joy, over the simple business of buying a few toys and decorating tat. He didn't think he'd ever properly understand women. And it was something of a miracle that, shopping done, they'd managed to get her an appointment in the salon on John Street. And he was doubly happy that he'd made his gesture, just from the shine in her eyes, as various mates from the market came up to say hello, fussing over Joey like he was a proper little prince. He knew just how hard she'd taken it when that old Harris bitch had mouthed off at her. So this was good. This was double good. His nausea had even lifted. He could even face having something to eat.

Still she fussed, though. 'Are you sure? I mean, it's such a lot of money. And are you sure you're all right having Joey for the hour? I can always take him in with me.'

'No, you're not taking him in with you. Last thing the lad needs is to be stuck in a bleeding hairdressers. No, he's coming to the Wimpy for some bloke time, with his uncle. Aren't you, fella?' he said, chucking Joey under his chin. And it felt pretty good, that. With his *uncle*.

In the end she was done in less than forty-five minutes, and they'd done bloody well. She looked transformed. Perhaps come-downs from coke were half in the mind. She looked as well as she'd ever looked. Like her old self. Better, even.

She slid into the seat opposite him, automatically checking on Joey as she did so, smiling the special Joey-specific smile he'd come to recognise, as he ordered her a hot chocolate before they set off for home.

'You look lovely,' he said.

'Yeah, yeah …'

'No, *really*. I mean it.' He leaned forward, the next question already forming on his lips. 'Are you happy, sis? I don't mean the haircut, I mean, in general like.'

She didn't answer straight away, looking like she was seriously thinking about the question. 'Let's just say I'm happy today,' she said eventually. 'Aww,' she added, looking again at her sleeping baby. 'But we got some lovely stuff, didn't we? I can't wait to see his face when he opens his little fire engine. And he's going to look the bee's knees in all his new clobber, isn't he?'

Her drink came, and she picked up the teaspoon and stirred furiously. Her eyes were shining when she looked up again, and Nicky had to fight back an urge to take her hand and squeeze it. She'd bat him away, for definite. Because he knew that, right then, it would probably make her cry. Fuck it. He was choking up himself.

'Come on, slack-arse,' he said instead. 'Get drinking that up. We've a long walk back and the waiter was telling me before that there's a dump of heavy snow on the way.'

'Snow? Oh, wouldn't that just be *brilliant*, Nick? Wouldn't it? His first Christmas and some proper Christmas snow!'

'Don't bank on it,' he said. 'More likely it'll be gone again by Christmas. Just piles of filthy slush by then. You wait.'

Christine buried her face in her mug and re-emerged with a moustache. 'Another tenner says it won't,' she said, licking the foam away. 'It's all going to be perfect. For Joey.'

It had started snowing on their way home and it didn't stop all evening. And it carried on snowing, for days after that. All week it fell, transforming Park Lane into a beautiful Dickensian winter scene, disguising all the dirt and rot that lay beneath. According to the news, it was set to last, too – was apparently going to be the worst winter on record. Which meant they were practically housebound, Nicky only venturing out if he absolutely had to. For drugs, or to get milk for the baby.

It was a happy kind of week, though, and, because Josie's Paula had gone down with chickenpox, Christine didn't have to venture back to the hated mother and baby group, and instead seemed to move almost serenely round the flat, carefully wrapping Joey's presents, constantly humming Christmas carols, and in raptures when Smiffy from upstairs turned up unexpectedly, with a gift of a little Christmas tree she'd shoplifted from Debenhams, complete with a box of posh baubles.

So it was only right – that's what Nick kept telling himself, afterwards, anyway – that they invited her, plus a couple of other mates, to a knees-up the following Saturday, once his stint with the probation officer – now recovered – was done.

And she'd come bearing gifts again – a litre bottle of vodka. Which went perfectly with the bit of Russian blow he'd procured, and got the party off to a flying start, while the snow continued to fall, forming drifts down in the car park, almost burying the few cars, frosting the windows and piling up prettily on the balcony.

It was the snow, Nicky decided, that probably did for them. That and the dope and booze that was soon coursing through everyone's veins. Either that, or he was back on some weird, surreal trip, because when the hammering began it came entirely without warning, muffled by the winter wonderland beyond the windows, and simultaneously drowned out by Olivia Newton-John on the radio – not to mention Christine and Smiffy and her gobby mate Claudia, all competing, it seemed, in some mad kind of dance-off, gyrating around the room as if possessed.

'Let's get physical' – those was the last words he heard before the hammering stopped and, with what sounded like a gunshot, the door suddenly burst open. And somehow there was a brace of coppers in the room.

The next thing Nicky noticed was the swirl of icy air, which had piled in all at once, like it was rushing through an airlock. How the *fuck* were there coppers standing in the middle of his living room? And then he noticed her, close behind them. Carol Sloper. And another woman. He didn't know who she was. He swallowed, realising he didn't need to. He'd know her anywhere, *anywhere*. With or without the Sloper woman. Everything about her screamed social services.

Then Christine's voice. 'What the fuck is going *on*?' He heard that clearly. Saw one of the plods grab her arm and try to talk to her. Instinctively, he went to her. Grabbed her other arm and held it tightly. Saw Carol Sloper come around, an expression on her face that scared him. He flapped a hand towards Claudia. 'Turn it off. Turn it *off*!' Then, trying to gather himself into some semblance of sobriety, turned to the copper.

'Hey, what's happening?' he said mildly. 'What's all this about?'

Carol Sloper took a step and also tried to put her hand on Christine's arm. Christine yanked it away, though, her eyes wild. 'I'm truly sorry, Christine,' she said. 'But this is it, I'm afraid. I've given you chance after chance, love. And I can't give you any more.'

She looked around her then, as if to fully register what she was seeing. The lads sprawled on the futon. The dope gear on the coffee table. The empty vodka bottle – how did it get to be empty so quickly? It wasn't even dark yet. And then she turned back to Christine, and now she did take her arm. 'I'm sorry,' she said again, and she looked like she meant it. 'But this is no life for a little boy. We've come to take him.'

Chapter 16

There was a moment – a long moment – when Nicky watched his sister and thought she might just keep it together. It was a strange moment, too, because he was already braced for the explosion. Did they not realise? There was no way in the *world* she'd let them take Joey. She would die before she let them. She might *kill* before she let them. If he knew anything – and, even in his drug-muddled mind, that thing he definitely *did* know – it was that Christine loved Joey with a love the likes of which he'd never seen. She was not like *their* mother. She would not let them take him.

So this stillness – the absence of reaction – felt strange. She was standing blinking at Carol Sloper, her features in relative repose.

But it was to be short-lived. Christine's brows drew closer together.

'Take him where?' she asked. 'Because if you think I'm going to let you take him to that bloody mother and baby group in this weather ...'

Shit, Nicky thought. *She doesn't realise. That's what it is. She's too far gone. She doesn't understand what the bitch means.*

Carol Sloper was already shaking her head. 'Christine, *listen*,' she said, the words coming out all clipped and sharp now. 'I've come to *take* him. Take him into *care*, Christine. Do you understand that?'

That did it. Christine gaped. Shook her head, almost as if to clear it. As if what she thought she'd heard obviously couldn't be true. Then she shook it more forcefully. 'No ...' she began. 'No, you can't. Not in this weather. No, you can't!' Seemingly ignoring the gaping door, she stabbed a finger towards the window. 'Have you seen what it's fucking like out there! You can't take a baby out in that! He'll die of cold!'

She began turning around then, this way and that, as if suddenly unable to get her bearings – a sick parody of the dancing they'd been doing only moments before. 'No, you can't,' she said, and it was now almost as if she was talking to herself. 'No, you can't. I won't let you. I'm his mummy – it's not happening.' Then she stopped. 'It's not happening!' This time a shrill, half-hysterical scream.

'Christine!' Carol Sloper again, her voice sharper still. Nicky wanted to punch her lights out. Anger was welling in him. Anger and a kind of horrified despair. He wasn't going to be able to stop this. He clenched and unclenched his hands. There was nothing he could – or should – do. It would only make it worse.

He placed a hand on Carol Sloper's forearm. 'Does this absolutely have to happen?' he asked her. 'Is there anything we can do? Joey's fine, honest ... he's fast asleep. I only checked half an hour back.' He tipped his head back. 'Go see if you like. He's fine. I don't understand why –'

It was the pity in her eyes that upset him the most. 'I'm sorry, Nicholas. It's happening. We're taking Joey into care. So the best thing you can do now is support your sister, okay? Now – Christine, love. Listen to me ...' And her attention was back with Chrissie, who, before Carol Sloper and the other woman could get a decent grip on her, keeled over onto the carpet like she'd been shot.

All three rushed to gather her up, the coppers standing back impassively. 'Please,' he whispered again to Carol. '*Please*, not like this. Not coming up to Christmas. Not now. It's too cruel. She's been really trying, too. We both have. Joey's *fine*.'

Now one of the police officers did step in, and tugged at his sleeve. Nicky fumed. He wasn't being pushy or aggressive or resistant, or anything, but even so ... *Fucking* coppers. It was hard to contain his rage.

'Leave it, lad,' he said. 'All right? It's a done deal. End of. Like the woman said,' he added, casting an eye around, taking in the damning details of their little gathering. Nicky was all too aware that one of the other lads – who'd been retching in the corner – had barely made it from the room before throwing up, wholesale, and knowing the sound of it, so obvious, since he'd not shut the bathroom door, would soon be followed by the sour, fetid smell.

He had another moment of clarity and it felt wretched. The copper was right, wasn't he? Bottom line. This wasn't any life for a kid. Why the fuck hadn't he seen that before now? Why? For all Chrissie's love for Joey, that he was safe, warm and happy was so much a case of luck over judgement.

Fuck, he thought, enfolding Chrissie in his arms while they went to take the baby. *Fuck.*

But Nicky had underestimated his sister's raw, physical strength. Apparently inert while some formal statement was made to her by the Sloper woman – about Joey being placed in a foster family until 'such date when social services have determined a final outcome' – *what?* – as the pair hurried off to the bedroom, it took her no time at all to escape his clutches, not least because he didn't want to hurt her.

'You can't fucking do this!' she screamed, lurching across the room in pursuit of the two women. It was the bigger of the two coppers – with no such concerns – who got a decent grip on her. Even then, it needed the other copper to help restrain her.

'Don't make this any harder than it needs to be,' the first one warned. 'It's not going to help you any to upset the baby.'

Christine made an animal kind of growl as she writhed to free herself from him. 'Not *the* baby!' she screeched at him. 'He's *my* fucking baby! Joey!' she screamed. 'Joey! It's Mummy! Joey, Joey! Baby! I'm here! I won't let them! I promise!'

Then her voice seemed to crack and she seemed to fold up in their grasp – a rag doll, lolling between them on jelly legs.

From the bedroom came the sound of Joey's bewildered, frightened crying then. It felt like being stabbed. Nicky dropped down in front of Christine, who was now knelt on the floor, face shrouded by her hair, the two policemen, presumably realising she had nothing left, having finally relinquished their grip.

He placed a hand either side of her head and lifted her face so he could look at her. 'We'll get him back, okay? There's nothing we can do now, but we'll get him back. Deep breath now. You've got to *think*, sis. Okay? Think about Joey. Keep calm now. But we'll get him back. I promise.'

Which broke his heart to say, because he'd seen the look in that Sloper woman's eyes. Seen what *she'd* seen. So he knew no such thing.

He had thought, in his naivety, that he was on top of it. That *she* was on top of it, as much as anyone could be in the middle of such a fucking nightmare. Perhaps it was the booze and drugs, both contributing to the dulling of her consciousness, that meant that, in the end, it had been quick and reasonably calm.

The two women had emerged from the bedroom, Carol Sloper holding Joey against her hip, the other woman cradling a bundle of clothes and cuddly toys, while Nicky was in a funk of indecision about what to do with his now silent and apparently passive sister. Did he heave her up, make her say goodbye to Joey? After all, fuck only knew when she'd next see him. Or did he lead her away, urge them to get the fuck out as soon as possible, thereby making the whole thing a great deal less upsetting for both his sister and his nephew?

He had no idea. But in the end he didn't need to make the call on it, because Christine, eyeing the two women, did something completely unexpected. She leapt to her feet, but rather than lunge for Joey, which was what Nicky expected, she went up to him, apparently calmly, placed a shaking hand on his head and kissed him. Then, glowering at Sloper, and then the other woman, stalked off past them into the bedroom, returning with Joey's crocheted cot blanket, and his beloved Eeyore, both of which she plonked onto the second woman's pile with a look of haunting despair.

He was as proud of her right then as he'd ever been.

He was also aware of Smiffy and Claudia stirring, as if they'd been in some kind of time lag, both of them muttering, none too quietly, about it being a fucking crime. About bitches and the social and how they had no bloody right … and to an extent and a volume that Nicky felt moved to turn around and tell the pair of them to shut the fuck up.

And then they left, the four of them, filing out into the hallway, the last copper making a big show of feeling around the now knackered door frame. 'There'll be someone along to fix that, lad,' he told Nicky. 'Within the hour, I expect. Not that we've an obligation to,' he obviously felt he had to add. He glanced at Christine. 'But, well, you know. In these kinds of circumstances ...'

Nicky had never felt the weight of responsibility press down on him quite so hard. The door was one thing, but what the hell was he supposed to do now? How did he deal with her? What was the plan?

But, actually, in the short term, it didn't look like it was going to be hard. He sent the guys and girls home – despite the vomiting one making a big fuss about not knowing where the fuck he *could* go – and all Christine seemed to want then was to lie on the futon in his arms, sobbing and sobbing, right through the man coming to sort the door frame, until eventually, at around ten in the evening, she went to sleep.

No, it was in the small hours when it all kicked off proper. He must have slept himself, and pretty awkwardly, as he had major pins and needles. When he was shocked into consciousness by the sound of screaming.

Christine was no longer beside him, but on her knees again, in front of the little Christmas tree, and he could see her reflection in the window. She looked possessed, and he struggled up and across the room to her.

The sight of them was enough to almost derail him. That and the conversation they'd had just a couple of days before about how Joey could roll over and might soon be crawling, and whether it was safe to leave all the carefully wrapped presents in such tempting reach. That and the drugs gear, she'd added. 'We'll have to sort that,' she'd said to him. 'Can't leave any of *that* shit around once he's up on his feet!' And they'd had a half-serious talk – no, a *proper* serious talk – about how they'd need to make some heavy-duty New Year's resolutions. *Fuck*, he thought now, sniffing tears away.

'Hey, sis, come on,' he urged, tugging on her shaking shoulders and pulling her back to lean against his chest. Her hair smelt of grease and smoke and cheap body spray. She felt tiny. Insubstantial. The proverbial bag of bones.

But it was like trying to soothe a terrified, captured animal. 'Oh, Nick, his presents! His presents! I never gave them his presents! I can't bear it. I can't bear it,' she said, sobbing, then jerking forward again suddenly and pounding her little fists into the carpet. 'I can't fucking BEAR IT! I CAN'T!'

In the end, it really seemed there was nothing else for it. She railed and screamed for so long and so desperately and loudly that he didn't know quite what else to do. But even as he poured the neat vodka and set up the line of coke, he wished, like he'd never wished for anything as much in his young life, that he had something more to offer her. That he *did* know.

Chapter 17

Christine couldn't remember a time when she'd felt so much pain. Waking up in the dark, in her bed, her breath clouding in front of her, her first thought had been that she'd dreamt it. That the events of the previous day were just a trick her mind had played on her – a sick joke, courtesy of the demons in her drug-scrambled brain. Then she'd sniffed – her nose seemed to constantly stream these days – and, reaching for the roll of loo paper she kept beside the bed for the purpose, her gaze fell on the empty cot and the fact of it hit her like an out-of-control juggernaut.

She'd sobbed herself back to sleep then, wanting only oblivion. She'd no idea where Nicky was, and couldn't summon the wherewithal to leave the bed and find him, and with so little light coming through the heavy old curtains she had no idea what day it was, let alone what time, when she felt herself being shaken awake.

'Sis, you've got to eat something.' It was her brother. She'd been dimly aware of some previous comings and goings, but had feigned sleep when he'd spoken her name. But he was now more insistent, and clearly not about to leave. 'Sis, you *have* to. It's been two days. You can't just hide in here for ever. You'll make yourself ill –'

'Like I *care*?' The response was automatic. Did he get it? Probably not. She wanted only one thing. To disappear.

'Bollocks,' he said, placing a mug and plate on the bedside table, shunting baby wipes and cream and wrinkled magazines to the floor. 'Absolute bollocks. Do you want him back or don't you? And what about his presents? What happened to that? I thought you were going to speak to that Sloper woman and get Joey his presents. Come on –' He yanked the curtains back, and an eerie pinkish glow filled the bedroom. 'You've stewed in here long enough. *More* than long enough.' His voice boomed in the space. 'Now, eat that and drink that. And we're going to go and *sort* it.'

Two slices of toast, thick with margarine. A cup of warm milk. Even in her agony, love for her brother suffused her thoughts. Even as her instinct was to tell him to fuck off and leave her alone, a part of her knew how much she needed him and cherished him.

She sipped, feeling nauseous as the milk flooded her mouth, and along with the bile came the same thoughts that had haunted her constantly. That some other bastard family had her Joey, that some other woman would be bathing and cuddling him, dressing and undressing him, feeding him and changing him, all the while thinking ill of her – she could see that *so* clearly – and thinking, in her ignorance, that he was somehow better off, ripped from the breast of the mother who'd given birth to him, and who loved him more fiercely than she ever, *ever* could.

The milk stayed down, and a tentative nibble on the toast confirmed that, actually, her insides were screaming for nourishment, even as her heart sobbed for Joey.

'What time is it, Nicky?' she asked his retreating back.

'Half past nine,' he said. 'Tuesday. And –'

'*Tuesday?*'

'It's Tuesday. And I got change for the phone box, and the snow's easing off a bit. So as soon as you've eaten and got yourself dressed, we're going down to the phone box. And put something warm on. It's absolutely freezing out there.'

Christine had never seen snow like it. Nick reckoned he'd heard on the telly that it was the worst winter of the entire century and she believed it. Never in her life had she seen the city so transformed. It was staggeringly beautiful. A wonderland, peopled by red-cheeked and joyful children – it being so bitter and, with the roads impassable, and the temperature still falling, there was no question of anyone getting to school. And, had it not been so cold – some twenty below freezing, so Nicky said – she'd have indulged herself with a constant train of distressing thoughts. Of snowmen and snowballs, of stalactites and stalagmites, and all the wonderful things she and Joey could be doing – Nick, too – in this sparkling white landscape. But as it was, as they trudged through the trodden path through the almost thigh-deep snow, she could think of nothing but the distance between them and the red roof of the phone box on Manchester Road.

That and Carol Sloper, the agent of her devastation. And who now – Nicky was adamant on this point – must be placated. Must be spoken to in a voice so at odds with the pain searing her insides that she wasn't sure she could carry it off. How could she stay calm when her child had been ripped from her? But she must not swear, or shout, or rant. Nicky was adamant on that point as well. She must simply ask, nicely – plead politely that she be given one last chance.

But, at the same time, she had to accept the grim probability that she would not get him back any time soon. So she must also beg Carol Sloper to be allowed at least to see Joey. At least to hold him and tell him she loved him and give him his presents. That surely couldn't be too much to ask, could it?

Nick was in step with her, his arm linked in the crook of her elbow, supporting her, though the snow was so deep there was really no danger of them slipping. Even if they did lose their footing they'd simply whump gently into a snowdrift. Which made it all the more wretched; it seemed so wrong for there to be so much beauty all around them, and a cold stone of dread in her gut.

She'd not realised how hard she was crying till Nicky told her. 'Hey, sis, you've got to stop that. Come on – chin up, before you go and set me off and all.'

She felt a flash of anger. And self-pity. What did Nicky have to cry about in comparison to her? She had fucked up so horrifically. She couldn't stop thinking about it. Even their own mother – she of Olympic-champion-standard non-mothering – hadn't messed up like she had. Nicky and Christine had never been dragged off into care, had they? The shame of it was so hard to bear. She hated that too – the inevitability of her mother finding out. Of her dry, bitter laugh – Christine could hear it in her head – and of her doubtless satisfied snort of 'I told you so'.

She wiped her nose on her sleeve, realising she couldn't even feel it. 'Don't you dare,' she told her brother. 'I'm relying on you totally.'

And even as she said it, she knew just how much that was true. Where exactly would she be without him now?

The phone box stank of piss but was at least a few degrees warmer, and though it took several attempts to fumble the phone number from her pocket, by the time she'd done so Christine had sufficient feeling in her fingers to dial.

She also managed to compose herself, via Nicky's stern directions. She must first ask what the chance was of a meeting to discuss getting Joey back and, if that wasn't a goer – for the foreseeable future, anyway – she was to ask if she could at least see him, to give him his presents.

The number rang for an age. Just kept on and on and on. But at last, the familiar click happened and the money clattered through.

But it wasn't Carol Sloper at the end of the phone. It was a woman who introduced herself as Jane something. 'I'm sorry, love,' she said, when Christine explained who she was and asked for Carol Sloper. 'But she won't be back in the office now till after the New Year.'

A few seconds passed before Christine was able to digest this. 'But that's over three weeks!' she said finally. 'How can I ... how can she be away so long? I need to *speak* to her.' She could feel her pulse thumping in her temple.

'She's on a course, love,' the woman told her, her previously clipped tone a little gentler. 'And she'll be off for Christmas after that. Is there anything I can do?'

The throbbing in Christine's temple increased. She was struggling to catch her breath now. 'My baby – what about my baby?' she asked. 'I need to talk to her about him. I need to *see* him. I ... When will I be able to see him? I know I'm allowed –' She felt Nicky's grip on her arm tightening, and realised she was gabbling. 'My friend was in foster care and she had visits. I know I'm allowed visits. When can I have one? I've got all his presents. Is there anyone else who can arrange that?'

She clamped her mouth shut and breathed the icy air in through her nose. How could Carol Sloper take her baby and just fucking *disappear*? How could she do that?

'Well, look, sweetheart,' the lady began. 'I understand how you feel. And it's me you want. I'm the one looking after Carol's caseload while she's away from the office. And what I can tell you' – her voice was all sweet now, like syrup

– 'is that your Joey is with a lovely young foster family, who are taking *extremely* good care of him, so you've no need to worry, okay? I've got it all here. He's settled in very well over the weekend and is happy. So, as I say, you've no need to worry about him. They've two little ones of their own, so I'm sure he's having a fine time.' Christine heard some papers being shuffled. She had a file. She had the business of Joey's happiness written down in a file. As if it could be *anything* like that easy to know if her Joey was happy. And she was *still* nattering on. 'Now, I'm not sure about all the ins and outs and what's going to be happening in the long term, but for now – just for now, love – I do have to let you know that there isn't any contact on the table.'

Contact on the table? What the hell did that mean? 'I don't understand,' Christine told the woman.

'Sweetheart, what it means is that you can't see him *just* yet.' There was another pause. 'Look, I tell you what I'll do. How about I leave a note on Carol's desk in case she calls into the office? And if she doesn't – though she probably will – I'll try to get a message to her that you need to speak to her, how about that? I do understand, love. And I'm sure Carol will too.'

'But I need her *now*,' she said, struggling to keep her voice level. 'I need him to have his presents. He needs to know I'm here. Needs to know I love him. Needs to have his presents to open on Christmas Day …'

'Like I said, sweetheart, you mustn't upset yourself. I'll do my very best to let Carol know that. But, if it works out we can't get them to him quite then, no matter. After all, he's only a baby, isn't he? It's not as if he'll remember and hold it against you or anything, will he?'

Christine wasn't even aware that she was falling. Not consciously. Not of dropping the receiver, or of the cry that came out of her. Only of Nicky's grip and how, as she ended up wedged with her back to the glass, he let go, and took up both the receiver and the thread of the conversation, the words 'won't remember' stabbing at her heart.

All hope was lost, clearly. Every vestige.

'Babes,' Nicky said, grunting as he pulled her to her feet again. 'Listen, stop that, okay? Are you still dizzy? Come on, lean on me. Let's get home out of this fucking cold. She's doing her best, okay?'

'Best?' Christine shook him off. 'Best? They've stolen Joey!'

'They have *not*,' Nicky said, pushing the phone box door open and allowing in the swirl of icy cold. 'She just promised me, okay? Promised faithfully that she'll get hold of Carol Sloper. Says if she doesn't come in by tomorrow night, she'll pop round her house on the way home. She can't do more than that, now, Chris, can she? *Can* she? That's above and beyond, that is. Come on. Let's get you home. And stick those hands in your pockets before you get frostbite. Hey, and make sure you cross your fingers, kid.'

As if that was going to make any difference.

* * *

Bad Blood

Christine was barely aware of the days passing. The snow eased off, but still lay, growing harder and greyer, as if determined to match the darkness in her soul. The run-up to Christmas came and went in a haze of booze and drugs, Nicky, rightly or wrongly (and all out of ideas), having decided, despite his earlier resolution for them both to ease off a bit, that what his sister needed was a distraction. And Christine was only too happy to be dragged from one pub to the next, in an anaesthetising haze. She hardly even noticed the people they were with, let alone whether she liked them – she just made sure to get in sufficient a state that all thoughts of Joey stayed deep down in the depths of her mind. If she never sobered up, or so she reasoned, she wouldn't have to come to terms with any of it. No more hurt. No more anguish. No more pain.

No more fucking *Christmas*. Which she more or less achieved, at least, because the day itself came and went unremarked. They'd been up in Smiffy's flat on Christmas Eve – Christine was ever more disinclined to stay in Brian's – and it had been dark before either she or Nicky had even woken up. And as the first thought that came into Christine's mind was that Carol Sloper had abandoned her, she wasted no time in badgering her brother to roll a couple of enormous joints, to ensure that what was left of it would be gone again as soon as possible, and the image of the presents, still gathering dust in front of the stupidly cheerful tinsel tree, sent its marching orders too.

* * *

'I am *so* sorry, love. I *really* am.'

Christine stared at the apparition currently outside the flat door, wondering if she was hallucinating or something. Logically, she knew she wasn't – since that one time, which had frightened her, she'd not been anywhere near the mushrooms – but at the same time, she had just smoked a joint on an empty stomach, so who knew?

She knew what day it was, at least. It was the day after Boxing Day and she and Nicky were getting ready to go out. There was a party on at the Spicer Street Club, a proper Canterbury Estate knees-up that half the estate flocked to every year.

But no, Carol Sloper was very real. Christine could smell her, and she smelled almost exactly like she looked; unremarkable, floral and vaguely sweet. 'Can I come in, then?' she said then. 'Have a chat? See how you're doing?' She looked past Christine, into the living room, towards the tree. 'Pick up Joey's presents, maybe?'

It was the way she said it. Apologetic, yes, but in the same mildly rueful tone she might use wishing someone a belated happy birthday. Not of someone who'd taken a beloved child away. That was what really set Christine's hackles rising.

'Where is he?' she wanted to know, having allowed Carol Sloper to follow her into the living room. 'Where have you taken him?'

Carol stepped politely into the room, looking momentarily as if she might be about to pass comment on the tree, but obviously thinking better of it. Instead she placed her briefcase on the carpet beside her and looped some stray hair behind her ear. She was wearing a raspberry-coloured beret. Christine wanted to rip it from her head. 'Christine, love,' she said, 'you know I can't tell you that. The foster carers have a right to privacy, as I'm sure you understand. So I'm obviously not at liberty to give out their address.'

'What about *my* rights?' Christine said. 'Don't I have any?'

Carol Sloper sighed. 'Of *course* you do,' she said, sounding like it was a tedious fact of life she had to deal with. 'But you must be aware, there are reasons why we have to respect foster carers' privacy. After all, some of the children placed with them come from ... well, *some* of them ... A few of them ...' She tailed off then, seeming to think better of saying anything more about that subject, as well. 'Anyway, the main point,' she continued, 'is to apologise for taking so long to come and see you, and that you'll be pleased to know that Joey is well, and that his foster family tell me –'

'Don't call them that!' Christine couldn't stop the words tumbling out of her. 'Don't call them that. Not in front of me. They're not his family!' She stabbed her own chest. '*I'm* his family. Me and my brother are his family! They've just taken him from me because you – you and whoever that other woman was – you just came and *took* him! How could you *do* that? And you cared so little – so fucking *little* – that you couldn't even be *arsed* –'

Carol Sloper raised a hand, as if directing traffic. 'Please don't swear at me, Christine.'

'Don't *swear* at you? Have you any *idea* what you've done to me?'

'Christine, don't think for a moment that I find any of this easy.'

'But you manage it just fine, don't you? Can't be that hard, can it? Just march in here, with the fucking pigs, just up and take him – for no *reason*! Why did you do that? Just come in like that? When he was fine. When he was *sleeping*. When he was fucking *happy*. WHY? Because you don't have a fucking *heart*, that's why!'

'Christine!' Like a whip crack this time. She was vaguely aware of the sound of Nicky coming out of the bathroom. Carol Sloper was looking daggers now. Well, let her.

'Look, young lady,' she said, 'you can consider yourself very lucky that I'm here at *all*. I'm on holiday, as you well know, and if you're determined to take that attitude –'

'Attitude?' Christine couldn't help herself. 'You have taken my baby. How else am I supposed to be? Jumping for joy? *Grateful*?'

'Sensible. And a hefty dose of humility wouldn't go amiss either, young lady. The courts will decide if and when you will be allowed to see Joey, based largely on what I report to them, and you need to accept that. You had chance after chance – it's not like you weren't warned. But your lifestyle, and choice of so-called friends, has obviously always come first. *That's* what I wanted you to be thinking about, Christine. That and how you might conceivably turn things around. Though judging from what I'm seeing here,' she added, looking pointedly towards the mirror on the coffee table, the pack of Rizlas, the torn-up strips of card, 'you've already made your choice in that regard.' She then pointed to the presents under the tree. 'Now, do you want Joey to have these?'

Christine was aware of Nicky behind her now. And of a rustling sound. He stepped past her and went towards the tree, a brace of carrier bags in hand. 'I'll get them now,' he said, stepping past Carol Sloper and gathering the presents into the bags.

Carol Sloper said nothing while he completed the task. Just looked on with what Christine belatedly recognised as sadness in her eyes. She felt a whump of remorse. She shouldn't have yelled. It was a horrible job to have to do.

She shouldn't have yelled. She'd just made everything so much worse for herself. 'I'm sorting myself out, honest I am,' she said. She wasn't sure what else to say now.

Carol Sloper's expression changed again.

'*Really?*' she asked, nodding towards the damning paraphernalia. 'I wasn't born yesterday, Christine. I think you sometimes forget that.'

'But I *am*. I want my baby back. So I *am*.' She knew she sounded like a baby herself now.

Carol Sloper took the bags from Nicky in one hand and picked up her briefcase with the other.

'D'you want a brew or something?' Nicky asked.

Carol Sloper shook her head. 'Oh, I don't think so,' she said, and in a way that made the rage rise again in Christine. Like she'd no more drink tea with her brother than fly.

'So you never told me,' she said. 'About when I can *see* him.'

'I didn't say you *could*,' Carol Sloper responded immediately, 'because I don't know if you can. Not with things like this.' She let out another long sigh. 'Christine, you know what? I am going to be honest with you. You want to know your rights – well, you certainly have a right to the truth. And the truth is that Joey's welfare is my paramount concern. Yours too, of course. But you're almost an adult. Joey, on the other hand, is just a baby. An innocent. And it's my responsibility to do my very best to see he has a chance. A decent start. With decent people. Who will put his needs before their own. I'm not seeing that here. I'm really not.'

Her eyes bored into Christine's. 'So I will be straight with you. As things stand now, the most likely scenario is that I'll be recommending Joey for adoption. And, as a mother, I hope you'll understand why.' The briefcase had a shoulder strap and she hitched it over hers now. '*That's* where we are, Christine. I'm sorry.'

Chapter 18

All Christine could think was just how much her chest hurt. It was the pain that had woken her, and all she could seem to make sense of; a sharp twinge and a tenderness every time she inhaled.

She didn't know where she was or why – and couldn't seem to summon sufficient consciousness to even wonder. She just knew that her chest hurt, as if she'd been punched – though she couldn't be sure, as she'd never been punched before. Or perhaps dragged along behind a car on her belly, at the end of a rope, like you sometimes saw in films. It hurt to breathe. That was all she knew. That it hurt to breathe.

'What a silly, silly girl you've been.' The voice startled her. It was a woman's voice, close by, and it made her snap her eyes open. A blur of navy. Was she back in the maternity ward, with Joey? She clung to the idea that was forming in her mind. That she might have dreamt all the terrible things that had happened to her since she'd had him. That this was all part of some terrible trip.

But she had lost him. She hadn't dreamed that, or conjured it via the crack pipe. That was *true*. The memory mushroomed inside her, and everything else with it,

211

making her catch her breath. Making her chest hurt even more.

The voice resolved itself now as coming from a nurse. She was a tall woman. Skinny. With heavy black hair – far too black to be natural – that was whipped up into a spiral above her pale, powdered face. She had taken hold of Christine's wrist and was checking her pulse.

'You girls,' the nurse said, and it wasn't even as if she was talking to her. Not really. Just talking. 'You girls.'

Christine didn't respond, not at first – what was to be said, after all? But then the nurse caught her eye. 'Welcome back,' she said, before glancing down at the watch she had pinned to her uniform. She released Christine's wrist to write a number on her chart.

Christine tried to think where she could be and how she'd got there. 'Welcome back?' she asked finally, wondering about the chest pain. 'Where have I been?'

She hadn't wanted to go out on New Year's Eve. That was the main point. Couldn't stand the thought of it – of being with people; of being looked at and whispered about and judged. Even if it was well-meaning, she couldn't stand the thought of being the object of anyone's attention. She just wanted to do some dope and curl up with the few scraps of bedding that still smelt of Joey. Find the oblivion she craved to get her through another night.

Carol Sloper haunted her. Haunted her by night, in terrifying but formless nightmares, and by day, in the replays her mind spooled over and over. She was done for. She was lost. There was nothing she could do now. There was no patching up the enormous rent in the fabric of her existence. From now on, every single day of her life would be a day when she would remember what she'd had and what she'd lost. She'd become a statistic. Another stupid girl, who'd no business getting herself pregnant. She'd become a headline about the perils of teenage pregnancy and young single mothers. She understood this with a clarity that surprised her. And something else. That there would be a couple somewhere – an older, wiser, more decent couple, for whom her loss would be the greatest gift imaginable. She understood that too. And she was powerless to stop them. Powerless even to hate them. Because they were going to give her Joey all the love in the world. And she was never going to see him again.

'Well, you're not staying here and that's an end to it,' Nicky had said. He'd become bossy since Carol Sloper had been. Terse and irritable. Snappy. And because there were no drugs in the flat and Nick had flatly refused to get any, she'd ended up – so, so much against her better judgement – pulling some clothes on, piling on some make-up, and trudging with him to the Listers, across the hard and uncompromising ice down in the streets, where she knew everything would be bloody awful.

Though, actually, for a while, it hadn't been so bad. Once she'd knocked back sufficient vodka, everything meaningful began to blur, and for a couple of hours she lost herself in dancing. But there was always someone. She'd known, because there was always, always someone. In this case, some young mum she barely recognised from the mother and baby group, who expressed her condolences – drunkenly, but not that drunkenly, because she'd a baby to think about, which only served to make it even worse.

She'd not said very much. She hadn't needed to. She was sorry. She was sad for them. She knew how she must be feeling. She put a hand on Christine's forearm and patted it sympathetically. And then she'd said what she must have thought was just the very thing to say. That Christine was young. That perhaps fate had a different plan for her. That perhaps, as with so many things, it was all meant to be. That she must be strong. That in time she could have another baby.

During a period when Christine had felt so entirely out of control, she surprised herself with how calmly she took this. She didn't rail or rant. She didn't tell the girl she didn't know what the fuck she was talking about, didn't point out the obvious – that you couldn't, ever, *ever* replace a child that way. Instead, she smiled politely through the haze of vodka, agreed that she must look to the future and then, as she watched the girl drift back to her partner, realised the solution to her pain was actually right there before her eyes. She didn't actually need or want a future.

It was easy then. She let the bells chime on the pub telly, and 'Auld Lang Syne' get under way. Made a special point of kissing Nicky – if she left before doing that he'd come looking for her, wondering where she'd got to. Then she donned her coat and gloves, and slipped away into the mild, cloudy night, raindrops raking her face as she hurried home.

Like all half-formed plans born out of impetuosity, Christine's could so easily have been derailed. And probably would have been, had she not been so determined. Had it not been for the diligence with which she searched the flat for pills, and Brian's previously unexplored, and very well-stocked, bedroom cabinet.

The pills amassed, she poured water, a whole brimming, freezing pint of it, and took herself back to the room she'd shared with Joey, and whose absence, tonight as all nights, made the tears roll down her face. After that it was easy, and she soon got into a rhythm. Pill in, slurp, swallow – till they were gone.

And as she slipped away – drifting off more peacefully than she'd done in many days now – her only thought was that, though she'd inconvenience Nicky greatly by dying without warning him, at least he'd get his bed back.

'*Been?*' The nurse gave her what her mam would call an old-fashioned look. She hung the chart back at the end of Christine's bed and popped her pen in a top pocket of her uniform. 'Been away with the fairies, is what you've been, young lady.' Then she smiled. 'How are you feeling? A bit sore?'

Christine's hand went automatically to her chest. She nodded.

'You will be. You've had your stomach pumped. I'll get some pain relief written up for you. And try to get some sleep. You've not had much of a night.'

'Can't I go home?' Christine suddenly wanted this desperately. To go home. To see Nicky. To gather her thoughts. Re-acquaint herself with the person she'd been last night. Was she still that person now, in the light of day, sober?

She wasn't sure yet.

The nurse shook her head. 'Not yet, I'm afraid. You've to see the psychologist.'

'The psychologist?' Christine wasn't even sure what a psychologist was. Were they like a psychiatrist? As if doing what she'd done had been the action of someone bonkers or deranged.

Which was ridiculous, under the circumstances. She'd never felt more sane. 'How did I get here?'

'How do you think?' the nurse said. 'Via a 999 call and an ambulance. And on a night when ...' She stopped and shook her head. She was trying hard, but Christine knew she was actually very cross. Impatient with her. Thinking her some silly teenager. Christine felt surprised by her clarity of thought. And by how much she wanted to explain to the nurse about Joey. How much she wanted to justify how little she valued her own life. But she found she couldn't. Because she'd failed. Even at that, she had failed. 'Well, as

I say,' said the nurse instead, 'I'll get you some painkillers organised. Try to sleep now.'

Christine watched the nurse walk briskly back down the ward, silent in her rubber-soled shoes. So this was how it felt, to try to die and fail. You woke up in hospital, having made yourself even more of a nuisance than you already were. Nicky. Where was Nicky? It must have been Nicky who'd found her. Where was he now? It wasn't visiting. Was he out on a corridor somewhere, curled up on a bench?

She resolved to try and find him. It felt imperative that she do so, what with everything. So she pulled the blanket and sheet back and, ignoring the potential indignity of the stupid do-up-the-back nightgown she'd been put in, swung her legs down and placed her feet on the floor.

The lino was warm underfoot. Much warmer than she'd expected, and as she stood up, she was relieved to find she didn't feel as bad as she'd expected to. The pain in her chest was actually less now she was standing, and her head felt surprisingly clear.

Perhaps she'd leave anyway. They couldn't stop her. Not if Nicky was around somewhere. There'd have put her clothes somewhere, surely. Perhaps they were even in her locker. Perhaps that was best. While the nurse was busy elsewhere, she would pull the curtain round and get herself dressed.

She was just reaching to grab it when she saw her mam.

The ward was on a high floor – fifth or sixth perhaps? Maybe higher. And the wall of windows looked down onto the hospital forecourt. It was murky out still, the snow of weeks almost melted to nothing in a matter of days, dissolved by both the mildness of the air and the relentlessness of the rain.

But, even hidden under her spotted brolly, Christine would have recognised her. It was her mam. She couldn't quite believe what she was seeing. It was her *mam*, coming to the hospital to visit her. So perhaps Nicky wasn't here. Perhaps Nicky had gone to *see* her.

Christine watched her mam all the way across the ambulance bays towards the hospital entrance. Hurrying along, legs encased in drainpipe jeans, tight denim jacket. Oversized handbag, full of God knew what – never anything remotely useful – till she disappeared out of sight underneath the window ledge.

'What are you doing out of bed, young lady?' Another voice. It was a different nurse, holding a small plastic pill cup.

'I'm sorry,' she said. 'I was just … I was just looking out the window.'

The nurse poured water from the jug that sat on top of the locker. 'Oh, there's nothing to see out there,' she said, placing the pill pot beside the drink. 'Welcome to 1982, I don't think. Nice weather for ducks. And that's about all, pretty much. That's the way, back into bed, lovey. How are you doing anyway?' Unlike the other nurse, this one's expression suggested she genuinely cared.

'I'm okay,' Christine said, folding the sheet back so it turned over neatly on top of the blanket. Her mam. It was her *mam*. Coming to visit her.

Christine had no idea how long she'd slept, only that the sky was beginning to darken when she was next shaken awake. She'd waited and waited. After half an hour she'd asked the same nurse, who said she didn't know anything about any visitors. So she'd continued to wait and wait and wonder, again toying with the idea of tracking her clothes down and going in search of her mam instead. But in the end she'd decided she must stay where she was, because perhaps, just perhaps, they'd not let her mam in yet, because it was New Year's Day, a bank holiday, and they were strict about visiting. Then the psychologist had come – a tiny woman, who asked her all sorts of stupid questions about her 'mood' (bloody wretched) – and once she'd gone, at some point she must have drifted back off to sleep.

But it wasn't her mam before her now. It was Josie.

'Where's Mam gone?' Christine asked her, once she'd properly come awake.

'Mam? What, *your* mam? I've absolutely no idea, mate. How are *you*, more to the point?'

'She didn't come, then?'

Josie shook her head. She'd obviously been out the night before, because her hair had been done. It was all spiky and bushy. She had bags under her eyes. 'Come? What, come *here*?' she said.

'I saw her. She came to visit me. Except she didn't actually get here. You didn't see her then?'

Josie shook her head a second time and perched on the edge of the bed. 'No, I didn't. Oh, Chris, I wish you'd said something. *Told* me. Christ, mate, I know you're down, but what were you *thinking*?'

'What about Nick, then? Maybe he was here and she went somewhere with him?'

Josie jerked her head back. 'Nick's down the pharmacy, picking up your prescription. The doctor's coming round in a bit to discharge you. I've got some clean clothes for you …' She nodded towards a carrier bag on the chair. 'So we'd best get you dressed, hadn't we? How are you feeling? Are you hurting anywhere? Not feeling dizzy? Oh, Chris …' she said again, grabbing Christine's cupped hands. 'What were you *thinking*?'

Josie was knackered. No, more than that. She was bone-weary. Exhausted. Whatever moment of lunacy had gripped her and convinced her that going out with her mam and dad would be a good idea, it had been short lived. Even as she cavorted around the Bull along with the next of the clan, she knew she would pay for her pleasures. Thank God for Eddie's parents, who'd had Paula sleep over. Because just the thought of having to deal with her mile-a-minute toddler made her feel weak at the knees, especially not now she was in hyper-drive after her chickenpox.

And it wasn't just Josie who was paying for it big time. So was Eddie – even her sensible, cast-iron-stomach Eddie, who'd spent half the morning chucking up like a teenager. Who'd been chucking up when she'd answered the door to find Nicky Parker standing on the front step.

She didn't think she'd ever seen Nicky quite so distraught. Or, she thought – and it was a thought that couldn't help but strike her – so articulate and sober. She'd invited him in and he'd explained all to her, breathlessly; how he'd finally noticed Christine's absence, and had just had a feeling.

'You know?' he'd said. 'Just that she'd gone and done something stupid.' And his expression as he'd told her this had spoken volumes.

He'd run all the way back to the flat, he said, his heart in his mouth, and, sure enough, Christine was unconscious on the bed, so he'd run to the phone box, and called an ambulance, and then dashed back and sat with her – doing nothing, because nothing was what he'd been told he must do. As long as she was on her side, and breathing freely, he must wait. So he'd waited, and the paramedics had finally come, wasting no time at all before transferring her to a stretcher, and somehow managing to get her down all those flights of steps without dropping her, and they'd sent him back up to collect all the bottles and packets and blister packs, because it was important to know what she'd taken.

'Fucking *shed loads*,' he'd said, and Josie had thought he was about to burst into tears. 'She meant it, Jose. She proper meant it. If I'd stayed in the Listers …' He cleared his throat. Wiped his mouth. 'And I'm not surprised, neither, what she's been through. I tell you, if I thought it wouldn't make everything worse, I'd punch that fucking social worker's lights out.' And then went on to explain how completely and apparently heartlessly Carol Sloper had removed every last vestige of hope his little sister had been hanging on to, and how completely it had destroyed her.

But not killed her, not quite. No thanks to her. 'She'd taken all sorts – including paracetamol, which could apparently destroy her liver,' Nicky told her. But because he'd come back when he had, they were hopeful there'd be no lasting damage. He'd stayed at the hospital for the rest of the night, only returning home to get some sleep, and some clean clothes for her, once they assured her she was sleeping it off and going to be okay.

'And now?' Josie had asked him. 'Did you want me to come and see her?'

And then he *had* burst into tears. 'I don't know *what* I fucking want,' he'd sobbed. Then apologised for swearing, not realising Paula wasn't around the house somewhere, playing. 'I just wanted to come and tell you. I don't know what to *do* with her, Jose, honest I don't. I just don't know what to *do*.'

So now Christine was home with her and Eddie – just for a day or so, while the dust settled and everyone got their heads together – and she was asleep in the spare room and Eddie had finally stopped chucking up, so, with a great deal on her mind, Josie decided she'd pop out. There was obviously nothing she could do about Carol Sloper till after the weekend, but she could at least solve the mystery of Lizzie's non-visit to see her daughter. Had she really had a change of heart? But how did she even know? Nicky'd already told her he'd no more go round her house than fly. So who'd told her? And having gone there, why hadn't she actually made the visit?

Josie wasn't stupid. Much as the thought of Lizzie taking Chris back made her happy, she wasn't born yesterday – the phrase 'pigs might fly' sprang to mind. But since Chris was so agitated about it, she might as well kill two birds with one stone, mightn't she? She had to walk down to Eddie's mam's to pick Paula up in any case so, on the way, she would pop in and see Lizzie.

Chapter 19

The social service offices looked as gloomy as Josie felt.
They were over on Killinghall Road, so she'd had to trek
right through the town centre to get there, which had been
a long slog through all the slush, despite the milder turn in
the weather. It had done very little to brighten her bleak
mood – any more than the stark row of grey Victorian
buildings. Cold and unwelcoming, they certainly didn't
look like the sort of place where you'd take children to get
a better start in life.

There was a part of Josie that knew this was not the best
time to confront Carol Sloper either. A Monday morning,
the first working day of the New Year. The woman probably had all kinds of shit on her plate and, in all fairness, she
should give the woman the benefit of the doubt – not go
wellying into her office all guns blazing.

She knew she'd have a struggle keeping calm, too. She
was still in shock – both about Christine, whose suicide
attempt had really shaken her, and about Lizzie – there
were no two ways about it. Lizzie added an extra layer of
darkness to an already bleak situation, and, if Carol was to
be believed, one she couldn't see lifting any time soon. Joey

gone, Christine wanting to top herself, and now this new and terrible news.

The strain of not knowing whether to tell Christine or keep it from her was beginning to take its toll, too. Truth be known, Josie had been glad when Nicky had walked round yesterday afternoon to take Christine home again, because she was finding it hard to look her friend in the eye.

Lizzie had answered the door two days earlier – less than twenty-four hours after Chrissy's overdose – and, for a moment, all Josie could do was gape. She looked terrible. Emaciated. Old. Rail-thin already, she'd lost an enormous amount of weight – and in an incredibly short space of time, too. If this was what happened when you had Rasta Mo in your life, Josie had found herself thinking, then thank God Christine had nothing more to do with him.

But Lizzie wasn't love sick. She was proper sick. She was seriously ill, in fact – it turned out that she had leukaemia.

Josie's second shock that Saturday afternoon was to find that her mam was round at Lizzie's too, looking much better than she'd any right to, given the party the previous evening – though, in comparison to Lizzie, who looked like a concentration-camp inmate, even with the roughest hangover she couldn't have come close.

'And yes, you're right. I was at the hospital,' Lizzie confirmed in answer to Josie's question as June had poured tea for them all. 'I had a turn. I've been on chemo and I had a really nasty turn. Makes you sick, it does – it's bloody horrible, but I'm used to that, sort of – but I woke up on Saturday with big bruises all over my arms and legs and I decided I'd better get down the 'ossy and get them checked out.' She looked down at her bony arm. 'Much good it'll fucking do me.'

For once, Josie found she wasn't even remotely irritated by the business of it being all about Lizzie. It was. She'd seen lots in her life, but she couldn't take her eyes off her. She'd heard the phrase 'death warmed up' – had used it many times herself. Actually seeing it – or what looked like it – chilled her. And when Lizzie went into the other room to get a cushion to put on her chair – 'Skin and bones, I am. Even hurts to bloody sit!' – the few words her mother was able to mouth to her seemed to confirm it. Lizzie was dying. Not even forty and she was *dying*.

'So what brings you round here?' Lizzie'd asked on her return. And after a moment's hesitation, Josie had told her. At first, given what she'd just been told, she'd thought perhaps she shouldn't, but the rational part of her brain soon overruled the emotional. Perhaps, for all Lizzie professed to have expunged Christine from her life, the seriousness of her illness, and the kind of thoughts that would presumably go with it, might mean she'd had a rethink. Though knowing her as she did, Josie was under no illusions. Even if she had, she would be much too proud to say so.

Bad Blood

So she'd explained about Christine's overdose and the chain of events that had preceded it, and though Lizzie's questions about the outcome were perfunctory at best, she'd thought she'd seen something. She hoped so.

Josie took a moment to compose herself before pushing open the double doors. Here it was, already Monday, and she still couldn't take it in. Couldn't get past how appalled she was about the unfairness of it all. The thought of Lizzie dying – she couldn't seem to process that at all, and had kept Eddie up half the night – both Saturday and last night – going round and round in circles, trying, and failing, to properly accept that, however cruel, it was happening nevertheless.

Which was why she'd felt doubly angered by Carol Sloper. Yes, she knew she had a job to do and she understood why she'd taken Joey. And a part of her still agreed it was the necessary course of action, however unpalatable that was for her to live with.

But the weight of the thing Christine *didn't* know weighed very heavily. Josie obviously couldn't second guess how she'd react to her mam's cancer, but on one point she was clear. And that knowledge coloured absolutely everything, up to and including how she might react when Josie *did* tell her about her mam – that Carol Sloper had encouraged her to try and take her own life every bit as surely as if she'd poured the pills down Christine's throat herself.

Not that Carol Sloper knew. Carol Sloper knew nothing about any of it. Knew nothing about the events that had followed the visit in which she'd not only taken Joey's presents but had taken all Christine's hope, and as a consequence was lucky that she was still left with her life.

And once she'd shown up to Carol's office – which she shared with several other social workers but was, thankfully, currently empty – Josie, who told her only that she wanted to chat about her friend, wasted no time in filling her in.

Not that Carol was one for preamble anyway. 'How is Christine doing?' were the first words she uttered, even as she gestured to a seat.

Josie didn't sit down. 'She's alive,' she said. 'Just.'

Carol Sloper hovered behind her desk, obviously uncertain about sitting down herself now. 'I beg your pardon?' she said. Now she did sit on her swivel chair, sweeping her heavy woollen skirt beneath her as she did so.

'She took an overdose,' Josie added. 'On New Year's Eve.'

Carol Sloper stood up again. '*What?*'

She glanced past Josie then, and she wondered if her first thought was to throw a coat on, grab her briefcase and hotfoot it round there. Again she wondered at the sort of person you needed to be to have other people's lives on your mind – and on your conscience – in that way.

'She tried to kill herself,' she clarified. 'Was that what you wanted?'

'Was *what* what I wanted?' Carol Sloper's voice was small.

'Her death. My friend's *death*. Is that really what you want on your conscience?'

Despite all her promises to herself that she'd keep calm, Josie couldn't seem to stop the words from spewing from her mouth. '*Is* it what you wanted?' she went on, fixing her furious gaze on the startled social worker. 'Because, my God, you pretty nearly got it!'

Carol Sloper's blouse was the perfect choice of work-wear. Buttoned up to the throat, and tied off with a little bow. Sensible and unostentatious, just like she was. Next to the women of her age Josie more usually came into contact with, she could so easily fade into the distance, unseen. Become a wallflower – go completely unnoticed.

How wrong she'd been to judge her on something so superficial. The woman was as hard as they came.

'What are you talking about?' she said, in her soft, approachable, but not quite believable accent.

Josie was only too happy to tell her.

And as she did so, the woman's eyes widened and the colour drained from her. She now looked as grey as the cardigan she wore.

'But *why?*' she asked. Josie's expression made her regroup and qualify. 'I mean what prompted it? What specifically? Did something happen?'

Josie rolled her eyes. 'All due respect,' she said, 'but *you* were what happened! The one hope Christine had of drag-ging herself out of this spiral was the hope that she'd get to see her baby again! What were you thinking, telling her all those things you told her? Christ! What did you *expect* to happen? You just destroyed her last hope! She tried to top herself because she's got bugger all to live for now, has she?'

The words had been swilling round and round her brain all the way here, but now they were out she felt none of the satisfaction she'd expected, as she watched the rosy glow disappear from Carol Sloper's face.

There was a silence then, a long one, as Carol Sloper digested what Josie had spelled out for her. 'Oh, God,' she said finally, clicking and unclicking the top on her cheap ballpoint. 'Where'd you say she is? I need to see her ...'

Josie put a hand up. 'Trust me, you are the *last* person she needs to see right now. "Oh, hi there, person who just told me I'm never going to see my baby again ..." Yep, I think you can imagine just how well *that's* going to go.'

She stopped then, becoming aware that Carol Sloper was beginning to grimace. No, not grimace, exactly. That her face was just bending slightly out of shape. She lunged into her bag, pulling out a pocket pack of tissues and opening it. She was crying, Josie realised. That was what she was doing – she was *weeping*.

She slumped down into her seat now, and Josie felt all at once both furious with the woman and sorry for her. Furious at her for snivelling – she'd no business to be doing that; she'd bloody caused all this, hadn't she? And also sorry for her. For the shit job she did, day in day out. Much as social workers were viewed with fear and suspicion on Canterbury, she hadn't forgotten the decision Carol Sloper had been forced to make. Wouldn't forget. Still couldn't find it in herself to disagree with. But what had happened since ...

She sighed, put her bag down and plonked herself down on the chair opposite. 'Look,' she said. 'I'm sorry. I didn't mean to shout at you. Well, okay, I did. It's not been the best weekend ever, as you can imagine. Look, I just couldn't ...' She sighed again. 'I just couldn't get my head round why you'd *tell* her something like that. I really can't. I mean, even if it's true, did she need to know that when she was – *is* – so frigging vulnerable? Christ ...'

She could feel her anger rising again.

'That wasn't what I said, Josie. *Genuinely*, that was not what I told her. Yes, I came down hard on her – I know I did, I accept that – because she was stoned, and I wanted her to take what I was saying seriously.' She paused. 'Because it *is* serious, okay? But at no point did I tell her Joey would definitely be put up for adoption. At no point. I just told her that if she carried on the way she was going the likelihood of that happening would increase. Because it *would*.'

She blew her nose. Did it delicately. Deliberately. Like a lady. And Josie found herself wondering how much she really understood about the lives that she held in her unvarnished hands.

Her eyes were still shining. She was clearly still very upset. 'I just wanted to shock her,' she said again. 'No question. I felt I needed to. It was a shock to me, too. I thought

231

she was getting her act together. I thought with you on her case – well, she listens to you, doesn't she? I thought she'd turn it around, what with Joey getting that bit older. But you have to understand, Josie – and I know you of all people do –' The inference was plain. 'I can't just sit there and let things ride. That would be a dereliction of duty. If people flag something up, then I've a duty to act. As you – as would anyone – would want me to do, if you thought a child was being mistreated.'

Josie raised a hand. 'Hang on. *Hang* on. What are you on about? What d'you mean, "flagging up". What's been flagged up? By who?'

Carol Sloper blew her nose. Shook her head while she was doing so. 'I'm sorry?'

'You said if people flag something up you have a duty to act. What do you mean? You say "people". Who?'

'Josie, don't play naïve here. You've been closer to her than anyone. Not to mention the fact that you were *there*.'

'The baby group? You mean the baby group? Yes, I was there. And I promise you, Christine did absolutely nothing out of order. Nothing at *all*. Who told you all this? Was it that woman who runs it? Because, believe me, Christine did nothing – *said* nothing – that could give you cause to do what you did. Nothing.' She sat back. 'That's why you came and took him, was it? Because some jumped-up old cow had it in for her? And you *believed* her? Jesus Christ!'

Carol Sloper stiffened. 'Actually no, Josie. It wasn't "just that" – though brawling at a mother and baby club is hardly what I'd call acceptable behaviour. But of course it wasn't just that. She's been living as a virtual junkie –'

'But Joey's been *fine*. She'd never hurt him. Never neglect him. I've been there. I've been with him. And no, it's not ideal' – she stopped short of swearing about the housing – 'but he's been *fine*!'

'No, he *hasn't*!' She'd properly shouted. 'No, Josie. Not by any decent standard. I don't know what *you* see, but I've seen something else. Filthy clothes. Filthy body. Reeking of smoke. Under-stimulated. And being cared for by a mother who is *not* fit to care for him. Now, you know perfectly well how much I wish things were otherwise but, seriously, Josie –' She lifted a hand and pointed a finger. 'Would you take your little one to a playgroup when drunk?'

Josie's eyes widened. 'That's ridiculous. I –'

'No it's *criminal*, that's what it is. And the last straw. There is *always* a last straw, and Christine chose to ignore it.'

It hit Josie then. Bam. Like a child's wooden mallet. That's what had done it. The woman's bile. The woman's vile malicious bile. She'd been unable to stop herself, even knowing Josie could tell anyone otherwise. Just slipped it in. She was drunk. She'd been drinking. She *reeked* of it. 'Sylvia Harris,' she said, pointing her own finger. 'Sylvia *Harris*.' She didn't need to say more.

* * *

233

Perhaps because of that – all unsaid, because social workers never revealed their sources – Carol Sloper was even more mortified. She was making excuses, yes – wouldn't Josie lose her temper seeing Christine in the state she was on that grim December morning? Already having smoked a joint? Already done for the day? But she was also contrite, because, actually, she understood perfectly. She'd taken Joey, without warning, based on the malicious, and spurious, reports from a woman who positively revelled in the opportunity to settle the score. Who'd done the one thing Canterbury people never did – been a snitch to the social.

Josie knew she could – and would – deal with Sylvia Harris later. Right now, more importantly, had the situation changed any? Was there any way Carol Sloper could give Christine an ounce of hope?

Carol sighed long and loud as she laced her slim fingers. 'You know I'd love to be able to tell you that,' she said, and she looked sincere. 'I'd love to be able to tell you that this – what you've disclosed – changes everything. That if Christine turns her life around – and she would have to do that wholesale – there would be hope for contact and, at some point, for a reassessment of the situation. And one thing I can at least tell you is that he's still with the same foster family and there are no plans to put him up for adoption in the short term.'

'Contact?' Josie seized upon it. 'That would make all the difference in the *world* to her. With that at least to hope for …'

Carol Sloper raised her hand for a second time. 'Don't give her that hope, Josie. I cannot in all conscience let you. I understand what you're saying and I know how much this matters. But since Joey went into care I've seen nothing to reassure me. And now a drugs-related overdose as well.'

'Not drugs-related,' Josie corrected her. '*No*. Not that at all.'

Carol Sloper looked sympathetic. 'In the scheme of things it makes little difference, Josie. It's not the sort of distinction the panel will care about a great deal. It's still an attempted suicide.'

Josie leaned forward. 'Please,' she said. '*Please* let me give her some hope. Some contact. One visit. Is that so much to ask? Is it *really*?'

'I can try,' Carol Sloper said. 'But don't make her any promises. I can't work miracles.'

But you still all play God, Josie had the wisdom not to say.

Chapter 20

It was the back end of January and, once again, bitterly cold. It had come out of nowhere – the icy air swept down from the far north, but far from prettying the place up with fresh snow, it just re-froze what was left of the last lot. Piles of banked sludge, grey and filthy, blocked the pavements and narrowed the roads, and created a very different kind of Dickensian scene now – one that seemed to accentuate the poverty and grime, highlighting all that was wrong with the neighbourhood.

Christine, however, was happy. Well, using her new definition of what constituted 'happy', which was easy to achieve if you followed one simple prescription. Spend as much time as possible pissed or stoned. She knew it wasn't sustainable – there was a part of her brain that knew that very well, even without Josie's constant badgering and nagging. But, for the moment, it was a way of living that made living bearable, which was presumably why so many people with shitty lives embraced it so readily.

That her life was shit was no longer in any doubt. It had been shit before – even with Joey, it had been bloody difficult. But there had always been that glimmer of hope that, eventually, it would get better. That a flat would be found for her, that she could get back to some kind of work, even that her mam would one day stop being such a bitch to her.

But the glimmer was gone now. Not only extinguished but trampled on, too, via the news that a sour, middle-aged woman had been the main agent of her current misery – and more than that, that she'd absolutely no redress. No right of reply. Not a vestige of power. That *she* held the power – that malicious old witch. Which she obviously did because Carol Sloper had proved it. Just swept in and stolen her Joey. It was just like Josie's mam had always said. You couldn't trust anyone, especially the social. They were a law unto themselves.

Well, fuck them all. Fuck the lot of them. They had ripped out her heart and they would all have to live with it. While she took herself off to a place where the pain couldn't reach her.

And today, her heart gone, she felt happy. Because today was the day that Brian was being released from Armley Jail, after serving just half of his sentence. He had kept his nose clean, and, courtesy of an HMP travel warrant, was getting the train across from Leeds. He was planning to meet Christine and Nicky in the Listers at some point in the afternoon, where she assumed he'd waste no time in reacquainting himself with the business of getting his nose dirty again. A proper party. And Christine was definitely in the mood to party. What else was there left, after all?

'Come on, Nicky!' she yelled as she banged on the bathroom door. The pub was calling, there being nothing to drink or smoke in the flat. 'What you up to in there? Putting on my mascara?'

Nicky opened the door and put a hand on his hip. 'Why, of course,' he said, fluttering his eyelashes. 'How do I look?'

'It's not so much how you look, Nick, it's how you smell – like a whore's bloody handbag. Now, are you done? Let's get going. I'm gagging.'

Nicky wriggled a hand into his jeans pocket and pulled out a small wrap. 'Don't be in quite such a hurry, sis. I've got this, to take the edge off. Nice bit of Lebanese Black.'

She'd been wrong, Christine realised. Perhaps she hadn't been quite as happy as she'd imagined. She clapped her hands and grinned at Nicky. *Now* she was.

They shared the joint en route, huddled close together, linking arms to help keep the cold out, as they weaved through the maze of flats and out on to Manchester Road.

It would be a while before Brian arrived but there was no point in waiting. They'd both had their giros – Nick had saved up a bit from the last one as well – and it made a lot more sense to sit in the pub and drink than waste money putting the fire on back home.

It also felt good to be a proper part of something. For all the wretchedness of the last few months, there were these small pockets of gladness – she was a part of the group now, felt more a part of the estate. And when one of their own came out of nick – which seemed to be a regular occurrence – a piss-up of epic proportions was always the order of the day. And she was a part of that. It felt good to be included.

The mood in the Listers was jovial. Already half full with regulars, it was welcoming and fuggy, as all the workers from the mills and factories drank with enthusiasm and commitment, trying to down as many pints as they could manage before legging it back to work.

Not that work was a concept Christine currently had much use for. Now and then she thought wistfully of the life she no longer had – and could, she knew, return to, if she could work up any enthusiasm. But the feelings never lingered; they were washed away all too readily, by the vodka bottle, or a nice comforting joint. Nick did his bits here and there – nipping out at odd hours to do things she never asked about, and invariably coming home with an unexpected take-away, or a couple of bottles, or some dope or some coke – but there seemed no pressing need for her to do likewise. Not any more.

They had a drink and then another, shouting at each other over the blare of the juke box, and feeling the warmth of the alcohol seeping into their bones. Nick had a thing about one of the barmaids, which was endlessly entertaining. He was quite a looker, no doubt about that, and had an impressive range of chat-up lines, too, but he was also handicapped by his penchant for large middle-aged women – the 'maid' in question wasn't only old enough to be his mother, she *was* a mother – of ten-year-old twins. 'It's Oedipus,' Josie had explained to Christine a while back. 'No doubt about it. He's looking for someone to mother him.'

Christine smiled to herself, watching him in action. If that was the case, it was buried deep in his subconscious. He certainly wanted her to do something for him, but 'mothering' wasn't it.

Weaving back with their third drinks, Nicky's expression had changed, though. From one of unrequited lust to one of obvious displeasure.

'What's up?' she asked as he put her drink down in front of her.

He gulped an inch off of his. 'Guess who's in?'

She craned her neck to try and see, but there was a solid wall of people in front of them, the pub having really filled up now. It was still mid-afternoon, but it was also a Friday, and with Brian due shortly, plenty of locals would have managed to skive off work.

'Who?' she said, taking a glug of her own drink. The bubbles from the Coke tickled her nose.

'By the bogs,' Nicky said, gesturing with a nod. 'Rasta Mo. I never feel quite comfortable when he's knocking around. You never know quite what might go down.'

'*You* don't feel comfortable?' Christine turned, and now she saw him too. The effect on her was physical. Though not in the way Olivia Newton-John was always bloody singing about. It was visceral. A fury. The yanking of an internal knot. He was with one of his drug-dealing mates – an older man, thickset and very black – almost tar-black – who went by the unlikely name of Troy.

She put her glass to her lips again and drank it down in one. Then rummaged in her pocket for a five-pound note.

'*Fuck* him,' she said, enjoying the way the word felt on her tongue. 'Here,' she said, 'work your charms on Rita over there. Get us another vodka. I'm going to need one.'

Nicky took the note and held it aloft. 'Just ignore him. Let's not let him ruin our day, eh?'

'Not a chance of that,' she pointed out, feeling tearful all of a sudden. That's how it went. She thought she was safe from herself, then something would break through, from deep inside her. She sniffed. 'Since he's already ruined my entire fucking *life*.'

Nicky gave Rita their drinks order, and then squeezed Christine's arm. 'Come on, sis,' he said, as the drinks were banged down in front of them, then led her away, over to a table on the far side of the bar.

Hidden by the cigarette machine, Christine continued to watch Mo, taking satisfaction that he couldn't see her doing so. He looked as dapper as he always had, flashing his pearly-white teeth, his hair in its perfect dreadlocks, swaying in time to the rhythm of the jukebox, his clothes – always colourful, always perfect, always pristine – shouting his status above the lesser noise of dun and grey and rust. She tried to remember what she'd seen in him, as a person she'd once liked and looked up to. And couldn't. Just this huge welling of betrayal. Then he turned and she automatically shrank back in her seat, as if skewered, and though he'd not seen her she felt exposed and small and hurt.

She downed her third double vodka almost without realising. Her head was buzzing now, her temples throbbing to the soundtrack of Bob Marley. 'Funny that,' she observed as Nicky returned with yet another drink. 'D'you think he clicks his fingers and the record changes?' She realised she was having difficulty turning her thoughts into words.

'I think my luck's in,' Nicky told her.

'What, with Rita?'

'She only winked at me, didn't she?'

'You're deranged.'

'Honest, I swear, sis. *And* she had that look on her face.' Then he nudged her. 'He's seen you.'

Christine stiffened. She risked a glance. He was staring straight at her, looking as if he'd just stepped on a dog turd. 'So fucking what?' she said. 'It's not his fucking pub. We can go where we like.'

She stared back, conscious that Mo had pointed her out to his friend now. Then they laughed, sharing some joke. She stood up.

'Hey,' Nicky began, as she picked up her drink. 'Sit the fuck down, Chrissy. I mean it. We don't want trouble, not today.'

She registered his obvious reading of her mind, and with a strange pleasure. 'There won't be any trouble,' she said. She was angry now. Very angry. What with the Leb and the vodka she was flying, and she knew it. She skirted the table. Why exactly did they call it Dutch courage? What did the Dutch have to do with it, anyway?

She felt her brother's hand tugging at her jumper. She ignored it. She felt unstoppable; suffused with a drive to speak her mind the likes of which she'd not felt since her baby had been taken. Her beautiful baby. *Their* baby, who had deserved so much better. She turned and smiled at her brother, oddly pleased with the anxiety etched on his face. 'I just need to have a word, Nick.' Now the words came out effortlessly, clearly. 'I think he has a right to know, don't you? That his son's gone into care? His son who he doesn't give a fuck about. *Don't* you?'

'No, Christine, I don't,' Nicky said, reaching to grab her free hand now. 'Don't spoil it today, sis. Sit back down.'

Christine lifted her hand and held it up in front of her, palm facing him. 'Don't, Nick. I mean it. I *need* to do this.'

He rolled his eyes, but let her go. And it was as if a sea parted to let her across the floor to meet her nemesis.

Who looked at her with contempt now. 'Just fuck off back to your druggy brother, love,' he said the instant she approached him.

Troy sniggered, and Christine felt the colour rising in her cheeks. But it was anger. Not embarrassment. She was a long way beyond that now. 'Not before I've said my piece,' she said, her voice level and low. 'Your son has been taken into care, you piece of shit. Just in case you were wondering.'

Mo looked her up and down, slowly, taking in every detail. Once she might have cared what he thought of her tired jeans and grubby jumper. No more. 'Son? I don't have a son. At least, not with you, girl. I mean, who in their right mind would lay down with this? You get me, Troy? This tramp must have me mistaken with some other black man, eh?'

The words bounced off, like rain on a newly waxed car. 'You weren't calling me a tramp when you were desperate to get inside my knickers, you black bastard. You black *raping* bastard.' There. She'd said it. 'Nothing big about that. Having to *force* yourself on girls. No wonder my mam told you to fuck off. You're nothing but a useless, lying ponce.'

Mo laughed. Long and loud. Swishing his hair around, like a woman, his big white teeth mocking her, he laughed, but she knew she'd struck a nerve.

'You're a funny fucker, you are, girl,' he spluttered, rolling his eyes at her. 'Your mam fucked *me* off? Did she? Let me educate you, tramp. You know food? You know, like pizza? You know it has a sell-by date on it? Well, that's your mam, right? She was way, *way* past hers. Her fuck *me* off? Do me a favour. She tell you that, did she? Too fucking old. Too fucking ugly. Which is why she had to be shown the fucking door. I hear her new favourite place to be is the fucking chemist. Probably carrying a dose big enough to infect Yorkshire, the slag.' He hoicked a finger. Troy laughed again. Like a girl. Like he was Mo's adoring girlfriend. 'Now do me a favour and fuck off before I throw you out on your fat arse.'

Christine's glass seemed to rise all by itself. Not for her. Not even for Joey. No, this was entirely for her mother. And her aim was true. Despite the disparity in their sizes, she managed to dump the entire contents, very accurately, all over Mo's precious dreadlocks.

'You lying piece of shit!' she yelled, loud enough to startle even her. 'My mother was always too fucking good for you, and so am I! And so's my Joey! And you can stuff your fucking hair up your arse, to stop all the filthy shit that spews from it! *Bastard!*'

He'd have hit her, she was sure of it, even at the risk of cramping his style, but Troy leapt between them, throwing his arms out to form a barrier. She could smell him. Smell chip fat on his sick-brown leather jacket. 'Don't, mate,' he urged, in his thick Jamaican accent. 'She's not worth it. She's trying to play you, man. Come on, let's go.'

Mo managed to jab a finger into Christine's sternum. She saw with great pleasure that his happy yellow top was now a sad shade of old piss. 'Next time, girl,' he growled, 'you won't get off so easy. Keep out of my fucking radar or I'll fucking kill you. That's a promise.'

'You already fucking *did!*' she screamed as they stalked out of the door.

Chapter 21

The silence in Mo's wake was deafening. But only momentarily. Soon Christine was being back-slapped and congratulated – the subject of unexpected respect – and borne back to where Nicky stood, shaking his head and simultaneously clapping, on a tidal wave of unrestrained admiration.

She could hear it and see it but felt trapped in a bubble, in which all that existed was the sight of Mo's sodden dreads, and the look of hatred in his black, heavy-lidded eyes.

'I need another drink,' she told her brother, raising the empty glass she still held.

'You deserve a bleeding drink, love,' someone called from behind her. 'Have one on me!'

'And on me!' said another man, to the side of her. And suddenly everyone was laughing. She wouldn't have been surprised if she'd been raised up and carried down Manchester Road on people's shoulders, such was the pleasure with which her impetuous act of courage was received. It stunned her.

It also made her realise, through the ever-thickening veil over her thinking, that Mo cast a shadow wherever he went. She'd not properly appreciated that fact before, she realised. The Mo she'd known, growing up, had been a very different animal. Now she saw him for what he really was. A thug and a gangster. Just an animal. A vile, emotionless monster. She resolved to draw a line in her head under everything that had gone before. A fresh drink appeared in her hand. She downed it.

After that, a kind of joy soon set in. She had vanquished the beast, she was among friends – she was even dancing! And with Nick, who was regaling her with the important revelation that he'd heard Rita the barmaid would shag anything that moved, which put him right off. He had standards and all that.

The idea of Nicky having standards – Nick, who'd happily piss in the kitchen sink – was hilarious, so that when Brian arrived, shortly afterwards, she was laughing so hard that she was doubled up.

'Quit that, you dozy mare,' Nicky admonished. 'Look who's here!' And when she saw Brian she felt a powerful wave of emotion. A kind of loving loyalty that she hadn't realised she felt.

Brian looked so different that she almost didn't recognise him. Prison must have been good for him, she thought, as she stared. He just looked so clean. She'd never seen him that way before, *ever*. Shaven face. Short hair. Smart white shirt. Decent trousers. He'd put weight on as well. He looked transformed.

'Fuck,' Nicky said. He'd obviously seen the same thing as she had. A brand new, squeaky-clean Brian, like something off an advert, fresh from Her Majesty's Giant Person Laundry. The thought tickled her.

Brian walked straight up to her, and grinned. 'Cat got your tongue, you little divvy?' Then he reeled her in for a bear hug, which almost brought her to tears. 'Hey,' he whispered as he squeezed her. 'You know Vinnie? Vinnie McKellan? Josie's brother? Course you do. Well, he told me. He was inside with me and he told me. I was gutted. Proper *gutted*. I'm so fucking sorry, Chris. You okay?'

Christine liked this new Brian. She hoped he lasted. Odds on he wouldn't, but she hoped so. 'I'm okay,' she said, feeling shy under his scrutiny all of a sudden. She turned on a smile. 'Let's not dwell on it. It's your day today.' She squeezed his arm. 'Oh, I'm so glad you're home,' she said, meaning it. 'Come on, Nick. There's a bloke here whose belly thinks his throat's been cut. Do the honours.'

'I got money, I do.' Christine turned, already sensing the bulk behind her. Bri's mate Mally. 'I got money.' He was waving a wad of notes in his hand. The penny dropped.

'You're the tatie man!' she said. '*That's* where I've seen you. I *knew* I'd seen you about. What a small world. I didn't realise you were a mate of Brian's.'

Mally smiled, then looked down towards his feet, obviously shy of her. 'I'm his buddy,' he said proudly, 'I want to buy him a drink, I do.' he grinned, revealing a collection of complicated brown teeth. 'He's been away on his holidays, he has.'

Nick handed him a pint. 'There you go, mate.'

'But I got money,' he persisted.

'Get the next one in,' Nicky told him, slapping him on the back.

Christine sipped her drink, trying to remember how many she must have had now. Too many, clearly. Or, perhaps not quite enough. Though enough to feel a warm glow of camaraderie begin to envelop her. Now Mo had fucked off the whole tone of the pub had changed. Like it had been holding its breath, or held taut, like a just blown-up balloon. And now she'd pricked it, all the bad air had rushed out.

Fancy the tatie man being Brian's mate. He collected all sorts around him, but this was definitely an odd one, because Mally was a pretty odd guy. He was built like a bear – an amiable bear – and everyone knew him. He was simple. A bit retarded. Accident of birth, she remembered someone saying once. But he was strong and dependable, which was why the potato man used him – he could swing a sack of potatoes over his shoulder as if it was fluff. He was much older than Brian, though, so it was an odd kind of friendship.

'Meeting of souls,' Nicky explained when Christine asked him. Mally didn't look the type to do drugs. 'Lost souls,' he added. 'He lost his mum same as Bri did.' He twirled a finger at the side of his head. 'Not dead in her case, just loopy. He's in the same council flat I think he was born in.'

Brian was busy whacking Mally on the back now as well. 'That's absolutely right, mate,' he agreed. 'You're my mate, you are, serious! In fact, put that money away, will you? I'm going to buy *you* a drink for a change, okay?'

He turned to Christine then. 'Poor old fucker,' he whispered, as he pushed his way closer to the bar. 'You know where I found him? Freezing on a bench at the bottom of Manchester Road. And, well, he's poked up to fuck, and you never know how long our money will last, do you? Now, who's got the coke or the blow?'

Her beliefs about their kinship not so much shattered as confirmed, Christine helped Brian get the drinks for the now much expanded crowd and was only too happy to join the others in making trips to the toilet, in between hearing Brian's lurid tales about his short time inside. The drink flowed and in between visits to the toilets for a bit of coke, the group partied together, laughing at Brian's tales from the inside. She didn't doubt that they were embellished, but they were still very funny. *Everything* seemed very funny. And life felt so much better. Had Mo walked back in she might have slapped him on the back too. Kneed him in the testicles, too, but sod him. He was nothing. Not worth her hate even. She was among friends now. And as long as she kept drinking, she knew her mood would last, so she was as dismayed as everyone else was to hear the bell rung for time. There was nothing gloomier than having to sober up when it was still daylight.

And her sentiments were clearly shared. 'Fuck,' Brian said as they huddled in the freezing car park. 'Is that it?'

'Let's go back to the flat, mate,' Nicky suggested. 'Carry on there. Well, in theory.' He felt in his pockets. All of them, systematically. 'Or maybe not,' he said, frowning. 'I'm all out of cash.' He turned to Christine. 'Do you have owt left?'

Christine shook her head. 'Not a bean. Well, apart from these.' She carefully extracted the two joints she'd made from the last of that morning's Leb. 'But they won't last long, will they?'

'I got lots.' The three of them turned around. She'd half-forgotten Mally was even still there. As with almost everything by now, bar the no drink or drugs problem, he'd kind of melted away.

'What's that, Mal?' she asked him.

'I got lots,' he said again, pulling notes from his jacket pocket. 'It's my mate's party day and my flat's nice and warm. I can buy some cider if you want some,' he added shyly.

'That's my boy!' Nicky said as he slapped Mally on his giant shoulders. 'You're a proper good mate, Mally. You've saved the day!'

'Just like Scooby Doo!' Mally said, beaming. 'Mally's saved the day like Scooby Doo!'

* * *

As they slipped, skidded and stumbled down Manchester Road to Mally's flat, the January sludge didn't feel quite so desolate any more. And once inside, the flat was warm and welcoming, and cosy.

Though also strange, Christine decided, as she left them to use the loo. Simply and cheaply furnished, it was impeccably clean and tidy. Perhaps his mam had been discharged from her institution, or perhaps he had a woman round.

It certainly didn't look like a place where a man lived on his own. Not in Christine's experience, anyway. But it was nice. She was floating now, unsure whether she regretted the final vodka, feeling alternately dizzy and suffused with contentment, the latter one soon overtaking the other as someone put on a Blondie album, the cider was poured and the joints from her bag were passed round.

But it was short-lived. It took a while for her to register it above the blaring record player and accompanying singing, but she thought she could hear someone banging on the door.

'Shh!' she slurred. 'Shhh!'

Only Nicky, nearest to the door into the hall, took any notice. There was shouting now, too, and – fuck – was that Mo's voice?

Her previous courage deserted her. But Nick flapped a hand. 'Just ignore it. He'll go away soon enough.'

But far from doing so, he was making an increasingly loud racket, yelling through the letterbox and sounding like he was trying to kick the door in.

'Ignore it,' Nicky said again, crossing the room to turn the volume up further. 'How can he possibly know you're here? He'll go away.'

But Mally was looking scared now, and rocking anxiously on the arm of the armchair. They'd no business letting Mo kick his door down. It wasn't right. 'No! Fuck it!' she said to Nick. 'Of course he knows I'm here! He'll have hung around or something. Followed us –'

'You really think he'd bother?'

Christine recalled his expression, the dripping dreads, the blooming stain on his poncey yellow shirt. 'Of course he'd fucking bother!' she snapped. 'Thanks to me, he's lost his precious street cred! I might as well have bitten his fucking dick off!' She felt scared but decided, and headed for the hall. 'And he's not fucking bullying Brian's mate as well as everyone else.' Grimacing, Nicky followed close behind.

Mo looked fit to be tied. And also very drunk. He had to hold the door frame to keep himself straight. 'You horrible little cunt!' he barked at Christine. 'Thought you could get away scot free after showing me up in the pub, did you?'

Christine gripped the latch. Troy was leering at her from behind Mo. 'What, like you thought you could get away scot free after –'

'Mate,' Nicky said, elbowing his way half in front of her. 'Can we leave this for today? I know you and my sister have some issues, fair enough. But the lad who lives here' – he gestured backwards – 'isn't right in the head, and he's getting scared.'

253

Mo threw his head back and laughed, his gold fillings winking. Three of them, all on the top, as familiar to her as were his dreads. 'Lad? That's rich. Lad? D'you hear that, Troy? Lad? And "not right in the head" – that's a brilliant one, that is! I've heard 'em called lots – let me see now – nonces and paedos, fucking scum of the earth – but this "not right in the head" is a fucking new one.'

As much tired of him as angry now, Christine squared up to him. 'Listen, Mo, why don't you just bugger off, eh? Okay, so I fucked you off in the pub. So what? You were slagging me off – me *and* my mother. And you got what you deserved. Now just *leave* it.' She tried to close the door then, but he had a hand on it and shoved it back, hard, almost sending both Nicky and Christine flying.

'You stupid mare,' he growled, lunging for her throat, and simultaneously shooting a warning look at Nicky. Then, as suddenly as he'd gripped her, he let her go. He laughed again. 'You know what, mate?' he said to Nicky. 'I reckon I will. You don't want to get involved, mate. That in there is a fucking straight-up nonce. Likes little kids. You get me? Everyone fucking knows it.' He looked at Christine, and there was now a different expression on his face. One she recognised. 'The kid's in care, you say? I get it now. No. Fucking. Wonder. Kind of people you associate with –' He glanced behind her, to where Mally had stood trembling, seeing it all. 'Jesus,' he said. 'Absolutely *no* fuck-ing wonder.'

Chapter 22

Nicky poured Christine a cider and ruminated on Mo's words. He'd known *of* Mally for years. No, not well, but enough to have a sense of him. He was just the numbskull who carried the potatoes around, wasn't he? The same Mally who all the kids teased and tormented when they saw him on the streets. Surely to God Nicky would have heard if he was a kiddy fiddler.

Christine was busy brushing it off, reassuring Mally, who was clearly shaken, that it was just Mo being Mo. As was Brian, though, as by now he couldn't even see straight, most of what he was saying was garbled rubbish. He was also more intent on necking as much cider as he could, which, after his months of abstinence, was knocking not only him for six, but also, as a consequence, Mally's furniture.

Still, it niggled. Nicky knew Mo. Knew him quite a bit better than the others thought. He'd done plenty of dodgy deals for him in the past, and knew him well enough to know that, whatever the circumstances, it wasn't like him to accuse someone of something if he didn't know for sure. He just wouldn't. It wasn't his style.

Brian soon jollied him out of his reverie. 'Oi!' he called, as Nicky returned from getting another bottle of cider from Mally's fridge. 'I've got a little confession to make!'

He was standing in the middle of the living room, bending unsteadily to roll up one trouser leg. He had a plastic bag sellotaped to his shin.

Nicky gaped at it, his mouth starting to water automatically. 'Don't tell me you've been squatting some bleeding coke all afternoon and keeping it from us!' he said. 'You sneaky little fucker! Didn't you learn *anything* in Armley? Share and share alike, mate!'

Brian laughed. 'What the fuck else do you think I'm doing now?' He then held a finger to his lips as he hopped about comically, trying to rip the bag off his hairy leg with one hand.

'Anyway,' he added, having finally freed the bag, plus a few hairs. 'You're wrong. No, my friends, this isn't coke. This is the finest H that money can buy.' He giggled boyishly. 'Even if I did nick it from under Geordie Paul's mattress before I left.'

Nicky whooped, delighted at this pleasing new turn of events. 'Well, what are you waiting for? Get it sorted! I'll just head up for a piss and then the party can really start.' He turned to Christine, who was swaying to the music, staring glassily into the middle distance. He felt a pang of anxiety. He knew it was hypocritical of him, given that he'd introduced her to this life, but he really hoped his sister would draw the line at heroin. He knew from experience that once you crossed that line there was no going back.

Mally told him where the bathroom was and he headed up the stairs two at a time, noticing as he did so how unusually clean the carpet was. Did he don a pinny and do his housework, just like his mam used to do on Saturdays? Mally really was an oddball, for sure. Or maybe he had a carer. That might be it. All right for fucking some.

The bathroom was similarly pristine. You could eat your dinner off the bog seat, Nicky mused while he peed. Even *out* of the bog, he thought, chuckling to himself.

He shook himself dry, zipped up and turned to the sink. Not so much to wash his hands as to splash some water on his face. And that's when he saw it; something he must have seen when he'd entered the room but not consciously registered. He registered it now. A small wicker basket of bath toys. Rubber ducks, plastic boats, tiny buckets.

Still extremely drunk, Nicky tried to clear his head. This was all out of kilter. This was *way* out of kilter. Why would a grown man have bath toys? He tiptoed out of the bathroom – even though the music still blared away downstairs – and glanced along the short, unlit landing. There were two other doors leading off, so he decided to have a nosey, discovering that the first opened into an airing cupboard – immersion heater, slatted shelves, neat pile of towels – which meant the second one must lead to Mally's bedroom.

Once again, it was a picture of efficient domesticity. A pair of burnt orange curtains were already closed for the night, so the room was in darkness, just a band of the darkening sky outside visible. There was a modern bedside lamp, and a matching ceiling lampshade, which Nick registered with some surprise – where he came from, light came from bare lightbulbs. He'd no more think of buying a lampshade than fucking fly.

Again, the room was cosy, and welcoming, all soft shapes and textures, including the chocolate shaggy rug that lay beside the bed. Nothing to see, then, until his eyes began adjusting – were there teddy bears perched on Mally's pillows?

He felt for the light switch and the room was bathed in a cheerful orange glow. And there were indeed teddies on Mally's pillows. But not just that. There was also a toy box under the window. Brightly painted with balloons and clowns – it looked like by hand – its blues, reds and yellows looked garish and distinctly out of place in the neat orange bedroom.

'What the fuck?' Nicky whispered to himself as he walked across to take a closer look. From his new vantage point he could see a great deal more. A train set. A box of Dinky cars. A two-storey garage, with a range of emergency vehicles neatly arranged on it. And dolls. Big ones. Five or six of them. All in different outfits and clearly – he felt nauseous – much played with.

He stared for a moment, swaying, wondering what the fuck he should make of it. Dolls? Why the fuck would Mally have all those dolls? Perhaps the cars … that he *could* get. Maybe they were relics from his childhood. Maybe he felt sentimental. Couldn't bring himself to throw them away. He did a mental head shake. But they were played with. They were out, and obviously used. There was no question. As with the ducks in the bathroom they were part of his life *now*.

But the dolls. He kept being drawn back to the dolls. And to the look on Mo's face when he'd said what he'd said. Why would a grown man be playing with dolls? Or were the dolls there for *others* to play with? Children he lured here and coaxed into his bedroom?

He flicked the switch again, shrouding the sickening tableau once more in darkness. Should he say something? If so, what? Or should they simply piss off? He lingered on the landing while he tried to think clearly. Think what to do, who to tell. Assuming it was true, which, given everything he'd seen now, seemed likely. A fucking nonce, right in their midst! His mental exertions bore fruit then, as he remembered the heroin. No, no point in doing anything – not today, not this evening. There was cider, and music and warmth and lots of *heroin*. No, he'd do the sensible thing and keep the weird fucker's secret for another day. First things first, after all. He hurried back down the stairs.

The party was already well under way. He was dismayed to see Christine already tooting the H from the foil with Brian, looking not in the least concerned at the step she was taking, despite having always, always promised him it was one she wouldn't take. But why would anyone be surprised, given the shit she'd been put through? She needed that bit of oblivion more than most did, no question.

Mally, too, seemed to find the whole thing fascinating. He was perched on the edge of the little sofa, rubbing his hands together and looking on intently, as if he'd never seen anything like it in his life. Which he probably hadn't, Nicky decided, looking at the big man with new eyes. Too busy fiddling with the kiddies. Well, maybe it was time to introduce him to slightly more adult pastimes.

He had to shout above the music to make himself heard. 'Hey, mate,' he yelled to Brian, 'give us a blast on that, will you? And don't forget our generous party planner over there,' he added, winking. 'I think he should have a bit of the powder, don't you? And a few glasses of jungle juice.'

Brian laughed and nodded, passing Nicky the foil. He heated up the heroin and grinned as Nicky took a big toot. 'Steady on, feller, this is strong stuff,' he warned. Then he glanced over at Mally, who smiled at him beatifically. 'Yeah, why not? Let's get Mally off his head, shall we? Be a laugh, that. Hey, Mal, mate – you want to try this? Course you do. Come over here.'

Chrissy was already well gone. Off her face. Which both concerned and peeved Nicky. He'd feel the biggest shit if she notched up a heroin habit too now, and that concerned him. And peeved that she was already in heroin heaven and he wasn't.

He went and joined her on the sofa, sitting down in the space Mally had vacated. 'All right, sis?' he asked.

'Fucking brilliant,' she slurred. 'Fucking *brew-i-ant*, young Rodders!' She tipped her head back against the sofa back and laughed. 'Love a duck. Cor, it's parky out. You plonkerrrr!'

'Shut up,' Nicky said, feeling a familiar warmth start flowing through him. That was the thing with H. The way it gave you that first sudden rush of adrenalin, an ecstatic feeling that only lasted for an exquisite minute or two, and was then replaced by a kind of blissed-up sedation where you were completely mellowed out and could see no wrong in the world. Then the drowsiness came over you, and slowed down your breathing, leading to the most fantastic, perfect, restful sleep. Until you woke up, of course, and that was when the real battle began. The desperate quest for more of the fucking stuff.

'Whasssup?' she managed. 'Whaaaaaaaas bleedin' up?'

'Shh. Listen. You know, I think Mo might have been right about Mally. In fact I'm pretty sure he was right. He *is* a fucking nonce.'

Christine pulled a face but could no longer seem to form any words. 'He's got a bunch of gear up there,' he whispered. 'Cars and trains and that. And fucking *dollies*. A whole bunch of them. I reckon he lures little kids to the flat and takes them up there, the filthy fucker. Promises of toys and that, and then he's all over them. A paedophile. A sodding paedophile. Can you believe it? Mo was *right*.'

Christine snorted and waved a languid arm. 'Not him again,' she drawled. 'Can't we just forget that black fucker for five minutes? Can't we? Just for today, eh. This is nice ...' She giggled. 'Look at him, Nick,' she said, pointing to Mally. 'Look at his face, Nicky boy – he's fucked and he's only had a bit.'

She was right. He was slumped on the carpet, in front of one of the armchairs, his eyes rolled back, his body slumped, a stupid grin across his face.

Christine was right. Out for the count. He could be dealt with tomorrow. In the meantime they would do what they'd set out to do to welcome Brian home. Get completely and enjoyably fucked.

Nicky got up again, and turned the record player up to the max, then grabbed Brian and swept him into a mock-waltz position. 'Do you believe in sex before marriage, darling?' he crooned, leaning Brian back across his arm.

'Only if it doesn't make us late for the church, dear!' Brian sang, as they swept around the room together, the Ramones, and the booze, and the H, and the warmth, all melting together into a happy heady nothingness.

Chapter 23

It was all very strange. That's what struck Christine first. Strange and impossible, when you thought about it. How could you feel as if your whole body was made of lead, on the one hand, and on the other, as if it was composed of jelly?

She pondered this conundrum for some considerable time. Or so she assumed. She had no sense of how fast it was moving. Had moved, for that matter, as there wasn't a clock in the room. It was fully dark, but that meant nothing. It could be seven o'clock in the evening or four in the morning. There was nothing to guide her but her own physical state – which was shaky – and, since she'd never done heroin (or would do again? Jury out) she had absolutely no idea how she *should* feel.

She was slumped in one of the armchairs, though with no idea when or how she'd moved there, and for a long while the sickly throbbing of her head made it clear that the armchair was where she should stay.

All the men were on the floor, sprawled in various degrees of abandon and dishevelment, looking a little like they were part of some weird children's party – the one where you had to play dead – *sleeping lions*, was it?

A thought came to mind then, and she fixed her gaze on Mally. The big lump whose hospitality they'd enjoyed. A wave of nausea made her clammy and she breathed it under control again, more because she didn't think she could walk anywhere where she might politely vomit than out of any reluctance to do so. In fact she needed to vomit. Her body screamed out for it. She felt poisoned and pickled; as if her gut were filled with swamp water. Just thinking that made her gorge rise again.

But it was Mally who fixated her. She remembered what Nick had said now. That he'd gone upstairs to his bedroom and the things he had seen there. And his absolute conviction that this benign-seeming lump was actually a paedophile; a man who sexually abused children.

He lay there like a dead man. A dead, supine weight. His body fat had kind of spread, and seemed almost to pool around him. He lay flat on his back, snoring lightly and rhythmically, a thin stream of drool inching stickily from the side of his mouth.

She needed to vomit, badly. She needed to pee. She needed to move. Placing a hand on each chair arm, she eased herself upright, then, confident her legs could hold her, stood unsupported for a minute, before walking gingerly out of the living room and, tread by careful tread, up the stairs.

The bathroom light was on, which made things easier. The toilet seat was up, too. And in no time at all it had come up, the lot of it, after which she felt purged and lightheaded. Her head thrummed now, and the sick stung and scoured her throat and nostrils. She felt she might faint. She needed to lie down now. Perhaps to sleep. She made her way into the bedroom.

And as soon as she walked in there, she knew. All thoughts of sleep left her as she gazed on Mally's kingdom. Teddy bears. The row of teddy bears, all looking up at her so innocently. And the dolls, looking more sinister – looking appropriately sinister, their eyes seeming to follow her as she made her way around the bed.

They'd been partying with a fucking beast. She felt sure of it. With a child molester. Like that Mucky Melvin, who, if the rumours were true, had been tortured and burned alive by Josie's Vinnie. Josie never spoke of it, *ever*. But there was no fucking justice in this world. Because Melvin might be gone – and whatever Vinnie had done to him had been too good for him – but Christine knew Josie would carry the scars of what he'd done to her for the rest of her life.

And here was another of them. An animal. A predatory animal, who clearly lured children here – young children, if the toys he had were a clue. Lured them to his bedroom and did God knew what to them. She'd felt sorry for him. Felt bad that Bri and Nicky had taken advantage of his well-stuffed pockets. Felt bad that they'd taken the piss out of him, because he was too slow to notice. Was too much the innocent.

Except he wasn't. He was evil.

265

She sat down on the bed, heavily, conscious that her nausea was already returning. She needed to lay her head down, even if it was on the bed of a filthy child abuser. And that was when she saw it – a tiny Eeyore, nestled among the bigger teddies. A tiny version of the Eeyore that Nicky had bought for Joey. That was with him now. Or perhaps not. Would his foster family even know how much it meant to him? Might it no longer mean much to him? Might he have forgotten it? Forgotten her?

Her eyes filled and misted, and her throat rasped as she choked. She lay down, her whole world disintegrating into pieces, ambushed by a searing, awful pain.

Sick and desolate, Christine pulled her knees up to her chest and cried her heart out. She cried for her Joey, her little boy, so cruelly ripped from her arms. She cried for all the babies that this man must have harmed. She cried at her own blind stupidity. Maybe she'd never deserved to be a mum in the first place. Maybe that was it. Maybe she'd no right to even *think* she could make a life for Joey. What had she come to? Lying on the bed of a fucking sicko, sick herself, from booze and drugs, sick inside – so sick inside – for what she'd come to.

When she woke up again, having slept long and dreamlessly, her first sensation was the taste in her mouth. She drew her tongue across her lips, gagging at the foulness of her breath, conscious that she'd made an impression on the thick, tweedy bedspread, and of the impression it had made on the side of her face.

She listened hard, gathering her senses, but the house was still silent, and a crushing sense of loneliness made the tears start again. This was no good. She had to move. Had to get herself together. She felt strange and disorientated, as if she was skittering on the edge of panic. She had to leave this place. Wake the boys up and free herself of it, even if it was the middle of the night.

With the nausea still present, she got up very slowly, and made her way gingerly down the stairs. Ignoring the living room, where, from the door, she could see her brother, prostrate, she headed to the kitchen, and more specifically to the sink where, despite the mug and bowl that were sitting in the bowl there, she vomited again, spewing water and bile.

Raising her head, she could see her reflection in the kitchen window, and it shocked her. She looked like a zombie, as if raised from the dead, incongruous against the sill which held a row of little plant pots, each home to an African violet. And between them, she noticed, more evidence of Mally's twisted mind, in the form of a second row, of plastic toys, this time more modest – the kind you'd get in Jamboree Bags, or Happy Meals – happy meals for *children*. A tiny aeroplane, a helicopter, a police car. Joey filled her head again. Memories of their first trip to McDonald's. First and, as it turned out, their only.

The toys seemed to mock her. Seemed to swim before her eyes. She closed her lids, trying to still the spinning universe inside them. Fucking heroin. She was never doing heroin again, *ever*. She hung her head, and was just trying to breathe her way to stillness, when a scraping noise behind her made her spin around.

It was Mally, blocking the light from the hall with his huge frame, and trying to steady himself by holding on to one of his flimsy, wooden kitchen chairs.

'Oh, it's you, Mally,' she said, raking her hands through her knotty hair. She realised she didn't even like the taste of his name on her tongue now.

He lurched towards Christine, grinning stupidly at her. 'Mally's a drunken sailor,' he said, clapping his hands now and trying to sing. 'What shall we do with the drunken sailor? Er-lye in the mornnnning!'

He almost fell then, but managed to grab the edge of the sink, effectively trapping Christine where she stood. He raised his other arm and reached past her to pull the blind down on the window. Gusts of body odour mushroomed up from his armpits. 'Mally is a *very* drunken sailor, Chrissy,' he told her, and then, without warning, reached a hand out towards her neck. 'Take this off,' he said.

'What the fuck?' Christine glanced down at her jumper.

'Take it off. You don't need it. Mally wants it.'

He'd pulled the blind down. And now he was asking her to strip? She batted his hand away. 'Get the fuck off,' she snapped at him.

'But you don't need it,' he persisted. And this time his fingers made contact. 'This,' he said, tugging gently on the thin loop of satin ribbon that, one of two, was sewn into the shoulders of the jumper so it could be looped over a coat hanger to stop the jumper sliding off.

'Mally,' she said, 'what the *fuck* are you doing? Leave me alone. I want to go find Nicky.'

His expression hardened slightly. 'But I *want* it. You don't need it. But I save them.' He was the most articulate she'd so far seen him. 'I got loads in my box. Please, Chrissy. Let me.'

Still he held it, and his proximity was making her gorge rise again. What the fuck would he want a silky piece of ribbon for? A new wave of disgust hit her. First the toys and now this. Did he tie ponytails for little girls with them? He was truly, truly bonkers. And dangerous. And far, far too close.

'Mally, *move*!' she yelled, right into his face. 'Fucking move! No, you can't have it, okay? What the hell do you even want it for, you retard?'

As soon as she'd said it, she devoutly wished she hadn't. It was like a spark to a touch paper – he gripped the ribbon even tighter, yanking so sharply on it that the jumper was pulled off her shoulder. She tried to duck under his arm, but his grip was too strong – all she did was yank the jumper even further to the side, causing the other to cut painfully into her neck. 'Christ, will you get *off* me!' she screamed, trying to push him backwards.

Which made him properly angry now. 'You're not nice!' he yelled back, spittle hitting her. 'You're bad!'

And then he lunged again, but this time in an entirely different direction. Twisting around awkwardly, because she was still pinned by her jumper, she saw a flash of metal and realised with a bolt of pure terror that he was reaching round her to the worktop, on which sat a loaf of bread and, beside it, a knife – a fucking bread knife!

'Fuck!' she screamed. 'No!' But his grip was like iron. 'You're bad and your horrible! You're mean and you're *horrid*!'

Their hands met the knife almost together. But Christine had it first and as she swept it up from the counter he jerked his own hand away from it as if stung.

'Keep away,' she said. 'I mean it.'

But he took absolutely no notice. 'Give it me,' he barked. '*Mine*.' He was still crowding and coming at her. With his foul, evil stench and his wild, staring eyes.

'I will,' she said. 'I will, Mally. Just you try it and I *will*!'

Still – even *then* – he made a grab for the knife. And suddenly it seemed quite the most natural thing ever. To avenge Joey. To avenge every kid he'd fucked up. To make things simple. To simply give him what he had coming to him. *Now*. She plunged the knife into his fat gut.

The cold of the kitchen floor seeped into Christine's bones. Weary bones, they were. So weary. She thought she could curl up and sleep for a year. She felt calm now, and watched him in only mild fascination. He was like a tree, she decided. A tree she'd now felled. Gone down like the sacks of potatoes he lugged around. His hands were round the knife, that still stuck, grotesquely, into his stomach, the body fat, just as she'd noticed before, spreading out from his sides on the lino. And the seeping, the red pool of blood that had appeared, and was now spreading inexorably across the floor. She shuffled away a bit, lest it creep out and touch her. She would hate that. Shuffled over into the corner, beside the big plastic swing bin, curled up into a ball. She could sleep for a year.

Chapter 24

Nicky needed something to drink and fast. He had woken up on the floor, twisted up and aching, and with a tongue like Gandhi's fucking flip-flop.

He turned over, awkwardly, to come face to face with Brian, who was also on the carpet, spark out. Of his sister there was no sign, however. And none of Mally either. Nicky grunted as he levered himself up to a sitting position. Probably taken himself off up to his creepy orange bedroom.

He stretched tentatively. What a day and a half that had been. But on the whole a good day, even with the Mally developments swirling at the edge of his mind, like the remains of a bad smell. Not his *problemo*, he decided, as he got on to all fours and finally stood. If Mo already knew, and he put it around and about, too, people would wise up to it. And after that – well, Canterbury people took care of their own. And those who were *not* deemed their own, for that matter.

No, they'd walk out of Mally's and not come back. That was a given. He scratched again. He was keen to get back to the flat now. Strip off. Have a cuppa. Go to bed. Even if he did have to go back to the ratty old futon. He'd sleep like the dead anyway, deffo.

Coming out into the hall he worked out what the time was. It was coming light now, so maybe six in the morning? He rubbed his eyes as he stumbled into the kitchen, vaguely registering the human form lying on its side on the floor as Mally's, then looking past him to the left where his sister was lying. He smiled – well, not so much lying as scrunched into a tight ball between a chair and the rubbish bin, like an alley cat after a bit of a bender.

Then the double-take. The terrible, rub-your-eyes-you-can't-be-seeing-this, horrified double-take, as he felt his foot slip – just a little, enough for him to grab the edge of the worktop to steady himself – and then looking down and seeing what he'd slipped on was blood.

Seeing the knife was like a stab in his own gut. *Shit*, he thought, immediately recoiling at the unmistakable truth it was telling him. You did not stick a bread knife in your own gut. *Shit*, he thought, *Chrissy*! He took a long careful stride towards her, then squatted down and checked her over for wounds. She seemed fine. No blood, no stab wounds. Sleeping like a baby.

He then turned to Mally, moving carefully so's not to dislodge the knife, put two shaking fingers to his neck to feel for a pulse.

He thought he felt something so put his head very carefully on Mally's chest. He was alive, but his breathing was laboured. He needed medical attention, and he needed it fast. *Gather your thoughts*, he instructed himself sternly. *Try and think this through. So your sister has stabbed Mally. Why the fuck? Why?*

He sat back on his haunches and considered. Then swung his legs around from under him and pulled his knees up close to his body, wrapping them with his arms and resting his chin on his knee caps, trying to recall what might have compelled her to do what she'd done.

It was all too much of a blur, though, and his head was really hammering. Time. That was the problem. That time was so much of the essence. He wasn't panicked, not quite yet, because the position of Mally's wound reassured him. He wasn't a doctor but he'd done first aid in his teens – ironically, given the run of his thoughts, when he was locked up in a pissing detention centre – and he had enough sense to know it couldn't have pierced any major organs.

But he'd lost a lot of blood and he needed an ambulance. Scrambling back across the floor, he started to shake his sister awake. He needed to know exactly what had happened.

'Chrissy!' He hissed. '*Christine*, wake *up*!' Her eyes flickered open and she half-smiled when she saw him, and his gut flipped at the thought of what was to come. He felt so fucking sorry for her. She looked so young and pale and helpless. 'Chrissy, mate,' he asked softly. 'What the fuck have you done?'

She sat up then, stiffly, and her eyes began to focus. He watched them widen in disbelief as she took in the scene. She started shaking then, violently, scraping her feet back towards her body, circling her arms around her knees, just as he had done, as if to ward it all off.

'What did I do?' she whispered. 'What did I *do*, Nicky?' Her words came out in bits, as she trembled. 'Did I do that?' She glanced again at Mally, and shuddered. 'I stabbed him, didn't I?' She put her hands over her face and moaned. 'Christ. I did, didn't I? I *stabbed* him …' She started plucking at her jumper. 'He was trying to cut it … he wouldn't let go of me … he was going to get me … he just looked so *angry* … And then he went for the knife. Oh my *God*, Nick, what have I *done*?'

Nicky pulled her towards him and held her tightly. So that was it. The fucking monster. So it wasn't just the kids, then. He had been trying to grope his fucking sister too? And at *knifepoint*?

He was just helping her to her feet when Brian shuffled in.

'What the fuck?' he asked, his mouth agape. 'Jesus, Nick, what's happened?'

A calmness came over Nicky then. He held his sister close against him, cupping her head, and letting her face burrow against his chest. 'Never mind that for now,' he said, his voice suddenly level. 'But here's what has to happen right now, okay? I'm going to get our Chrissy sorted in the living room and you're going to run to the phone box and phone for an ambulance. You got that? You tell them that you don't know what's gone on. That you've just woken up. But that there's a man stabbed and he needs medical treatment right away.'

Brian looked terrified. 'But what if they ask me what went off? They'll think I'm lying, Nick. What *has* happened? Just tell me.'

Nicky looked Brian straight in his eyes. 'Do you know what's gone off, Bri?'

Brian shook his head. Seemed to get it. 'Well, there you go, then,' Nicky said. 'Isn't it *better* that you know fuck all? All you know is that it had nothing to do with you. Now please, Brian, *go*, and hurry up.'

Brian gone, Nicky took his shaking sister into the living room and sat her down on the couch. He then went back and wet a dishcloth under the hot tap – one that had some actual hot water – and used it to wipe the splashes of blood that had dried on her hands and face. Her shoulders shook. 'Is it blood, Nicky?' she croaked. 'Is it *his* blood?'

'Shhh, babe,' Nicky soothed. 'No, it's not. And listen, don't even *think* about any of that any more, okay? That nonce bastard was going for you, mate. You had no choice. You hear me? Now I want you to promise me something. One thing. On your life.'

Christine nodded and made a small cross on her chest with her fingers. Like a ten-year-old. Like a child. 'I promise, Nick,' she said.

'You just sit here, okay? You sit here and say *nothing* when the ambulance comes. You are in shock, Chrissy, because of what you've been through, but you mustn't say *anything*. You got that? Anything at *all*, okay?'

She nodded again and, satisfied, Nicky went back into the kitchen. He knew time was short, so he worked quickly and methodically. He set the breadboard and the bread on the floor, half ripped down the blind, clutched at the knife still sticking out of Mally, gagging as he did so, then slithered down on the floor beside him, turning once, and writhing around a little, to make sure he was sufficiently covered to make it look right – like he'd slipped to the floor and rolled around with the stab victim for a while.

Brian appeared in the kitchen doorway just as he was clambering up again. His gaze darted around and he exhaled noisily.

'Oh *man*!' he said, hopping from foot to foot. 'Oh, this is bad, Nick. What the fuck is going on?'

Nicky gave him a tight smile. 'Try to keep calm, mate. Just know I'm doing what's best for everybody, okay?' he told him. 'And don't forget, you are clueless here. There was a party, we all got pissed up and you've just woke up to this. That's all you know. That's *all* you know, okay?'

'But, Nick, I only fucking got out yesterday!' Brian's face was contorted with fear and confusion. 'They'll fucking nick me again – just for fucking being here!'

'They won't, mate. I swear. Just let me handle it, and

you'll be fine. Now go sit in there with our Chrissy. She's fucked, mate. Her head's gone.'

'*Her* fucking head's gone? Jesus *Christ*.'

Nicky wasn't surprised to see the coppers had turned up as well as the paramedics. It was a stabbing, after all. He opened the flat door before they got to it, the sirens having alerted him, and showed them straight in to where Mally was still lying unconscious on the kitchen floor.

Then he stood aside, watching silently, while they did what they had to do, and while they did their bit to get the lump down the stairs to the waiting ambulance, signalled for the police to follow him into the living room. 'I didn't move him or anything,' he told them. 'And I left the knife where it was.'

'You're all heart, mate,' one of the coppers mumbled as they followed him in.

Three coppers had turned up – quiet morning down the station? – and one of them was female. 'And you two are?' she asked Brian and Chrissy.

'Brian Giles. I'm the one who phoned you,' Brian supplied. Then he pointed at Chrissy. 'And this is Christine Parker. She's a friend.'

'She's my sister,' Nicky added. 'I'm Nicholas Parker. And the guy they've just taken is Mally Brown. He invited us round for a party yesterday afternoon – you know, after the pubs shut.' He ran a hand over his stubble. 'And we all got a bit shit-faced.'

The female copper's expression could have soured milk. 'Anyway, a couple of hours ago,' he continued, 'I went into the kitchen. And found Mally attacking my sister.' He glanced at Chrissy, as did the two coppers – the third was in the kitchen, presumably still rootling around the crime scene. She was looking down at the floor, quietly sobbing.

The metallic tang of blood kept wafting up from his shirt. 'He was grabbing at her clothes,' he explained, 'and had that knife you saw – in his hand. She was really drunk and she couldn't get away from him. So I waded in, threw her out of the way and tried to get the knife off him –'

'Brave of you,' remarked the male copper. He had a pad out and he was scribbling in it.

'But he was like a raging fucking bull by this point – you've seen the size of him. A real handful. And as we grappled, he ended up getting stabbed himself.'

Bar the sound of his sister's sobbing, there was silence for a few torturous moments. 'And you say this happened a couple of hours ago?' the female copper said. 'Yet you've only just phoned for an ambulance?'

He could have kicked himself. Why'd he mention the fucking time? Basic error.

'I didn't keep track of the time,' he said, the irritation in his voice wholly self-directed. 'I was scared. It was fucking scary, man. And I didn't know how to deal with it. Brian here was sparko. My sister was fucking hysterical. I couldn't wake him, and I didn't want to leave her – didn't dare. And it took an age to wake him up –' He jabbed a finger in

Brian's direction. 'And then he went fucking mental, and Mally clearly wasn't waking up. I thought he'd be okay. I mean ...' He shuddered. 'I didn't know what to *do*. It was self-defence. I didn't *mean* to ... I just ... what a fucking *nightmare*. I just don't *know*.'

There was a cough from behind the policewoman and they all turned around. Just as Christine vomited all over the carpet.

Chapter 25

Had she not been so strung out and upset and scared, Josie would have found it funny. She'd been turning up at the bloody hospital more times in the last few months than in the whole of her life put together.

And perhaps she should try and see the funny side, she thought, as Eddie pulled into St Luke's car park. What did they always say? If you didn't laugh, you'd cry?

And thank God for it being a Saturday – and for Eddie. She'd have walked round but they'd told her they'd given Christine a sedative, so she'd need to be collected by car. 'You sure you're okay to wait for me, babe?' she asked Eddie, touching a hand to his forearm. She knew he wasn't altogether thrilled with this turn of events – to put it mildly – but what could she do? Someone had to step in and help, didn't they? And who else would it be?

Eddie nodded grimly and turned the dial on the radio up. 'I'm sorry, love,' she said as she climbed out of the car, 'but she's a mate and I've got to be there ... after all she's gone through just lately ...' She left the rest unsaid. She could have added *and all that she has still got to go through*, but she didn't. Didn't even want to think about what might happen now. Wasn't even yet fully sure what *had* happened, because apparently Christine didn't know herself. Just that there'd been some sort of drug-fuelled shenanigans which had resulted in a stabbing and that Nicky was helping the police with their enquiries. And everybody knew what *that* meant. What a mess.

Between entrance and ward, Josie took time to rearrange her features. What kind of state Christine might be in she had absolutely no idea, but the last thing she'd need was to be made any worse by Josie turning up wearing an expression that matched the bleakness of her thoughts. At what point was her friend going to stop falling? 'Mate, you look as rough as a bear's arse!' she said brightly when she reached Christine's bedside. 'You *sure* they said you can come home?'

Christine managed a wan smile, but it sat like an impostor on a face filled with terror. 'I'm sure, Jose. The doctor's just gone. Have you heard anything about our Nicky?'

Josie's expression softened. 'They arrested him yesterday and locked him up. But don't worry – everyone is saying he'll be out on remand by Monday.'

Christine looked close to tears. 'What have they charged him with?'

So it was true what she'd heard – that no one really knew what had happened. Christine included, clearly. Doubtless because she'd been off her bloody head. On what? 'Suspicion of assault and GBH,' she told her. 'But apparently, because it was self-defence, they'll have to let him out.'

Christine was pushing her feet into the boots she'd been wearing. They looked gross – spattered with stains – and smelt even worse. What the hell had they all been up to, for Christ's sake? 'Yeah,' she said. 'Self-defence. I remember that.' Christine bent, then, trying to tie her boot lace, had to reach out and grab the chair arm. 'God, I feel peculiar.'

'That'll be the sedative they gave you,' Josie said, grabbing her arm to support her. 'Though why they'd give you a sedative when they're about to discharge you is beyond me,' she added. 'You okay to leave? Seriously? You're looking really pale.'

Christine shook her head. 'It's okay. I was just in a bit of a state. I had a lady copper here for over an hour, grilling me. I woke up and there she was, sitting by my bed. Frightened the life out of me.'

'To make a statement?'

Christine nodded. 'Apparently I wasn't in any fit state this morning. Not that I'm clearer about anything now.'

'So what did you tell them? Chris, what the fuck happened yesterday? All I know is what Brian knows – which doesn't seem to be much. Other than that Nicky stabbed the bloody potato man. Which I am having some difficulty making any sense of. I mean, *Mally*? What on earth were you doing round his, for God's sake? And Nicky *stabbed* him? I mean, I know he's a bit of a boy, but *Nicky*?

Stab someone? It just makes no sense.' Josie's frown deepened.

'Nor to me. Oh, *God*, Josie, I hope he's going to be okay.'

'What, Nicky?'

'No, *Mally*! I mean, yes, Nicky too. Of course, but ...'
She raised her hands to her face and rubbed it, as if trying to erase the memories.

'But?' Josie probed.

Christine was now bending down, tying her other boot.
She'd been put in a corner bed of what looked like a half-empty ward. No one near her, and the nearest bay was curtained. And perhaps with good reason. Christine stank, Josie realised. Of sick.

Christine raised her head. 'Eh?'

'What *do* you know, Chris? What did you tell the copper?'

'The truth,' she said, sighing. 'What else? Well, as much of it as I could really remember. Which isn't enough, like I say – oh, Josie, I'm not even sure I've got it right, either. I remember Mally going for me, and trying to grab the knife ...' She stopped, her face clouding. 'And the rest of it's all so confusing. I remember struggling with him – him trying to grab my jumper ... and I remember Nick coming in and shaking me. And being asleep on the kitchen floor. That bit I do remember. I remember the bin ...'

'The bin?'

'The rubbish bin. I remember I could see my face in it. I remember turning away from it so it couldn't see me.'

'Jesus, Chris, what the fuck had you *taken*?'

Christine's eyes filled with tears. 'I'd been drinking, and had a couple of joints, and …' Her hands flew to her face again. 'Oh, Josie –' She lowered her voice. Sounded desperate. Urgent. 'I did some heroin.'

'Oh, for f—'

'Ah, so you're off then?' said a nurse who seemed to have materialised out of nowhere. She looked as if a 'yes' would make her the happiest woman on earth.

'Yes, my husband's waiting downstairs in the car,' Josie told her. Who definitely wasn't going to be the happiest man on earth.

Eddie maintained a stony silence during the short journey home, and Josie thanked God it hadn't been any longer. It was like bringing home a character from *Oliver* bloody *Twist*.

'So you're staying here tonight. Not least for a feed-up – Christ, Chris, when was the last time you ate? You look like a Cambodian! Oh, and my mam's round – she's minding Paula –'

'Oh, God, Jose – what's she going to say when she finds out?'

'Finds out? What planet are you on? Most of the bloody estate know!' Then, seeing Christine's anguished face, she threaded an arm between the front seats and reached for her friend's hand. 'Which is a good thing, okay? Means you won't have to tell anyone, doesn't it? Anyway, bath, change of clothes, and you'll start feeling better …'

'Not possible,' Christine said, in a small, desolate voice. 'God, Josie. What have I done?'

'Nothing. You hear me? *Nothing*,' Josie told her firmly. She just wished she knew for sure it was true.

Eddie made himself scarce as soon as they got in, opting to walk down to the park with Paula, even though it was beginning to get dark. June had no such desire to escape. Indeed, no sooner had Christine come back downstairs after her bath than June was pressing her for all the gory details.

'So how did he do it then?' she wanted to know. 'Did he just stick him, like? Or was there a fight first?'

Josie's eyebrows shot up. Her mother was beyond belief. Except, actually, not so much. This was normal. 'Mother!' she snapped. 'Tame the frigging blood lust, will you? I'm sure the last thing Chris wants to do is give you chapter and bloody verse on it. In any case, she's not even sure what happened, is she?' She gave her mam a very pointed look.

'No, it's okay,' Christine said. 'I *want* to talk about it. I still can't believe our Nicky even confessed to it. I just can't believe he would have done it. I really can't. In fact I *know* he didn't. I have been racking and racking my brains and that's the one thing I'm completely sure of. That I never saw him hurt Mally. And what if he goes to prison for it? What if they send him to prison for years?'

Christine's chin was wobbling again. She was clearly extremely traumatised, and Josie wished now she'd asked the nurse if she could take something home for her to take. She put her mug down on the coffee table and put her arms around her friend. 'Course he didn't commit a crime, mate. Everybody knows that. He was defending you. He was doing what all big brothers do – just like mine did for me, remember? He was protecting you. Maybe it just kind of happened, in the struggle. That's what everyone's saying must have happened.'

Josie thought for a moment that her mam was going to make the sign of the cross, so much did she deify Vinnie.

She didn't quite, but she did one of her special Vinnie sighs. 'Only the bastards made him pay for it in the end, didn't they?'

'Mam, that's not helpful.'

'Well they *did*! And him a hero. My poor boy a bleeding hero! Oh, it's a messed-up world, kid, but your Nicky will be all right. *Course* he will. It was a clear-cut case of self-defence and that's all there is to it.'

Josie wished she could believe that, but she wasn't sure she could. He already had a suspended sentence, and what with the drugs they'd taken and everything … And they'd been at Mally's flat – which hardly looked very good, did it? Given Mally was what he was …

'I think you're right, Mam,' Josie said. 'I do, honest, Chris. It'll be fine. You'll see. Anyway, how about some food, eh? You'll feel much better once you've got something in your stomach.'

'Speaking of which,' June said rising, 'I'd better get off round to see to Lizzie.' She then pulled a face, presumably realising her mistake, and looked at Josie apologetically. *Great*, thought Josie. Just the thing she *didn't* want to have to discuss today. Surely her mam understood that?

It had been hanging over her, big time, the whole thing with Lizzie. She'd been round to Brian's flat, what? Three times? Four? And every time the same. No frigging answer. So the last time she'd left a note. When had that been? Tuesday, or Wednesday? And no response to that either.

And it was now all so clear why. She might not even have seen it, let alone read it. She could imagine it floating down onto the pile of junk mail – and important mail – that habitually sat on the hall floor, and was habitually walked over, too, unread. There was no getting away from it. Christine was living the same life as Nick now, and, if it was true she'd taken heroin, as the newly released Brian.

How bloody ironic. Her constant fretting about not having told her about her mam yet, but it was the *last* thing Christine needed to deal with today.

Christine's head snapped up. As she'd known it would. 'See to? See to *Mam*?'

And the words said it all. It was a daily thing with June now, Josie helping out when she could. If she didn't go round with a meal or made some soup, Lizzie simply wouldn't eat at all – the chemotherapy saw to that. She felt constantly sick and her mouth ulcers hurt too much. And all for nothing? Increasingly, it looked like it.

Josie sat back down again. There was no keeping it from Chris now. She wasn't that stupid. And, besides, perhaps now *was* actually the right time for her to know. When she and Nick were both in trouble. Just perhaps – and it was by no means certain – the brittle carapace Lizzie had erected to protect herself from their rejection might reveal itself to have a weak spot. You never knew. No, perhaps this was the perfect time, especially with Nick currently languishing in a cell, however nonchalant everyone seemed to be about his prospects.

'What's *wrong* with my mam?' Christine said, turning from one to the other. 'Tell me, Josie. *Please.*'

But it was June who spoke. 'Look, sweetheart, your mam didn't want you to know, that's the bottom line. But I think you have a right ...'

'What do you mean, Auntie June? Is Mam okay?'

June sighed again. 'She's not, love, no.'

'There's no easy way to say it, Chrissy,' Josie said. 'But I'm afraid your mam's got cancer. It's called acute myeloid leukaemia,' she added, enunciating the now familiar words slowly. 'It's a kind of blood cancer. And, Christine, lovey, I'm sorry, but you might as well know this as well. They're not going to be able to cure her. It's too advanced.'

Christine couldn't look any paler than she already was, but now she started trembling, violently. Josie cursed her mam again – and herself. They should have got some food inside her before landing her with a bombshell like this. She put her other arm around her and gripped her tight.

But June, for all her faults, had the sort of way about her that Christine, right now, badly needed. She took over. Pushed her sleeves up and took control of the situation. Indicating that Josie should let go of her, she took Christine's hands in her own. 'Look at me, love,' she told her. 'Look straight at me, okay? You're going to be fine. You're just in shock. But you're going to be fine. And you're going to be strong. You're going to be strong for your mam, okay?'

'*Me?*'

'Yes, you, love. Now, I'm a good mate of your mam's, but I can't pretend I was happy at her keeping this from her kids. But, well, the truth's out now, isn't it? So why don't we *all* go round to see her, eh? So you can ask her why the bleeding hell *she* didn't tell you. Because falling out over something stupid is one thing, but the big bleeding C, well, that's another thing.'

'But she's dying? My mam's *dying*? Oh, God. Does our Nicky know?'

June shook her head. 'No, mate, he doesn't. Not as far as I know. She didn't want either of you to know, because she's that bleeding proud and pig-headed. Thought it'd be easier on the pair of you if she just left things as they were. And she's adamant she doesn't want your sympathy. Is not deserving of your sympathy, like it ever works like that, eh? She's your mam and you love her, don't you? Anyway, how the fuck she's worked all that out I doubt I'll ever know, but there you go. She was always a stubborn mare. And now she's feeling sorry for herself as well, so she's a right bloody princess.'

June smiled – trying to inject some levity, and Josie loved her for that. Loved her loyalty. She too would grieve when Lizzie went. They were like sisters.

But tears were rolling down Christine's face now. 'She hates me *that* much?'

'What?' June said. '*Course* she doesn't! Downright bloody mad at you for a bit there. But then she was under the spell of that monster then, wasn't she?'

'But she must do – she'd even *die* without making up with me?'

'No!' June said sharply. 'No, love. She doesn't hate you. She loves the bleeding bones of you.'

Christine pulled her hands from June's. 'No, she *doesn't*. If she loved me she'd have *told* me. She'd have *shown* me she loved me. She hates me. Hates both of us. We've never been anything but a nuisance to her – she's always wished she'd never had us. She's said so often enough!'

'You're wrong, love, believe me. She's stupid, pig-headed, and she's a pain in the bloody proverbials. But she loves you. She just doesn't have a clue how to begin to *sort* things. She feels so bad. So *guilty*. As she might well do, too. But you've got to remember, mate, she's never had any kind of a childhood herself, has she? And she knows exactly how *she* feels about her own so-called parents. Why wouldn't she expect you and Nick ...' June stopped and tutted. Then she grabbed Christine's arms again, and hauled her to her feet. 'Come on,' she said, and Josie quelled an urge to hug her mother. 'Enough talking. Let's go and see her, okay? And you can tell her how much you love her. How about that?' She stroked Christine's hair back from her forehead and kissed it. 'And we'll get some bleeding soup in you as well.'

Chapter 26

June held her hand all the way from Josie's house to Quaker Lane. Held it firmly within her own, with its manicured fingers, occasionally squeezing it, turning her head, and going 'Okay?'

She had a key. Which was the first shock. Had it already come to this? She became scared, then, wondering quite what she was going to see.

It felt strange entering her own home, with June and Josie, as a visitor, and for a moment she had to fight an urge to run away. She wasn't sure where it had come from – or even why, since she'd been so desperate to make things up with her mother. But it was powerful enough, with the memories of her last visit clamouring, to stop her in the hallway, frozen in the coloured light of her mam's Tiffany-style lampshade, wondering, while June went 'cooey' and Josie strode purposely towards the back living room, if it was altogether too much of an emotional meltdown to even contemplate.

She shook it off. She felt the pull now, smelling the familiar polish, the familiar air freshener, though noticing straight away that her mam's rabid cleaning schedule had fallen a bit by the wayside. The house wasn't dirty, or even particularly messy. There were just little indicators that she had slightly different things on her mind. A pile of post on the hall table. A couple of pairs of shoes on the stairs. One of the photos on the wall – the one of her great grandmother – slightly askew.

She swallowed and followed June into the back room.

'Look what the cat's dragged in!' she quipped gaily as they entered.

Josie, on a different mission – or perhaps keen to duck out of anything too emotional – went straight across to Lizzie and asked her what she fancied to eat.

Christine could only stand in the doorway and stare. Even in the gentle light from the couple of lamps and the telly, her mam looked ravaged. She felt a tightness in her throat.

But that was what you mustn't do, she knew – snivel and whine on self-indulgently – so she sniffed hard and told herself to pack it in.

'Right,' said June, as she and her mother's eyes met. 'Get the kettle on, Jose, love. I think we all need a brew.' Then, glancing back and forth to the pair of them, 'So am I going to need to bang your bleeding heads together or are we going to do this nicely?'

She followed Josie then, throwing 'I'll warm up the oxtail' over her shoulder, and, left alone with the woman who had caused her so much pain, Christine couldn't find a single thing to say. And the same was true, evidently, of her mam. Which was no surprise, given that Christine was probably the last person she'd been expecting, but she flapped a hand beckoning her over.

She was sitting on the little sofa, her feet up on an embroidered footstool that had never not been there, and, not knowing quite what else to do, Christine sat down beside her. They had not touched each other in so long. It felt weird to be so close.

'Oh, Mam,' she began.

'No,' her mam said. 'Enough of that.'

'Enough of what?'

'Enough about *this*.' Her mam raised an arm which had a plaster across the inner elbow, and Christine realised she must have some sort of permanent line in, presumably in order to give her her chemotherapy. 'I don't always look this shit, so you don't need to look like you've just seen Methuselah's fucking auntie. It's just the drugs. They go in cycles and when it's a drug week it's bloody shitty. Couple of days, though, and I'll be good again. It's just temporary.'

'I thought you'd come to see me,' Christine said. She had this urge take her mam's hand. 'Back at New Year. I had no *idea*.'

'So I heard,' Lizzie said. 'And I'm sorry about that.' She looked into her lap. 'If I'd known ...'

She fell silent then and it took a few moments for Christine to realise that she wasn't speaking because she couldn't speak. Because she was trying very hard not to cry.

It struck Christine that she'd been doing that half her life, one way or another. Setting things up so she wouldn't cry. Never letting the mask slip. Like crying was the worst fucking thing you could ever do. Like you could help it. You could not. She could not, anyway. Since losing Joey she'd cried enough for the whole fucking world.

She took her mother's hand. 'Mam, it's okay.'

'No, it's fucking not!' her mam snapped. But she didn't snatch her hand away. She gripped Christine's tighter. Like she'd never let it go again. 'Where's that bloody soup?' she said then. 'God, you can't get the bloody staff.'

Hate was a strong word. One with which Christine had always had a very clear relationship. It was a word she used, just as everyone did – I hate this, I hate people who, I hate when, and so on. But had never felt, not in the sense she understood the emotion. She had never been sure she was capable of it. Hate was for other people; people who had a reason for such a handicap – people much more done wrong by than her.

She wondered if Josie hated Mucky Melvin, who'd raped her, which was surely good reason. But, knowing Josie, and how strong she was, she wasn't sure even then. Why waste time hating someone who was dead?

But walking back to Josie's, there was hate burning in her. For Mo, and what he'd said in the Listers, which she had only just fully processed. The way he'd stood there and told her that her mam was past her sell-by date – how

Christine had been misinformed. That, far from being dumped by Lizzie, he'd cast her off like a fleck of dirt. Like she'd never, *ever* mattered. And how, to her shame, Christine had completely believed him. Believed, at a stroke, that her mother had lied to June. That she'd not kicked him out as a result of what he'd done to them all, but had clung on, pathetically, disowning her own daughter, rather than believe he had pursued, seduced and, finally, taken her.

No, it hadn't changed anything at the time – she'd still been almost hysterical with rage and grief about it. And the last time she'd rejected Christine – and Joey – still stung.

But the hate she felt for Mo now was a positive thing. Like a runaway steamroller, it ploughed over everything, and made her strong. He would not prevail. He could no longer hurt them.

Chapter 27

It came back to her in the small hours of Sunday night, once she was back at the flat. 'Home' again, despite how much the concept had been skewed now. It came back properly, and in detail. In so much technicoloured, ghoulish, grisly detail, that she woke up sobbing and sweating and terrified. The stupid ribbons. Mally grabbing the knife. Shouting at her. Pulling her. Then the sound of him falling. *Like a tree that had been felled* – the memory of her thinking that had even come flooding back to her. She could not let Nicky take the blame for it. She just couldn't.

She lay awake for an hour, constantly wondering if she should go and wake Brian. Not so much for comfort – though, strangely, she knew that Brian would be able to do that; just him being home again was an unexpected comfort. But more to ask him what the hell she should do. Should she just take herself to the police station and confess to them? Phone them? *What?* And if she did so would she get Nicky into even more trouble for lying to them? And what if they didn't believe her? What then?

* * *

She was still in shock about her mam, too. Not quite able to take it in. That she'd even been inside her home again – oh, the *ache* of that, now all this horrible shit had happened. No, she corrected herself. Not happened. That she'd *done*.

And she knew she had. Didn't matter how much anyone banged on about her keeping her trap shut. How could she live with herself if she didn't tell the truth about what she'd done?

'You've done fuck all,' her Auntie June had told her, as they'd all walked back from her mam's, and she'd confessed she thought it might have been her who'd used the knife. 'You're a victim in all this and don't you forget it. That fucking cretin attacked *you* with that bread knife – what the bleeding else were you supposed to have done? Anyway, it's done now. And if you were off your head, how can you remember what the fuck happened anyway? Trust me, do as Nicky says. This is the best way, Christine. Especially with everything that's going on with your mam.'

But they didn't get it. Any of them. It was *because* of her mam that she felt so driven to tell the truth. Even if it was only the truth as she remembered it. Because telling the truth felt like the most important thing in the world now. She was a mum herself now. It didn't matter that she'd lost Joey. For his sake, she had to do the right thing.

* * *

But she'd been beaten to it and, being her brother, Nick obviously knew what she was up to. She could see from his expression. He just *knew*.

'Off out, sis?' he'd said when he'd appeared as if from nowhere, just as she was putting on her coat. She cursed inwardly, despite being so relieved and pleased to see him – she'd lain awake so long that it had been light before she'd drifted off to sleep again. She should have just got up and *gone* – camped out on the station steps, if need be. Now she was trapped.

'I was popping round mam's,' she improvised, without even quite meaning to. She'd agonised over that, too – whether she should tell Nick about the cancer. He had so much on his plate now, because of her – because of what she'd done. But would he even care that much? She realised she had no idea.

Apparently not. She gave him a quick summary of the events since he'd been arrested and his response was to simply shrug and shake his head.

'Well, that's obviously a bummer for her,' he said. 'But such is life, eh?'

'You don't want to even come round and see her? She really wants to see you, Nick. To say how sorry she is …'

He raised his eyebrows, perhaps knowing intuitively that she was over-egging it somewhat. Which she was. Her mam had said no such thing. But she *did* want to see him, and she knew she was sorry. 'Yeah,' he said. 'I'm sure she does.'

'No, really, Nick – I *mean* it.'

'Well, it's only to be expected, I suppose. That's the kind of thing people do when they're dying, isn't it? Repent and that. How long has she got anyway?'

'She's not sure. Matter of months, they reckon. Nick, seriously, she's' – she struggled for the right word – 'broken.'

'Yeah, well, so she should be – the way she's treated you.' There was a flash of real anger in his eyes then. 'And Joey. Don't forget Joey. Because I haven't. If she hadn't –'

'Oh, Nick, *please* don't say stuff like that.'

'But, Chris, it's *true*. Anyway,' he said, changing his expression, 'where's Bri?'

So that was that, then. At least for now. She began taking her coat off. 'In bed. Least, I suppose so. I'll go and see Mam later, since you're here now. D'you want a cup of tea?'

Tea. It was always tea that made everything all right, wasn't it? But even as she drained hers, sitting next to Nicky on the futon and watching the clouds scud past the window, she felt nothing would ever be right ever again. Not now she'd remembered. Not now she understood what he'd done.

'I can't let you,' she said. How many times had she said it now? 'I just can't.'

He was beginning to get cross with her. First over their mam, and now about this. 'Listen to me, Chrissy, because we're not discussing it again. The statements have been made and are signed and with the police. Yours, mine and Brian's. All three of them. Now, what do you think would happen if it came out that, actually, there was another version of events that night, eh? What do you think?' He paused to let her answer but she knew he wasn't anticipating one. 'I tell you what would happen, mate,' he went on. 'All three of us would be banged up, and you would never, *ever* stand a chance of getting our Joey back, *that's* what would happen.'

'Nick, I'm never going to get him back anyway, so it makes no difference!'

He looked at her just as he often had when they were little. Sternly. As if exasperated. As if she knew nothing about anything. And perhaps she didn't. Not in things like this. 'Why are you getting your knickers in such a fucking twist about this, Chris? It's dealt with. It's nothing, okay? The man is an out-and-out nonce, Chrissy – a beast of the highest order. The police *know* that. This'll be just box ticking for them. Trust me, he got exactly what he deserved, *however* it was he got it. And will probably get it again when the neighbourhood finds out. So can we just *leave* this?'

Brian shuffled in then, and it hit Christine very hard that the dapper version of him that had turned up at the Listers not much more than forty-eight hours previously was already being eroded away. And not just from the shadow of stubble now becoming evident on his lower face. No, it was the look in his eyes – as if he were thinking

'What the *fuck* happened here?' And it was all her fault. All of it. It felt like she was walking around with a house brick in her gut. Why couldn't Nicky *see* that?

He must have heard them arguing. At least some of it. 'Mate, you know, you are so wrong about all that, okay?' he said to Nicky. 'That stuff that goes round about him – it's all bollocks.'

'How the fuck would you know?' Nicky countered. 'You bum chums now or something? Oh, and nice to see you too mate, after my spell in clink. Cheers.'

'Don't be a div, man,' Brian said mildly. 'And leave it out, okay? He's just a friend.'

Nicky snorted. 'Friend? Seems to me he's only your "friend" in the sense that you never waste an opportunity to be in the company of his trouser pockets.'

'No, mate – *really*.' Brian's face expressed rare irritation. Here they were again, the three of them. Happy days. She felt she could scream. 'They're his *own* toys,' Brian was saying. 'He's just a big kid. He's not *into* fucking kids or anything. He wouldn't hurt a fucking fly.'

'How'd you get to be so sure, mate?' Nicky persisted.

'Because that's what they're *like*. My mam's mate had an older brother who was retarded and I knew him well. We used to go round there for tea and that, and that was the thing that always struck me. That he lived at home with *their* mam and he was, like, pushing thirty. And he had a bedroom like a kid's room and I used to be allowed to go and play with him. You know, proper train set, and this enormous Scalextric. An' he had teddies on his bed an' all. It was just like he'd never grown up. Seriously, mate, you're *wrong*, okay.'

Nicky was still wound up like a watch spring, and Christine felt even worse. 'Since when were you the expert on fucking simpletons? He's still got the grown-up equipment, ain't he?' He gestured towards his crotch.

'Mate, you're *wrong*,' Brian persisted. 'You gotta understand the psychology –'

Nicky scoffed. 'Psychology? Jesus *Christ*. What did they do to you in fucking jail?'

'You know what Mo's like. How he operates. He wanted to get at Christine, didn't he? And he's bright, he is. *Way* bright. Knows the buttons to push, doesn't he? Great bit of mischief I'll bet that was to him, winding her up.'

Just the thought of how thoroughly Mo might have fucked Nick's life up made Christine feel sick. If she could have hated him more, she would have. Only that wasn't possible. 'Oh, God,' she said. 'Oh, please *God* let him be all right.'

Nicky stood up. Glanced at Christine. Gave her shoulder a squeeze. 'Well, thanks for making us feel *so* much better, Bri, I don't think.'

'Mate, I'm not trying to make you feel bad, I just thought you should, like, know that.'

Nicky raised a hand. 'Fair enough. Anyway, it doesn't actually change anything, does it? He still went for Chrissy with a fucking bread knife.'

Brian spread his hands. 'I know, mate. I know. Shitting *sodding* business.'

'It'll be fine,' Nicky said. He kept on saying it, over and over. 'Mally'll recover, and under the circs – brandishing that bread knife, threatening Chrissy – it'll be straightforward. I've pleaded guilty to the stabbing and no one can argue that I didn't do it in self-defence. Christ, he's almost a foot taller than me, and double my weight. And I'll get a suspended sentence –'

'You already *have* a suspended sentence,' Christine pointed out.

'For something entirely different. Trust me, they won't lock me up, sis.'

'They won't,' Brian chipped in. 'How could they justify it? Really? It was an accident. They get that.'

'I wish I had your confidence, Bri,' Christine said.

'It's just logic,' Brian said. 'You'll see. Anyway, who's for a cuppa? Since there's shit-all drugs in this fucking place.'

They both nodded. Tea. The cure-all. He ambled back out again.

'Oh, shit, shit, *shit* – I can't *bear* this!' Christine hissed once they were alone again. 'You keep telling me it's all going to be okay, but I can't bear it. I know it was me stabbed him. I just know it.' She thumped her fist against her chest. 'I keep seeing bits of it. I know he was on the floor … and there was all that blood … and you weren't there, Nick. You weren't! I can't let you do this.'

'I've already done it. And that's the end of it. Seriously. *Leave* it.'

It was like slamming her fists into a wall. 'But what if they send you to prison?'

He swivelled round on the futon, the better to look at her. 'Look, s'pose they do? It's not the end of the world.'

'How can you *say* that?'

'Because it's true. It would only be a matter of weeks, after all. Few months, tops.'

'You have an in-depth knowledge of sentencing, do you?' she said, remembering his own jibe to Brian. 'How do you know it wouldn't be for more?'

'Because it can't be. That can't bang me up for GBH for defending you against an attacker, sis. The only reason, the way I see it – and remember I've spoken to the brief about it – is because of the H and the fact that I've got drugs previous now. So even if they do – which they won't – it'll be for no time at all. And I'm really not bothered. I've thought it over and I'm *really* not bothered. Decent bed, decent kip, decent food – proper cooked food. It'll do me good. And best of all, no drugs.'

'Oh, like you're looking forward to the idea of that?'

'No, but I know myself, don't I? No willpower. That's always been my problem. All the backbone of a pile of fucking blancmange. So it'll be *good* for me. And I know if I can get myself together, there's work for me afterwards, sis … you know, when I get back.'

'You mean doing *more* jobs for bloody criminals? I'm not an idiot, Nicky.'

'And what of it? It's still work. And meanwhile, you can, well, you can get yourself sorted … maybe work a bit harder on that bloody social worker about getting Joey back, for starters …'

Christine stood up. 'I'm not listening to any more of this,' she said. 'I can't let you take the blame for this. I *know* what I remember.'

'Then stop *thinking*,' Nicky countered. 'Because you're remembering it all wrong. That's heroin for you, sis, which is why you need to avoid it like the plague.' He stood up too. 'Just leave it now. It's done. Leave it alone now. Ah, the tea, mate,' he said to Brian, who was returning, bearing mugs. 'Now, who's hidden the biscuits?'

It all felt so much worse now. Not only was Nicky in trouble for something he didn't do – it was for something that she'd done not because she had been driven to it out of desperation – but because she'd been so stupid and naïve. Had she not taken the heroin, had she not listened to Mo – God, how different it all looked in the cold light of a murky January morning. Mally had wanted nothing more than to snip the bloody ribbons out of her jumper! Not rape her. Or beat her up. Or any of that ridiculous nonsense. He wanted the bread knife to cut a length of bloody *ribbon*. What would he be thinking now?

Another stab of guilt ambushed her. Mally would be

lying there in his hospital bed thinking he'd been attacked by a heroin-addled mad woman. She had to come clean. Explain herself. Explain how frightened she had been of him. Which she had. That part was *true*. She'd been terrified. But due to an enormous, wretched, shameful misunderstanding.

Though she wasn't necessarily planning on coming clean to Carol Sloper.

Christine was used to Carol Sloper turning up unannounced – on one particular occasion that she'd never forget either – but she was the last person she expected to see, under the circumstances. She had taken Joey now. Wasn't she done with Christine?

Apparently not. It was early on Tuesday morning – only a few minutes past nine – and, after a peculiar evening in which Bri and Nicky had downed plenty of cider but no drugs, they'd all gone to bed early, exhausted.

Nick had a twice-daily appointment at the police station to keep – one of the other, equally odious conditions of his bail – and had left with Brian only a few minutes previously. He was hoping that he'd be dealt with fairly quickly, as was usually the case with a charge such as his, and affected an air of it all being an inconvenience and nothing more, but his brisk and bright demeanour didn't fool Christine for a moment – any more than did his dismissal of his sick mother. He *must* be terrified of a custodial sentence, however much he professed not to be. She well remembered how anxious he'd been after their party had been raided. However much he played the hard man, he simply wasn't. Not in that way.

'So how are you bearing up?' Carol Sloper wanted to know, after Christine had grudgingly invited her in. For once, there was nothing in the way of drugs paraphernalia littering the coffee table and after Nicky and Brian had left she'd even felt moved to do some tidying and washing-up – not so much for pleasure as from an inability to sit still.

Bearing up. What a ridiculous term. How on earth was she supposed to answer?

'All right, I suppose,' she said, 'under the circumstances.'

Carol Sloper nodded. 'I'm, so, *so* sorry about your mum, Christine. But' – she raised a hand as if to pat Christine but apparently seemed to think better of it – 'I'm so glad to hear you've been round to see her. Start patching things up.'

How the *fuck* did she know that? It was only Tuesday, for God's sake! But then the penny dropped. 'Who told you all that?' she asked. 'Was it Josie?'

'We've been keeping in touch, Christine,' Carol Sloper said. She smiled. 'Look, I know you see me as your enemy, but I'm really not. And what's happened this weekend … well, let's just say how glad I am that you and your mum are trying to make a go of it. Josie tells me she's quite sick –' Christine had to try hard not to sneer. 'Quite sick'? What kind of language was that? 'And, well, all this business,' Carol Sloper went on. 'You must be reeling. What a terrifying experience for you. And your brother –'

Julie Shaw

'How's Joey?' Christine said. Why wasn't she telling her about Joey? 'Have you seen him? Is he okay? Is he still with his foster parents?'

Carol Sloper nodded. 'Yes to all of that,' she answered.

'So he's not being adopted yet?'

'No, not yet, Christine, but –'

'But that's none of my business now, right?'

'Christine, Josie tells me your mam would like to see him. She –' She paused. And just as Christine was about to ask her what the hell was going on between her and Josie lately, and how the hell did she know *that*, she did touch her arm, and said, 'Can I be frank with you, Christine?'

Christine nodded.

'I feel terrible about what happened over Christmas. I can't tell you how much. I thought I was doing the right thing in trying to jolt you into some sort of action. To stop you going down the … well, I don't need to spell it out. I regret it *terribly*.'

'Why are you telling me all this?' Christine asked. She really couldn't fathom.

'Because, as you say, Joey is still with his foster family – and likely to remain there for the foreseeable future. Look, I'm not going to paint it better than it is. But under the circumstances, with your mum and everything, I think I could probably arrange contact. Which is not to say it's definite, obviously, but given he's still so small … But it might not be what you want, Christine. That's why I'm here. To ask if you want to think about it. Because it

310

might make it all the harder ...' She trailed off. *When you take him off me again*, Christine thought. *For ever*. 'But with your mam, and how she's, well, so poorly ... It's something to think about. Something I *might* be able to do for you.'

Christine felt like the girl who was first in the queue for the ice-cream van, only to find her pockets were empty of cash. *But I stabbed Mally*. That was all she could think. *You don't realise. I did heroin and listened to lies and did a terrible, terrible thing. I didn't mean to. I didn't want to. But it happened all the same. Here you are, offering me something I want more than anything, but at precisely the point where I no longer deserve it. Unless I come clean. Unless I cleanse myself of this ugly stain.*

It suddenly felt as if Carol Sloper was, in fact, the very best person in the world to unburden herself to. To understand.

'Oh, don't cry, love,' Carol Sloper was saying to her. 'I know. There, I know,' she added, pulling a little pack of tissues from her capacious briefcase.

She hadn't even realised she was crying. 'I'm sorry,' she said, blowing her nose. 'It's just – well, such a shock. And what with everything that's happened, and what's going on with Nick and that –'

'Oh, ho. Speak of the devil!'

And there *was* Nick, Brian behind him, bringing the cold air in with them.

'Ah,' said Carol Sloper.

'Ah, indeed,' quipped Nick, as though it was all terribly funny. Except his eyes said otherwise. 'So, spill, then. My ears have been proper burning.'

Carol Sloper had left soon afterwards, Christine having promised her she would very much like it if a contact meeting could be organised, even if it made no difference in the end. It didn't matter if he didn't have a conscious memory of it when he was older. Or, indeed, her mam. A part of him would know, no matter how deeply buried. He would know he'd been loved and would always be so.

'You see, that's it, *right* there,' Nicky said to her, when she returned to the living room, her plan thwarted. He'd heard it all, seen it all, knew exactly what had been in her mind, clearly. '*That's* why you have to shut the fuck up about what happened Friday, okay? *Her*. She has the power to help you get Joey back, sis. And how the hell would you feel if you go blabbing and lose him for ever? Because that's precisely what would happen. You understand now? That would be *it*.' He grabbed her hands. 'Stop it, Chrissy, okay? The best thing you can do, for *Joey*, is to *stop it*.'

'Anyways, the good news *is*' – Brian added cheerfully – 'that we saw a mate of mine from down the Listers on the way back from the cop shop, and he was saying there was no two ways about it, under the circs – it's either going to be a suspended sentence or a very short one – just a rap on the knuckles kind of thing. No more. And he should know, because he had almost the exact same thing happen to him just last year. They can't be arsed, that's the thing.'

'With what?' Christine said, not at all convinced she was being told anything but a load of nonsense.

'With the kind of everyday shit that goes on round these parts. Better things to do, what with IRA terrorists and so on ...'

'Seriously, Chris,' Nicky said. 'You've just got to let me deal with this, okay?'

She sighed. 'God, I know, Nick. A part of me does know, and with what Carol's said ...'

'Exactly,' Nicky said firmly. Or would have done, anyway, but for the end of the word being drowned out by a loud staccato knocking on the flat door.

Brian grinned. 'Speak of the devil. A copper's knock if ever I heard one!' He trotted out to answer it, entirely unconcerned. They weren't exactly rare events, coppers calling, after all.

But when Brian returned, followed by the two large policemen, he didn't look so cheerful any more. 'Nick,' he said, his voice small now, 'seems they're here for you, mate.'

And in no time at all, as Brian might have put it, all previous bets were off.

The first copper cleared his throat, then stepped up to Nicky. 'I'm arresting you for the manslaughter of Mally Henderson,' he said. 'You have the right to remain silent ...'

Chapter 28

'You'll have to jump through a few hoops.' That's what her Auntie June had told her. 'Might be a month. Even more.' And Christine had believed her. Because her Auntie June would know, having done more prison visits than most.

But as Christine walked up to the entrance of Armley Prison to set things straight with her brother, it had, in fact, been less than a fortnight. Luckily, remand prisoners had less restrictions about visitors, and thankfully they'd been able to arrange it pretty quickly. Just as well, as she felt she might explode.

She'd never been inside a prison before and had no idea what to expect. To her untutored eye, approaching the enormous building felt like walking straight into the pages of a particularly scary fairy tale. It loomed above her, ticking all the imaginary boxes. The high stone walls, the huge turrets, the ridiculously giant door. And the clouds massing above it, as if pausing there for effect, only added to the sense that, once inside, all hope was lost. All of which was good, she decided. Because it only served to strengthen her resolve.

* * *

She could, she knew, just have gone and done it anyway. It had only been Brian, who knew exactly how desperate she'd felt, who'd stopped her from marching straight down to the police station, explaining again and again, and again, how it would only make things even worse for her brother.

No, he'd impressed upon her, she had to go and speak to Nicky first. If she didn't, he would simply deny everything she'd told them, and make out – and do it convincingly, Brian pointed out – that, due to her guilt that she'd put him in the position of having to defend her, she was talking bollocks, and entirely off her rocker.

She shuddered, thinking of the bulk of the walls that separated them. It had all happened so quickly – the copper reading out Nicky's rights as he arrested him, the other explaining to her that there was no point in making any sort of a fuss; that her brother was going with them and that was all there was to it.

And her breaking down then, inconsolable. Just screaming and screaming. She'd taken a life. Killed a person. Whether she'd meant to or otherwise. And no amount of reasoning by Brian could help. And he did try to reason with her, endlessly. About Mally having the knife, about Mally terrifying her the way he had, about Mally being a grown man, who was off his head on drugs as well, about it being a tragic accident. All of it glanced off. Every single excuse. None could so much as dent, let alone prick, the huge bubble of self-hatred that had blown up inside her.

Well, today, she would set things straight, and there was nothing Nick could do. Clutching her precious paperwork, she made her way to the entrance on steady legs. Today she was going make things right.

'No. Not under any circumstances. Do NOT go against me on this.'

Nicky looked so different, yet, at the same time, so eerily familiar. It took her straight back to the Listers – a place she hated to return to – and seeing Brian, fresh out of his own incarceration. He was wearing a prison bib and an expression that immediately made her wary. He looked furious with her, in a way she'd never seen before.

'I mean it,' he said, leaning forward across the small Formica-topped table that separated them. He put his warm inside hands over her cold, reddened, recently outside ones, and it came to her just what a big thing being locked up must be. Was he ever allowed out in the fresh air? She had a vague memory come to her, of hearing about 'exercise yards', but the image that accompanied it, of angry-looking, boiler-suited American mass murderers, did nothing to make the idea cheer her up.

'I can't do it, Nicky,' she said again, keeping her voice as low as possible, away from the hearing of the prison officers who stood at the room's edges.

'It's not a question of "can't",' her brother told her. 'It's a question of not being a fucking idiot. Look, I've spoken to the brief, and it doesn't look too bad, on account of there being so many extenuating circumstances. Nothing's changed, okay? Nothing about what happened during the struggle. Nothing about what started it, or how it ended. All that's changed is that there's different mandatory sentences when it comes to manslaughter – poor bloody fucker, when all's said and done, so quite right too.'

'But it means you might go to prison for years, Nick – for something *I* did!'

'No, you *didn't*!'

Christine shook her head. 'Stop it, Nick! Why do you keep on and on like that? You *know* I did!'

'For *fuck's* sake! Keep your voice down!' he hissed at her, grabbing her hands and squeezing them. 'Why do *you* keep on and on like this? I need to *do this*!'

Christine had never seen her brother cry, any more than she'd seen her mother, and she recoiled from it initially, because it was like the bottom falling out of her world. The way his handsome face contorted. The way his eyes became so glassy. The way all her security – all that was constant and safe, scant though it was – was suddenly, violently, stripped away.

He fought it. Like her mam did, he fought it with all his might. But it was too powerful and a racking sob escaped him. She glanced across at the nearest guard, but he was apparently unseeing. Completely passive. And it occurred to her that he must see so many tears shed by men here that one more weeping inmate was of no consequence. Either that or he was being respectful. She preferred that.

317

Her hands trapped, she couldn't do anything but whisper, however. 'Please don't cry, Nick.' She said the same thing over and over.

But still he cried, albeit quietly now, for a good minute and a half. Then he wiped his face on his sleeve, sniffed and sat back. Then again, forward. 'Right,' he said, his voice finally under control. 'For the last time, here's the thing. I have to do this. I'm not being a martyr, so you can shut the fuck up about that one. I'm doing it for me, right? So I can hold my head up when I'm out again. So I can clean up, get my life together, and lots of other worthy bollocks like that. But mostly I am doing it because I've fucked you up royally –'

'Nick, you –'

'Shut it. I've fucked you up royally. I've stood by and done nothing while you started on the drugs, I've stood by and done nothing when it all kicked off with Joey, I've stood by and done nothing while you bloody *imploded* – and if you think I'm going to stand there and watch you go to *fucking prison* as a consequence, then you are even more deranged than I shall convince whoever I need to if you say a single bloody word more about all this shit, okay?'

He took his hands off hers and moved them up to her cheeks. And she realised she had never felt so loved.

'Okay?' he said again. 'You've got to promise me, here and now. This is the end of it. My sacrifice. My choice. My redemption. Now make it worth it, for fuck's sake, sis. Get my nephew back.'

Chapter 29

Leeds Crown Court, 1 April 1982

Christine wasn't sure if it had been the right thing to do, bringing her mam all the way on the train to Leeds for the hearing. It wasn't that it was that cold, but she was so thin and frail now that she looked like a breeze could blow her away. Still, the fact that she'd insisted spoke volumes. As the nurse at the clinic had said – and she'd said it like she'd meant it – there was still plenty of life in the old girl yet.

But half the day had already passed, and Nicky hadn't been up yet, so, with the court broken for lunch, they were now at a loose end – time they were filling by sitting on the low sandstone wall, smoking, till the solicitor came to get them to go back in again.

'Only your Nick,' Brian was saying. 'Only your bloody brother could do that – could cop for a sentencing hearing on bleeding April Fools' Day.' He blew out an expert stream of smoke rings. 'What a frigging plonker, eh?'

Christine nudged her mother. 'Have you heard him, Mam? Talking about your son like that. I'd belt him, I would.'

She and Brian exchanged smiles, as her mam did as instructed – albeit weakly, with her not-at-all-hefty handbag. And Christine thought for the umpteenth time since she'd last seen her brother how, apart from whatever glimpse he got of her in court, the likelihood was that he'd never see his mother again. She'd already said she wouldn't burden him with a prison visit. Was completely adamant, in fact. 'What bleeding good is that going to do him?' she'd pointed out, more than once. 'Having a picture of me in his head looking like this?'

No, she was happy enough, she'd said, to come here, to be here, and to support him. Because that was what he'd want. For them to pull together for Joey now.

Not that her mam knew the whole truth. She was principally here knowing only the public version of it, and that was something Christine knew she'd have to learn to live with. All Lizzie knew was the version that had been read out in court the previous week, when her brother had been found guilty of manslaughter, with extenuating circumstances. How did *she* feel, right now, with it almost certain, given she wouldn't visit him, that she was never going to see her son again?

Christine pinged her cigarette butt away, remembering she was giving up tomorrow. Actually, there were no 'buts' about it. Despite refusing a hospice place, on the grounds that 'being with a bunch of dying people' would finish her off for certain, Lizzie, in reality, only had weeks left, and was looking a couple of decades older now than she really was.

People stared at her in the street now, which made Christine want to slap them. Like she was mutton dressed as lamb, that she'd been dieting too much. No one ever thought. That was the thing. That no one ever *thought* she might actually be dying. Or was it some weird denial thing humans had mastered – to not even *think* the 'C' word, let alone say it?

Her mam was shivering in the weak April sunshine. 'You all right, Mam?' Christine asked. 'Do you want my cardi?'

'I'm okay, love,' she answered. 'Just haven't took my jungle juice this morning, have I?'

'Jungle juice' was what Lizzie affectionately called her morphine. She was on a self-administering dose, and it usually sent her off her head. Or 'away with the fairies', as she called it – somewhere Christine never wanted to be again. But today, understandably, she had wanted to be lucid, so despite the pain that must have been coursing through her body as a consequence, she had refused to take any meds today.

Brian nudged her out of her reverie. 'Eh, up,' he said, throwing his own cigarette away. Nicky's solicitor had come out looking for them and was gesturing that they should return. The courts were back in session and it looked like he was first up. *Please God*, Christine prayed. Please God, let them be lenient. There wasn't a day when Mally's death didn't sit like a stone in her gut, and the thought of her brother being incarcerated for years on top of that was almost unthinkable. But she had to brace herself, because the solicitor had predicted three or four years minimum. And there was nothing – absolutely *nothing* – she could do to change it.

But she could tell straight away that it might not be that bad, just by the expression on the presiding judge's face. She couldn't explain why, but as Brian linked hands with her, she felt hopeful. And, glancing across at Nicky – this new, bulked-up, straight-back-and-sides version of her brother, she felt it again.

And she'd been right. He was given two years. 'It might have been shorter,' explained the judge, looking regretful, 'due to the unfortunate series of events leading to this man's death.' He turned to Nicky. 'That is, had it not been for you already being on a probationary period when the incident took place.'

And Christine could see that, just like her, Nick was relieved rather than disappointed. But she reined in the beginnings of a relieved smile on her face. Mally was dead, she must never, *would* never, forget that. And, thanks to her brother, she had been given another chance at life. For Joey. And he'd given it to her willingly.

Their eyes briefly met as he was ushered from the box. 'I'll do it on my head, sis,' he mouthed as he was led away.

It was only when they were out in the brightness of the spring afternoon that Christine set eyes on Carol Sloper. Slipping her hand out of Brian's and unlinking her other arm from her mam, she hurried across the concourse to catch her.

She turned just as Christine caught her up. 'Ah, there you are,' she said, smiling. 'Not too bad in the end, was it?' Then she smiled. 'I'm so glad, Christine, really I am.'

And Christine knew it to be true. Along with another truth that had been living with her since back in late January. That, in all likelihood, Carol Sloper knew of the real course of events that had led Nicky here. And though they never spoke of it, and probably never would now, Christine had this profound sense that Carol Sloper wasn't her enemy. That, just like Nicky, she believed in redemption. She had also proved it. Had been tireless in helping Christine since. Drug and alcohol support programmes. Constant support. A kind of friendship. Mutual trust.

She'd even gone to Mr Weston down the market and got her her old job back.

And, despite her never quite allowing herself to believe it might happen, Christine and her mam were seeing Joey next week. Which meant nothing in the big scheme, but at the same time meant everything. It meant hope. She couldn't wait to tell Nicky.

'I didn't realise you were coming today,' Christine said now. 'You should have said. You could have sat with us.'

Carol Sloper shook her head. 'I hadn't planned to. But it's in the nature of my job that I spend rather more time down here than most. So, as I was here, I thought I might as well pop in and see. You'll be relieved, I'll bet.' She looked back towards where Brian and Lizzie were waiting. 'How's Mum?'

'A little weak today, but nothing a few doses of her jungle juice won't be able to sort once we're back. She'll be fine for next week. Plenty of life in the old girl yet.'

'I don't doubt it,' Carol said. 'And now I'd better get off. And you'll be wanting to see Nicky before he leaves, I imagine.'

Christine shook her head. 'I'm going to see him once he's settled in,' she told her. 'His call. And now we need to get Mam back.'

She looked back to where Bri and her mam were still standing, arms linked, by the low sandstone wall. She waved, and Brian looked at her the way he often did now. Funny how things worked out. Who'd have thought?

She set off, mentally correcting herself as she returned his shy smile.

Not 'back'. What she should have said was home.

Acknowledgements

Forever grateful to the team at HarperCollins, who continue to have faith in the stories I have to tell. I'm also so thankful for my partner in crime, the lovely Lynne Barrett-Lee, who continues to make silk purses from sows' ears without any complaints, and of course, as ever, I have to thank the UK's leading literary agent, the wonderful Andrew Lownie – a true gentleman and a friend.

Moving Memoirs

Stories of hope, courage and the power of love…

If you loved this book, then you will love our
Moving Memoirs eNewsletter

Sign up to…

- Be the first to hear about new books

- Get sneak previews from your favourite authors

- Read exclusive interviews

- Be entered into our monthly prize draw to win one of our latest releases before it's even hit the shops!

Sign up at

www.moving-memoirs.com